D0725214

The Woodfinishing Book

The Woodfinishing Book

MICHAEL DRESDNER

The Taunton Press

for fellow enthusiasts

First printing: September 1992
Second printing: June 1993
Printed in the United States of America

A FINE WOODWORKING Book

FINE WOODWORKING ® is a trademark of The Taunton Press, Inc.,
registered in the U.S. Patent and Trademark Office.

The Taunton Press, 63 South Main Street, Box 5506, Newtown,
CT 06470-5506

Library of Congress Cataloging-in-Publication Data

Dresdner, Michael M.
    The woodfinishing book / Michael Dresdner.
      p. cm.
    "A Fine woodworking book" — T.p. verso.
    Includes index.
    ISBN 1-56158-037-6
    1. Wood finishing. I. Title.
TT325.D74   1992   92-14899
684.1'043 — dc20   CIP

This book is dedicated to Chris A. Minick,
my patient and stalwart guide through the jungles of darkest chemistry.

CONTENTS

ACKNOWLEDGMENTS

You ought to know that it is next to impossible to write a book all by yourself. In spite of the fact that my name appears on the front, I am not the only one responsible for this work. I owe a lot to those who joined me in putting this together.

First and foremost, I have to thank my "first reader," M. Jane McKittrick. If this book is even remotely comprehensible, it is because of her influence. She spent an enormous amount of time and effort helping me rewrite the text until my garbled explanations started to make some sense. Once she had straightened out the text, she turned to the illustrations, creating the sketches that help translate my scattered descriptions into visual reality.

Thanks, Jane!

The others are listed below, in no particular order. They include my editors, photographers, artists, and people who were there for me in a hundred different ways: Andy Schultz, Sandor Nagyszalanczy, Bob Flexner, Phil Hostetter, Bruce Schneider, Jim Crook, Johnny Candurra, Nat Loupus, Susan Kahn, the BR Boys.

Finally, I'd like to thank my parents, who pressured me into apprenticing as a finisher so many years ago.

ABOUT THIS BOOK

It's no secret that finishing can be a frustrating and confusing endeavor. Paint and hardware stores have an astonishing array of finishing products crowding their shelves. On top of that, the field of finishing is riddled with old wives' tales and other absurd notions, all of which come from a lack of basic information concerning what finishes are and how they work. I guess it's not surprising that many woodworkers become so frustrated that they find one finish that works well for them, and then never try anything else.

This book is designed to take the guesswork out of finishing. By dividing finishes into categories based on characteristics such as appearance, durability and ease of application, it will help you make an informed decision about selecting the best finish for any given job. There is even a pull-out wall chart in the back of the book that will serve as an invaluable shop tool for quick reference.

The book will also help you get past the gobbledygook of product labels with a no-nonsense approach to understanding what is in the can. A "Key to Brands" at the back of the text will offer some guidance in matching familiar brand names with the type of finish you are seeking.

Most important, this book will walk you through the steps of preparing a surface and applying just about any coating you choose. And for those operations that you really have to see to understand, there is a companion video that will let you watch some people who have a solid hold on all sorts of finish-application techniques.

CHAPTER 1
Choosing a Finish

Daydreaming is a favorite occupation for most twelve-year-olds, so I was probably in good company the afternoon I sat alone at my desk gazing at the side of my dresser. The problem was that while my mind had been on sabbatical, my hands had been busy: there, like a series of white scars scratched into the dark finish of the dresser, were my initials. "Did I do that?" I thought in horror as my attention snapped back to the present. Like most adolescents, I knew nothing of finishing, but my natural instinct for self-preservation kicked in as I spied a can of hair spray. "It can't get any worse," I reasoned as I sprayed and wiped the oily aerosol across the scratches. The gods must have been with me; I was elated as the white marks blended back into the color of the surrounding wood. It wasn't a perfect fix, but the scratches were barely noticeable.

And so, like most woodworkers, I started my finishing career using what was available—a simple oil finish. In that case, my choices were limited to the confines of my room. But since then I have met all too many adult woodworkers who face their first finishing decisions with the same fear and confusion that accompanied mine.

All that is about to change.

What's in the can? Product names and advertising claims can be confusing if you don't understand the characteristics of the various finish types.

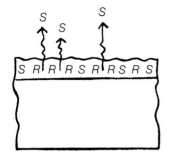

Final film

As the solvent (S) evaporates, the resin (R) left behind forms a film on the surface of the wood.

What is finish?

Like a good friend, finish is defined not so much by how it looks, but by what it does. A wood finish can protect, enhance, preserve or color a piece of wood, and often does all four. Finishes protect wood from scratches, dirt, stains and wear. They often enhance wood's natural beauty, bring out color, figure patterns and grain, and add depth with their lens-like quality. Finishes also preserve wood from the unrelenting ravages of nature: water, oxidation and the ultraviolet rays of the sun. And to top it all off, they can add color, hide defects or even totally change the wood's appearance.

Technically speaking, finish is a mixture of materials in liquid form that can be spread out to cover a surface of any shape with a very thin film. How that film is formed can be very important, and it supplies us with a means of categorizing finishes. In the simplest assessment, finishes all fall into two broad categories: evaporative and reactive.

All finishes contain resin, and most also contain solvent. The resin is the portion of the finish that remains behind to form the film. The solvent is a liquid added in to make the resin flow. It is the solvent that evaporates during drying.

When an evaporative finish forms a film on wood, the only action taking place is that the solvent evaporates. The resin itself is exactly the same as it was in the can, only drier. In fact, if you pour the solvent back onto the resin, it will once again become the liquid that was originally in the can.

By contrast, in a reactive finish the resin actually undergoes a chemical change. As the film is formed, the resin becomes an entirely different material than it was in its liquid form in the can. Consequently, it will not redissolve in its original solvent.

This primary difference is vital in understanding how finishes behave. It can offer us clues to how the finish should be handled during application, and what we can expect of it once it is cured.

Evaporative (solvent-release) finishes At the heart of an evaporative finish are one or more resins and one or more solvents. There may also be other ingredients—pigments, dyes, plasticizers and other additives— but the basic film-forming action is controlled by the solvent and resin. As the solvent evaporates, the resin is left behind to form a coating on the wood. The resin has not changed other than having gotten thicker and drier through losing its solvent. This means that the finish can be redissolved by its own solvent.

Shellac and lacquer are examples of evaporative finishes. Putting alcohol on dried shellac or lacquer thinner on cured lacquer will cause them to revert to their liquid state. Furthermore, each coat of solvent-laden finish melts the coats before it. No matter how many coats are applied, they all meld together to form one thick layer. This single characteristic explains many of the traits that we have come to associate with shellac and lacquer. For example, each coat has outstanding adhesion to the previous one, and there is no need to sand between coats. If the finish is rubbed or buffed, it all acts like a single coat, no matter how unevenly it is sanded or rubbed. The finish never shows halos or witness lines—those fine outlines that indicate a sand-through from one layer to another.

Evaporative finishes are easily repaired, since you can "re-enter" them with the correct solvent and spot-spray just an area and have it blend into its surroundings. By the same token, touching an evaporative finish while it is wet will destroy it right down to the wood surface, and dyes that share the same solvent as the finish are likely to bleed up through each coat.

White-gloved ladies

Out of earshot, we called him Jimmy the Hacker; although he was the senior finisher in the shop, he had a reputation for requiring two or three attempts to get a finish right. Still, when he was sober, he did some beautiful work, and the neophytes like myself enjoyed learning from this profane ex-marine in spite of his rather short temper.

One Friday, Jimmy was putting the finishing touches on a tabletop that had been keeping him busy all week. The finish was a fake-grained lacquer job with at least three separate color glazes used to mimic red oak. It was a bear of a finish to do, and this was Jimmy's second shot at it. His first effort was undone by a local flying insect. After the final coat of lacquer was applied, a palmetto bug flew into the wet finish, and its death throes undid all of his fine efforts. You see, each coat of a lacquer finish redissolves all of the previous coats, so that the last coat again melts all others into one thick layer cake of translucent colors. That bug ruined the finish right down to the raw wood. There was nothing to do but strip the finish off and start over.

Now in its second incarnation, the table once again went into the booth for its final coat. Just as Jimmy wheeled the top out into the drying room, the shop's owner came by with two potential customers in tow—Southern matrons who still wore white gloves despite the eroding etiquette of the 1970s. The look of the still-wet lacquer under bright lights must have been too much to resist, for as she walked past, one of the women gently ran her fingers across the glistening top. To her surprise, the lacquer moved aside, leaving a furrow down to the wood. It looked like the icing on a two-year-old's birthday cake after an unofficial tasting.

Those of us who saw the incident let out a collective gasp, convinced that we were about to witness the shop's first justifiable homicide. Jimmy turned beet red, and barely containing his fury, blurted out, "That finish is wet!" "Oh, it's quite all right," replied the offender, holding up a clean, but now gloveless finger, "I had my gloves on."

How a Reactive Finish Works

As the solvent (S) evaporates, the resin (R) undergoes a chemical change that creates a new film (X) on the surface of the wood.

R S R S R S R S R S R S

R   R S R   R   R
S   S   S

X X X X X X X X X X X

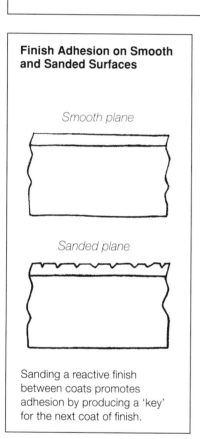

Finish Adhesion on Smooth and Sanded Surfaces

Smooth plane

Sanded plane

Sanding a reactive finish between coats promotes adhesion by producing a 'key' for the next coat of finish.

Reactive (thermoset) finishes

Reactive finishes may consist of a mixture of solvent, pigments and other additives, but the only critical ingredient is the resin. Some reactive finishes (linseed oil and tung oil, for example) may consist of nothing else. A reactive finish forms a film when the resin goes through a chemical change that causes its molecules to link up and form larger molecules (see the drawing above). All oil-based varnishes, catalyzed lacquers and conversion varnishes are reactive finishes, as are two-part crosslinked and epoxy coatings.

A reactive finish may contain solvents to dilute and thin the mixture for ease of handling, but these evaporate off first and do not play a part in the film-forming process. Because an entirely new molecule is formed during the cure, reactive finishes are not generally dissolved by their own diluents. For example, mineral spirits will thin out an oil varnish, but once it has cured, the mineral spirits can not redissolve the film. For this reason, each coat of finish acts like a separate layer, adhering to the previous one without actually melting into it. Because adhesion is based on available surface area, it helps to scuff reactive finishes between coats, an action that increases the surface area and provides a greater "key."

Reactive finishes are more difficult to repair than evaporative finishes, and the repair generally shows more readily. Spot-spraying or sanding through during rubbing is likely to result in halos and witness lines. On the positive side, since each coat cures before the next is applied, there is usually little or no bleeding of colorant or contaminants.

Finishes: Evaporative or Reactive?	
EVAPORATIVE FINISHES	REACTIVE FINISHES
Shellac	Oil-based finishes
Lacquer	*Alkyd varnish*
Acrylic	*Danish oil*
Cellulose acetate butyrate (CAB)	*Linseed oil*
Nitrocellulose	*Oil varnish*
Urethane lacquer	*Polyurethane/alkyd varnish*
Vinyl	*Spar varnish (oil/phenolic)*
Water-based one-part varnish/lacquer emulsions	*Tung oil*
Acrylic	Crosslinked finishes
Acrylonitrile	*Catalyzed lacquer*
Nitrocellulose	*Conversion varnish*
Polyurethane	*Polyester*
	Moisture-cured polyurethane
	Two-part epoxy coatings
	Water-based two-part coatings
	(with aziridine or carbodiimide hardener added)

Compromises and trade-offs

Choosing a finish is a lot like buying a car, only cheaper. Let's say you are trying to decide among four vehicles: a sporty two-seater that corners well and appeals to your racy self-image, a pickup truck for hauling wood and tools, a station wagon that would hold the whole family (including the dog), and a four-wheel drive jeep for icy roads and mountain camping trips. Strictly speaking, all of them perform the same basic function—they get you from here to there. But each has obvious advantages and disadvantages.

Similarly, all finishes do the same thing—they coat wood. But whereas finances may force you to choose only one car, you can afford to buy the most appropriate finish for each woodworking job. You'll need to know what you expect of the finish, as well as how each one performs, in order to make the right choice. Most of the considerations are fairly straightforward; whether you require high heat resistance (in the kitchen, for instance) or solvent resistance (a dressing-room vanity) and what you prefer the coating to look like are easy decisions.

Q: I'm looking for a durable finish for a dining table. The finish needs to be wet sanded and polished to a high gloss. I'd prefer a lacquer-based product, but the lacquer that is on the table now is very susceptible to heat damage. Can you recommend a product that is more heat and scratch resistant?

A: Although most lacquers are affected by heat, some are more sensitive than others, depending on the resins chosen for the formulation. Of the hundreds of lacquer formulations on the market, you'll be able to find mixtures covering a vast range of heat and scratch resistance.

If you prefer a brushable finish, try a polyurethane varnish. Although you could coat right over the lacquer, you'll get more durability and a nicer appearance if you remove the old finish first.

If you want to use a sprayable finish, consider catalyzed lacquer. Catalyzed lacquers offer astonishing heat and abrasion resistance, but are very difficult to remove should that ever be desired. These systems generally require a crosslinker to be added to the base material just before it is sprayed. The finish cures over time to form a very durable film. Speak to your finish supplier about the options—some lacquers will go over an existing finish, but most catalyzed systems will not.

One variable that deserves more discussion is the issue of brittleness vs. flexibility. Which is more advantageous? That depends on what the wood will be used for. A flexible finish is more likely to tolerate a wide range of wood movement due to moisture changes, so exterior finishes are always very flexible. Floor finishes must also be flexible. No matter how strong a floor finish is, it is still only a thin film. A floor finish that will follow a dent instead of chipping off is clearly advantageous. On the other hand, a freestanding indoor table or chest that does not require a highly flexible coating might instead benefit from the depth, clarity and abrasion resistance of a more brittle lacquer. You absolutely must have both? That's where crosslinked or catalyzed finishes enter the picture, but be aware that they are generally less user friendly, more dangerous and more expensive (see pp. 19-20).

Finishing, like life, is full of compromises and trade-offs. In a perfect world, you would select a wood coating solely on the basis of the finish's long-term performance characteristics. Although that is still a very large consideration, other factors balance in as well: drying and curing time, relative safety of the material, application requirements (do you need a spray gun or can you use a brush?), ease of use and even cost. In order to be in a good position to make these decisions, you need a thumbnail profile of each type of finish that explains what it is, how it behaves and wears, what it looks like and how it handles.

To make this massive range of options more manageable, I've grouped the thumbnails into three categories based on method of application: brushable finishes, wipe-on finishes and sprayable finishes. This is the most logical starting point when deciding on a finish material; there is no sense in finding the perfect wear and drying features in a sprayable material if you don't own a spray gun. Several finishes, shellac for example, show up in more than one group. At times, the only difference is the drying speed or the viscosity (thickness). Bear in mind that terms like durability are relative, and any finish applied very thin will offer significantly less protection than the same material brushed on thicker. Charts on pp. 24-27, and the pullout wall chart at the back of the book, summarize the finish thumbnails in each category, and will help you compare the attributes of various finishes at a glance.

For most finishes, the resin controls the character and durability of the final dried film, and the vehicle (solvents, additives and other liquid portions of the mix) affects handling characteristics, drying time, and so on. These characteristics are largely determined by the formulator, and are quite variable. Consequently, the guidelines presented here are only generalizations, and may vary considerably with specific materials. It is always a good idea to read labels, and if there is a discrepancy between the product label and what you read here, trust the label. After all, the manufacturer knows what's inside the can.

Brushable finishes

For the most part, finishes designed to be brushed are slow drying to allow the finish time to flow out and eradicate the inevitable brush marks. This is not to suggest that you can't brush fast-drying finishes, but don't be surprised when they don't lay out as well. Many brushable finishes are reactive, not evaporative, and the reason is simple: reactive finishes don't redissolve themselves. A finish that did would be difficult to brush out, since it would drag around the previous coats on the last ones. As always, there are exceptions.

Shellac

One of the oldest and most adored finishes, shellac is a fast-drying evaporative coating characterized by exceptional clarity and depth. Shellac is refined from the secretions of *Laccifer lacca,* an insect indigenous to India and Southeast Asia. Until 100 years ago, it was one of the two most popular wood finishes for high-quality interior work, and it is quite common to find antiques finished in shellac. It is revered for its ability to bring out the beauty of wood as well as for its compatibility with most other finishes. An excellent wash coat for sealing refinished as well as new wood, shellac seals in fish-eye-causing silicone (see p. 137) as well as many other contaminants.

Shellac consists of resin and alcohol only, and is sold both premixed as a liquid and as dry flakes, granules and buttons. The concentration of the premixed liquid is identified by the number of pounds of shellac per gallon of alcohol (e.g., a 3-lb. cut means 3 lb. of shellac in 1 gal. of alcohol). Once the shellac mixes with alcohol, it immediately begins a process of esterification, in which the resin converts to a very flexible plasticizer. The process goes on indefinitely until the entire volume of shellac is converted. The liquid shellac does not look any different as the reaction progresses, but the film it forms gets more rubbery and eventually reaches the point where it simply will not dry at all. For this reason, it is very important to use fresh shellac. Never work with material more than six months old.

Most finishing aficionados solve the short shelf-life problem by buying shellac flakes and mixing finish as they need it. To mix shellac, add it in any proportion you choose to denatured alcohol or ethanol. Let the mixture sit overnight, and stir or shake it occasionally. If there is any residue (dirt, twigs, etc.), strain it through cheesecloth. Add denatured alcohol or ethanol to thin it to a good working consistency. The resin comes in a variety of grades that range in color from light golden to dark orange-brown. Dewaxed flakes tend to be clearer and more brittle than unprocessed seedlac material, and generally don't require straining. White shellac has been bleached, a process that causes it to lose clarity and age even faster.

Lacquer

Like its more common sprayable counterpart, brushable lacquer is a fast-drying evaporative finish that boasts outstanding clarity and durability, and will rub up to an excellent gloss. The major difference is that it contains solvents that slow down the drying time to allow it to flow out and correspond to brushing speed. Visually, brushable lacquer is probably the closest thing to shellac, and shares with it the traits of brittleness and poor solvent resistance.

Oil varnish

Wood appears to get slightly more translucent when it is impregnated with oil, and the shimmer that results is one reason that traditional brushed-on oil varnish looks so good. Most interior varnish uses alkyd resin to add body to the film, along with soya, linseed or tung oil. The word "alkyd" comes from the way the resin is manufactured; it is an oil that is modified by reacting first with an alcohol, then with an acid (<u>al</u>cohol + ac<u>id</u> = "alcid," or more phonetically, alkyd). Oil varnishes are slow-drying reactive finishes that are flexible, durable and quite solvent resistant. They handle best with moderately stiff natural bristle brushes like badger and China bristle (see pp. 32-34), and clean up and thin with mineral spirits.

Polyurethane varnish

Adding polyurethane resin to an oil varnish creates polyurethane varnish, another reactive finish. Polyurethane is a modified oil that contributes durability, abrasion resistance, and quite a bit of heat resistance to what is, in spite of its name, simply a buffered oil varnish. The relatively thick resin adds body to the material, but also makes the varnish a little harder to handle than other oil varnishes.

Enamel

Finishing terminology is complex (see the sidebar on pp. 12-13), and occasionally a term gets so widely employed to mean so many different things that it ends up meaning nothing at all. Enamel is one of those words. At this point, it is generally taken to mean some colored coating, so that oil enamel is colored oil varnish, lacquer enamel is colored lacquer, and so forth. Enamel has also been used to define a type of coating and a level of gloss, among other things.

Spar varnish (oil/phenolic)

Spar varnish is a reactive finish that is used mostly for exterior surfaces. It generally contains phenolic resin and has the ability to resist ultraviolet degrade from the sun's rays (see pp. 20-21). Although the extreme flexibility of spar varnish allows it to tolerate the wide range of movement typical of wood that stays outdoors, a certain amount of abrasion resistance is sacrificed; as a consequence, spar varnish tends to wear away rather than chip or peel. It shares with its other oil-based cousins the traits of excellent adhesion and the ability to go over most other finishes.

Water-based one-part varnish/lacquer emulsions

The easiest way to get a handle on water-based varnish/lacquer is to think of it as a clear version of latex paint. Although the addition of different resins may result in a variety of film characteristics, water-based varnishes and lacquers share a lot of the same handling properties. These are not water-soluble resins (if they were, the film formed would redissolve with water), but emulsions (mixtures of two incompatible liquids forced to co-exist) in which little droplets of some type of resin are dispersed throughout a volume of water. Because the water surrounds the resin, the water is called the "continuous phase," and the resin portion is the "dispersed phase," or "discontinuous phase."

Whether a water-based coating is evaporative or reactive depends on the discontinuous phase, but they all share the same first stage in the drying process. When the coating is spread on wood, the water evaporates, forcing the droplets of finish to bunch up against one another. A group of slower-drying solvents (called "tail solvents" or "co-solvents") remains after the water is gone to help the resin droplets merge to form a film. Thus, water acts as a diluent to thin out the material, replacing some, but not all of the solvents in the lacquer. The result is that because of the presence of the water, the mixture has significantly lower solvent levels and is much less combustible.

Unfortunately, the film-forming process works much better in theory than in practice. The low solvent levels account for several problems and one advantage in virtually all water-based coatings. Most significant among the problems is the reduction in inter-coat adhesion; even though most latexes are technically evaporative finishes, the relatively low solvent level prevents them from melting into the previous coat the way high-solvent lacquers and shellac do. Instead, the coats form discrete layers similar to what you'd expect with several coats of reactive finishes, a situation that can lead to witness lines if the finish is buffed. This problem is even more severe when the finish is applied with a spray gun instead of a brush.

Water-based coatings demand tight controls on the workshop environment (see pp. 142-145). If the relative humidity is too high, you can experience crossover, where the tail solvents, which are less affected by humidity, evaporate before the water. If that happens, the resin droplets will never coalesce into a film, but will simply dry as separate particles that scrape off the surface easily. Temperature also plays an important role. All coatings have a Minimum Film Forming Temperature (MFFT), the lowest temperature at which a coating will form.

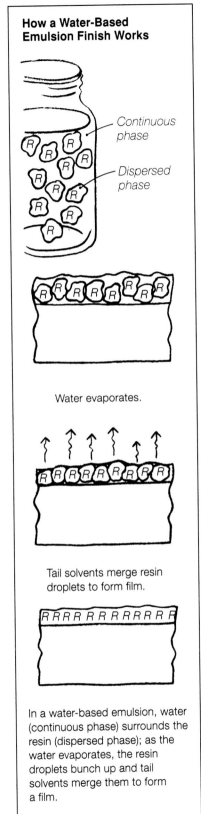

How a Water-Based Emulsion Finish Works

Continuous phase

Dispersed phase

Water evaporates.

Tail solvents merge resin droplets to form film.

In a water-based emulsion, water (continuous phase) surrounds the resin (dispersed phase); as the water evaporates, the resin droplets bunch up and tail solvents merge them to form a film.

Water-based coatings generally have a much higher MFFT—usually above 60°F—making these finishes inappropriate for use outdoors or in unheated garages during the winter.

On the other hand, water-based coatings boast the advantage of a higher Moisture Vapor Transmission Rate, the rate of speed at which moisture vapor is able to cross the finish barrier in and out of the wood. All finishes allow moisture to move in and out of wood (that's why we let solid wood raised panels float in their frames), but some slow it down more than others. If the moisture is held too long on its way back out of the wood, as is sometimes the case with certain oil-based coatings, it will force the finish away from the wood in the form of blisters. When house painters switched from oil-based exterior coatings to latex paints, there was a corresponding decrease in blistered and peeling finishes. I suppose the moral is, "If you can't stop the moisture from entering wood (and you can't), then stay out of its way when it wants to leave."

*F*inishing terminology: What do the words mean?

If it often seems as if you can't get a straight answer to what appears to be a simple finishing question, chalk it up to that classic problem, "a lack of communication." It's not your fault. The folks who aren't communicating are those choosing the terminology. You see, there are no simple divisions of finish into descriptive terms, and there is an enormous amount of crossover. On top of that, some finishes are described by their resin (polyurethane), others by their usage (spar varnish) and still others by their solvent or diluent system (latex). Let me give you a few examples.

Almost any finish can be called a varnish. It is a lot like "motor vehicle," a term that can refer to a motorcycle and an 18-wheel tractor trailer, and everything in between. Varnish simply means a liquid that forms a film—which is what coating and finish mean, too. Varnishes are subdivided into three traditional classes, and several more modern ones, but the subdivisions are based on various different criteria. Oil varnish describes the resin film-former (oil), as does polyurethane varnish. Spar varnish is also oil varnish, but it uses a different oil and resin so that it is suitable for exterior use. Spirit varnish doesn't describe a material component or the place to use it, but instead refers to the fact that the material is evaporative instead of a reactive oil. Shellac, a specific evaporative resin finish, is often correctly called spirit varnish. But the term "lacquer" also means exactly the same thing as spirit varnish—an evaporative coating. Water-based polyurethane is an evaporative coating, but oil-based polyurethane is usually a reactive one, though both are described by their labels simply as polyurethane.

Confused? You're in good company. We all are. And we're likely to remain that way until the manufacturers all agree on a consistent set of terms. Then again, I suppose we woodworkers are in no position to complain about terminology, considering all of different names we use for the same wood, and all the different woods we call by the same name (in various parts of the world, over 109 separate woods are all called ironwood).

Acrylic   Characterized by a colorless clarity and good handling properties, acrylic resins have become popular in water-based coatings. Their resistance to yellowing makes them useful as top coats over white or light-colored paints, although some finishers miss the warm amber tint characteristic of oil varnish, shellac and lacquer over wood. Acrylics have good ultraviolet stability (see pp. 20-21), good stain resistance, and are quite durable, but have only fair solvent resistance. As they come from the can, acrylics are evaporative finishes. Most can be made into reactive coatings by crosslinking them with carbodiimide or aziridine additives, which are sold off the shelf as "hardeners" (see p. 20). Carbodiimides are much less hazardous to health than aziridines, if you have a choice. Like all water-based coatings, acrylics dry fast and can be handled in a few hours, but take about 30 days to cure fully.

Polyurethane   As with oil varnishes, adding a polyurethane resin to a water-based varnish improves its heat and scratch resistance, and the resulting mixes are called polyurethane coatings. The polyurethane

---

To make things a bit easier to decipher, here are some of the descriptive categories used, with examples. Some terms (polyurethane for instance) show up in several spots.

Resin types (some resins are used in both evaporative and reactive systems): acrylic, alkyd, cellulose acetate butyrate (CAB), nitrocellulose, oil (all types), phenolic, polyester, polyurethane, shellac, urea, vinyl.

Evaporative film-forming systems: lacquer, shellac, spirit varnish, water-based acrylic, water-based polyacrylic, water-based polyurethane.

Reactive film-forming systems: catalyzed lacquer, conversion varnish, crosslinked epoxy hardener (to be added to water-based systems or epoxies), moisture-cured urethane, oil

(most oils used in coatings are drying oils), polyester, any two-part system.

Some other terms that have specific meanings: Shellac is a natural evaporative resin finish. Latex is an emulsion or dispersion in water (the terms "latex" and "water-based" are synonymous). Enamel once meant a sheen, but is now taken to mean "colored opaque," as opposed to clear. Urethane used interchangeably with polyurethane is a misnomer. Technically urethane is the monomer that acts as one of the building blocks in the formation of polyurethane. It is impossible to have a urethane finish.

Like candy by the pound, you can mix and match finishing terms. For instance, if a paint can is labeled "Acrylic Latex Enamel," it contains a water-based (latex), colored (enamel), acrylic (the resin) finish. It will

form a film by evaporation (not reaction) and will clean up with water. The film will be opaque (not clear) and will have the durability and appearance associated with acrylic resin. You can also infer some things from the label's list of contents. A water-based (latex) polyurethane is most likely an evaporative system, but a polyurethane that contains no water but lists oil as one of the ingredients is a reactive finish. It's not easy, but by reading the label and playing detective, you can actually figure out what's in the can. You may not always get what you want, but at least you'll have some idea of what you are getting.

For more comprehensive definitions of finishing terms, see the Glossary on pp. 204-209.

Have you ever shaken up a bottle of oil and vinegar salad dressing and watched as the two translucent liquids, one atop the other, mixed into one cloudy emulsion? Have you ever put a pencil in a glass of water to see the image get visually distorted? These effects are caused by the same property that makes clear water-based coatings look milky in the can.

Light travels differently through air and various liquids, and this difference is measured as the refractive index of the liquid. If two or more clear liquids with different refractive indices are emulsified, the light going through is forced to change speed so many times as it enters or leaves each tiny droplet that the mix appears cloudy. Water-based finishes are just such an emulsion, because the clear resin has a different refractive index than water.

resin is generally combined with some acrylic or acrylonitrile to make a polyacrylic or polyacrylonitrile mix. These mixes are usually referred to simply as polyurethanes. In addition to forming a more durable film, the slightly bluish tint of the polyurethane resin adds a pale cast that becomes more apparent over dark woods like walnut. Acrylonitrile resin adds some amber back in when it is used in the formulation, so some water-based polys are less pasty-looking than others. Like the acrylics, water-based polyurethane is an evaporative finish as it comes from the can, but it too can frequently be crosslinked with the additives on the market.

Water-reducible (oil/water emulsion) finishes If the evaporative acrylics and polys are the lacquers of the water-based field, then the water reducibles are the varnishes. Because the resin is some type of oil, these reactive coatings act like oil varnish once the water has evaporated. Their film characteristics are the same as those of oil varnish, including the deep, lens-like quality and amber color that oil imparts to the wood. The most interesting aspect of water reducibles is that they go through phase reversal as they dry. When a certain amount of water has left the film, the coating reverses from being droplets of oil in water to being droplets of water in oil. At that point, the film momentarily turns white, then becomes clear again as the rest of the water leaves.

Wipe-on finishes

Wipe-on finishes are coatings that leave the wood natural-looking. Because they are very thin, they offer very little protection to the wood. Almost any finish can be wiped on, whether it is evaporative or reactive, but a few lend themselves more to this technique and are consequently marketed as such. The properties of a wipe-on finish are more or less the same as its brushed-on equivalent, except that they are often greatly diminished because the film is so thin.

Shellac

Shellac thinned with alcohol makes a wonderful wipe-on sealer coat, especially on solid wood. It can stand by itself, or be improved by topping it off with a coat of wax to make a traditional waxed shellac finish. On the other hand, if you carefully rub on lots of layers of shellac with a cloth pad, you are French polishing (see pp. 175-178).

Danish oil

Most Danish-oil mixtures consist of linseed or tung oil, sometimes buffered with some alkyd resin, with a tremendous quantity of mineral spirits added to make them handle easily. If you think of Danish oil as an ultra-thin oil varnish you'll be on the right track. Danish oil is a reactive finish, but it loses almost all of its protective properties because it is so heavily diluted. On the plus side, it is very easy to use, and it imparts that familiar oil luster to wood.

Linseed oil (raw and boiled)

Raw linseed oil is pure oil pressed from flax seed, and with nothing else added, is the simplest reactive finish in existence. Like most oils pressed from seeds or nuts, linseed is a drying oil and will form a film all by itself by combining with oxygen in the air. (Soya, tung, sunflower and walnut oils are drying oils; vegetable oils like corn oil and peanut oil are not.) Whereas most finishes shrink during drying as their solvents evaporate, solvent-free linseed oil expands as it takes in oxygen. (That's why the skin that forms on the puddle of oil around the can's pour spout is usually wrinkled. As it cures, the skin gets bigger than the still wet puddle, and having nowhere to expand, wrinkles up.) Linseed oil forms a film that is very flexible and has good solvent resistance, but it is too soft to afford much scratch resistance. It has a nice amber color and imparts depth to wood, but it darkens considerably upon long exposure to sunlight.

Linseed oil dries very slowly, so manufacturers add metallic driers to speed up the curing process. This faster mix is called boiled linseed oil, in spite of the fact that it is not actually boiled. Manufacturers thicken it by blowing air through it, making it appear like a pot of boiling liquid. Thus, it is likely to be a heavier-bodied oil than raw linseed oil. Both raw and boiled linseed oil form the same film, but because the driers may be toxic, raw is the better choice for coating wooden spoons and salad bowls.

Boiled linseed oil has the distinction of being the simplest catalyzed finish. The metallic driers, the only thing added to the oil, act as true catalysts, speeding up the drying action without becoming part of the molecules being formed. They get trapped in the matrix of the film, but are not part of it.

Working with linseed and other oils requires some special precautions. Oil-soaked rags or paper left in a pile will result in spontaneous combustion. As oil dries, it gives off heat, and even one crumpled rag can generate enough heat to ignite in less than two hours. If you cannot incinerate the oily rags immediately, either open them out and hang them up one layer thick until they dry, or store them immersed in water until you can incinerate them.

Tung oil

Like linseed oil, the oil pressed from tung nuts is an example of a natural reactive finish. Tung oil dries faster than linseed oil, and it does not require (or benefit from) the addition of metallic driers. To make it cure even faster and minimize the wrinkling, tung oil is sometimes heat bodied, a process that partially polymerizes the oil. The film it forms is similar to linseed oil, but tends to be a tad more durable.

Q: I am building a cradle with light-colored ash stock. I hope to finish it with several coats of tung oil, because it seems to cause little change in the natural blond color of this ash. Is tung oil a safe finish to use?

A: Pure tung oil is completely nontoxic and would be a perfectly safe choice for a cradle or crib finish.

Gel finishes—gelled oils and oil/polyurethane mixes

Oil too thin and runny for you? Well, you must be in good company, because lately, both pure and Danish oil finishes have been offered in higher-viscosity gels. The film is the same, but the handling properties are improved. Some manufacturers beef up their gel by adding polyurethane resin, just as varnish makers do.

Wax

If oil is the simplest reactive finish, I suspect wax is the simplest evaporative finish. In order to be manipulable, wax is mixed with a solvent (usually mineral spirits or naphtha) and will redissolve with it as well. As a protector of wood, wax offers very little moisture, solvent or scratch resistance, and no heat resistance at all. However, when it is put on top of another finish, wax helps deflect scratches by making the surface more slippery. Wax also repels water, causing it to bead up. This trait doesn't actually accomplish much, but it sure looks neat.

Water-based polyurethane

Although they are rarely marketed as wipe-on finishes, water-based emulsions can be sloshed on and wiped off just like shellac. Because of the way the film is formed, polyurethanes are a better choice than acrylics. One coat wiped on and off looks surprisingly like a light-colored Danish oil finish, and is at least a little more protective.

Moisture-cured polyurethane

Moisture-cured polyurethane, a one-part crosslinked finish, is something of an odd duck in the finishing world. It goes on like a thin oil, but uses the moisture in the air to form a surprisingly strong and clear solvent-resistant film. As its name implies, it cures faster in moist, humid air than in dry air. If you think moisture-cured plastic is a brand new concept, think again; that's the way cyanoacrylate glues cure. (Cyanoacrylate glues are fast-setting adhesives sold in tiny amounts under trade names like Krazy Glue and Super Glue.)

Sprayable finishes

Somewhere along the evolutionary line, the human urge for speed began to overtake some of our finer instincts, and the age of fast cars, fast food, and spray finishing was born. Placed against the currently emerging backdrop of concern about efficient use of our world resources, it is hard to believe that spray guns ever made it past first base. And yet, spraying is by a huge margin the most common method of applying finishes to everything from cars to wood. Common sprayable finishes are discussed below. For more on spray equipment and the techniques of spraying, see pp. 154-161.

Shellac

What, again? Yes, shellac makes it into all three categories, and no matter how you apply it, the film properties are always the same. It is least fond of spray guns though, and likes to creep and run, so spray it on thin and light. When you are finished, clean out your gun and run some lacquer thinner through it. If you leave shellac in the cup, it will eat any plating and pit the aluminum.

Lacquers

It is hard to think of a spray gun without thinking of lacquer. Both came of age in the 1920s, and they are perfectly suited to one another. Except for the crosslinked materials, all lacquers are evaporative finishes that are built for speed. They go on fast and dry fast. Unfortunately, they all contain goodly amounts of volatile organic compounds (VOCs), hydrocarbons that have been implicated in the deterioration of our air quality.

Nitrocellulose   The old man of the evaporative lacquers, nitrocellulose film is rather brittle with good scratch and moisture resistance, poor solvent resistance and rather poor heat resistance. These days, most spray lacquers have some other resin added in. Nitrocellulose films tend to chip easily and yellow with age, but their excellent buffing properties, high gloss, clarity and slight amber cast keep them popular for furniture and other woodwork.

Acrylic   Although solvent acrylics have long been used as automobile finishes, they are less popular with woodworkers, perhaps because these clear resins lack the warmth of the more amber nitrocellulose. The film is very similar to nitrocellulose, though it is usually less brittle and does not yellow as it ages.

Cellulose acetate butyrate (CAB)   The motion-picture industry nearly died in infancy due to a rash of theater fires caused by extremely flammable cellulose nitrate film. In addition to being very difficult to extinguish, the cellulose nitrate was so flammable that if the projector jammed, the heat from its light bulb was enough to ignite the stalled film. A then small company saved the industry and ensured its place in history by developing CAB as a less flammable substitute. To this day, that company—Kodak—continues to supply us with cellulose acetate butyrate resin, but its use is not restricted to Hollywood. It made its way into car windshields as the soft layer between the double plates of safety glass, and onto wood as butyrate lacquer. Similar to nitrocellulose, CAB is often sold as water-white lacquer since it is less amber. For the most part, its film properties are the same, except that it is less brittle and has better resistance to cold checks (fine cracks caused by rapid drops in temperature).

Vinyl   Used mostly as a secondary resin in sealers, vinyl is prized for its ability to seal certain resinous woods like rosewood. It is actually an entire category of resins with almost as many profiles as members, but most are fairly tough and flexible with fair solvent resistance.

Urethane lacquer   Urethane lacquers are made by adding polyurethane resin to a film former—lacquer—for improved durability, toughness and heat resistance. They may smell a bit different, but they handle about the same as other lacquers.

Sanding sealer   To make the first coat of lacquer seal better and sand more easily, manufacturers add soft, soap-like self-lubricating zinc, magnesium, aluminum or calcium stearates, then call the resulting mix sanding sealer. It is usually too soft to be used for anything except the first coat or two on raw wood, and then it should be sanded back.

Water-based lacquers

The film properties of water-based sprayable lacquers pretty much mimic those of their brushable evaporative counterparts. If anything, spraying them exacerbates some of the problems. Their high surface tension makes them very sensitive to fish-eye caused by silicone oil and wax contamination (see pp. 74-75), and atomizing the lacquers through a gun further weakens their ability to bite into prior coats. Witness lines are a common problem for those who try to rub these materials up to gloss.

Acrylic   Clear, colorless, fairly brittle resins with poor heat resistance, fair solvent resistance and good stain and scratch resistance, acrylics are the easiest of the water-based lacquers to spray.

Polyacrylic   Polyacrylic is a polyurethane/acrylic mixture that offers toughness and heat resistance, but as the level of polyurethane in the mix goes up, flow-out and stain resistance both go down, and the material gets bluer and hazier.

Polyacrylonitrile   By linking up three different types of resin onto one backbone, manufacturers can offer a combination of characteristics. Polyacrylonitriles are one of the hybrids of the finishing world, offering the handling properties and stain resistance of acrylics, the flexibility and strength of polyurethane, and the favorable appearance provided by the nitrile group.

Nitrocellulose   Water-based nitrocellulose retains most of the desirable traits of nitrocellulose lacquer without the high solvent content that makes the latter a serious air polluter.

Crosslinked finishes

The idea behind the crosslinked finish is that you can develop a combination of otherwise mutually exclusive properties by creating highly durable plastic films right on the surface of the wood. In many cases, you mix two different ingredients to start a chemical reaction, just as when you mix the two parts of epoxy glue to make a very strong, non-shrinking adhesive. In fact, finishes are remarkably similar to adhesives, from how they perform (they form thin layers that adhere well to wood), right down to their chemistry. All crosslinked finishes are reactive, not evaporative, and although most contain solvents that evaporate off quickly, they often have substantially higher solids contents than their solvent-release counterparts.

As with all things that seem too good to be true, crosslinked finishes involve trade-offs. Although they often develop a wide range of final film properties in one neat package, they frequently contain materials that are somewhat hazardous to work with; require tight control of the working environment (temperature, humidity, air flow, etc.); and have specific handling windows that limit the time between mixing and application (called "pot life"), recoat time and even the number of coats. These controls vary greatly among the various brands, so if you want to use a crosslinked finish, read the tech sheet or label carefully before you try it. And whatever you do, be certain you clean out your spray gun before the pot life of the finish has elapsed. Cured coatings adhere just as well to the inside of a spray gun as to wood, and considering the tight working conditions, are even harder to remove.

Catalyzed lacquer, vinyl, CAB   Many evaporative finishes we are familiar with can be made reactive by changing their formulation and adding an activator at application time. Generally the crosslinked versions are tougher, have better scratch, moisture and solvent resistance, and resist cold checking. The most common ones use an acid as the initiator, and although they dry to the touch as quickly as regular lacquer, they take about seven days to cure fully.

Conversion varnish   Very similar to catalyzed lacquers in the strength characteristics they develop and in their drying time, conversion varnishes maintain more of a varnish appearance and generally are somewhat more amber.

Polyester   Polyesters are popular only in industrial settings like finishing assembly lines because their crosslinking agent is hazardous enough to require considerable caution in handling, and because once mixed, they have a very short pot life. Their ultra-high solids content guarantees fast build, and they flow out to level any physical irregularities (like large pores). The result is an exceptionally strong plastic coating that maintains clarity even at high film thickness.

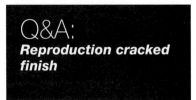

Q&A:
Reproduction cracked finish

Q: I have seen period-furniture reproductions with a "cracked" finish. I find this look appealing and I'd like to know the methods for achieving it.

A: The easiest way to mimic the cracked effect of an old shellac finish is with a special lacquer known as "crackle lacquer," available from some lacquer distributors. This finish handles just like regular lacquer and is sprayed over a smooth coat of gloss lacquer to allow the crackle to occur properly. The size of the cracks in the finish is controlled by the heaviness of the sprayed coat—heavier coats yield bigger areas of cracking. A fine pattern of cracks can also be obtained by coating a sealed or partially finished surface with a mixture of white glue and gilder's whiting that's thinned considerably with water. When the film has dried, exposing it to a heat gun or blow dryer will cause cracking. This method is somewhat more controllable than using crackle lacquer, but the film is milky instead of clear, so it is effective only with white or colored finishes. The glue/whiting mix can be colored with dry powder pigments.

Crosslinked water-based lacquers   Crosslinked water-based lacquers, the most benign of the crosslinked finishes, are simply any water-based materials to which an appropriate crosslinking hardener has been added. Crosslinking adds moisture, scratch and solvent resistance. Two categories of crosslinkers are common for water-based materials. The aziridines work with almost any formulation and are very efficient, but require the proper handling procedures typical of hazardous materials. Carbodiimides, on the other hand, are quite safe, but they seem to work well only on certain resins, so not all water-based formulations will exhibit significant improvements in film qualities with their addition.

Aziridine and carbodiimide hardeners share one lovely trait; they hydrolyze over time. That means that if you add them to a finish and don't use it all up, in a few days the crosslinker disintegrates and the finish reverts back to the solvent-release system it was before. You can use the lacquer at a later date as is, or add a new measure of crosslinker and start the process all over again.

Other considerations

Ease of application and durability are not the only factors to consider when selecting a finish. Some other significant things to take into account are the finish's tendency to fade when exposed to sunlight, its reversibility (is the finish easily stripped or repaired?) and the safety of its solvents.

Coping with sunlight

Just as too much sun causes damage to human skin, so it does to the skin of furniture — the finish. Specifically, the high-energy ultraviolet (UV) range of light causes dyes to fade and finishes to crack, peel and discolor. Ultraviolet rays smash into the molecular structure of the finish or dye, breaking off charged pieces called "free radicals." These free radicals in turn create havoc by breaking down other molecules, and creating even more free radicals in the process. The effect is self accelerating; once it starts, there is no stopping it.

Fortunately, not all finish materials are affected equally. Certain pigments, like red iron oxide, have an enormous resistance to UV degrade, or destruction. Similarly, various clear finish resins hold up to UV attack better than others. Acrylics fare better than nitrocellulose.

Just as we have sun blockers for our skin, there are clear materials that are often added to exterior finishes to slow down the destructive impact of the sun. These additives fall into two broad categories: ultraviolet absorbers (UVAs) and hindered amine light stabilizers (HALS). The UVAs act by absorbing UV photons before they have a chance to break up molecules and create free radicals. The HALS take free radicals out of circulation after they are formed. UVAs and HALS have a synergistic relationship; working together, they are significantly more effective than either one alone. As a result, formulators often allude to UVAs when they are actually talking about a combination of both UVAs and HALS. UVA and HALS additives extend the life of exterior finishes and allow finishers to work with less fade-resistant colorants. Unfortunately, manufacturers don't always tell you when they have added UVAs and HALS, but more have been doing it lately.

Why don't companies sell straight UVAs and HALS for you to add to your favorite finish? There are two reasons. The first is that certain additives work with only certain resins, and many finishers don't know what resins are in their favorite coatings. The second, and more troublesome, reason is that the amount that can be added to a coating is very specific. Too little additive and you don't accomplish anything; too much, and you get an exudate—a sticky, yellowish liquid that oozes out of the finish and sits on top. Not a pretty sight. To make matters worse, the amount required is based not on the total volume of the finish material but on the resin weight, expressed as the percentage by weight of the resin to the total mix. Most manufacturers do not offer this information to the consumer. Besides, the mathematical calculations and precise measuring needed to get the right proportions of UVAs and HALS into a given finish are difficult enough to guarantee plenty of foul-ups, and a proportionate number of lawsuits.

Reversibility

You might be tempted to do something about the deteriorated finish on "that highboy thing that used to belong to Great Aunt Beulah." If possible, resist the temptation, at least until you've had a chance to make sure that the piece is not a particularly valuable antique or collectible. Most antiques lose a large part of their value if the original finish is removed.

Even if you find out that the finish is not valuable—and it's usually not—there is still a good argument for reversibility (the concept that you should not do anything to a piece that cannot be reversed later). As far as finishes are concerned, that often means sticking to those that are easily removable, and avoiding very durable and hard-to-strip crosslinked coatings.

If you are going to refinish on top of an existing finish to save and protect it, it is a good idea to consider a finish that can be separated from the original without destroying it. French polish, which is actually just shellac, is often chosen to spruce up old oil varnish because it lies on top of the old finish rather than biting into it. The shellac can be revived indefinitely without being removed, and can be carefully lifted

Q&A:
A finish that doesn't yellow with age

Q: I have just received an order for kitchen cabinets that are to be finished with a white pickling stain. I have been told that all finishes of this type turn to a yellowish color after a short period of time. We are hoping to avoid that so that the white floor and appliances will remain compatible.

A: Most pickled finishes do yellow with time, but the culprit is not the white pigment. The yellowing is a discoloration of the clear binder and/or top coat used as the matrix to hold the white pigment in place on the wood. In some cases ultraviolet light may also cause the underlying wood to discolor, adding to the amber effect.

To avoid yellowing, use clear binders that are "water-white," which means clear transparent (non-amber), and that are ultraviolet (UV) stable. As an extra measure of protection, choose a material that also contains UV absorbers. Several of the water-based polyurethanes and acrylics would work, as would some solvent-based acrylics (primarily auto finishes) and some cellulose acetate butyrate (CAB) lacquers.

from the old varnish at some later date if the need arises. Finally, if you decide to strip and refinish a piece completely, you might want to choose a finish that is appropriate to the design and period of the furniture. A new super polyurethane on the market may be more durable, but there is a lot to be said for recreating the look that the original craftsman had in mind when the wood was young.

Solvent safety

You'll notice that the charts on pp. 24-27 list the thinning solvent for most finishes—at least, those that can be thinned. There are a lot of hazardous materials on the chart, and it is worth talking about them if we are going to use them.

Probably the greatest danger from finish solvents is the most immediate one: fire. Most of the thinners used in solvent coatings will ignite at fairly low temperatures, so it is important to keep your work area free of sparks or open flames. It is also a good idea to avoid exposed heating elements, like those found on inexpensive portable electric heaters. Even though they don't spark or flame, they are hot enough to bring the solvent fumes to their auto-ignition point (the temperature at which they will ignite without a spark).

With some solvents, explosion is a threat. The smallest concentration of solvent fumes in air that can cause an explosion is called the Lower Explosive Limit (LEL). Good ventilation is the key to avoiding reaching the LEL. As you design the air flow in your finishing area, bear in mind that most solvent fumes are heavier than air, so they tend to collect at ground level. If the floor is wood or wood over a plaster ceiling, think about what is below you. Fumes can easily pass through the floor and get trapped in the basement below, waiting to surprise anyone who walks in and throws an electrical switch or lights a match. Fume concentrations should be a particular concern if your furnace is below your work area; furnaces kick on automatically.

Less immediate, but still important, is the way solvents affect us biologically. Individuals react differently to chemicals. Some people react violently to certain materials that others barely notice. It goes without saying that if a solvent bothers you, avoid it and the finish it thins. There are plenty of other options in these pages so that you can enjoy finishing without discomfort. But even when you don't notice it, certain solvents can have a deleterious effect on our health. Luckily, most of the materials we come in contact with are quite safe. Even those that are more dangerous usually cause trouble only in large cumulative doses, and pose little worry for the occasional finisher or hobbyist. Still, it is a good idea to wear protective gear—gloves for solvents that enter through the skin, respirators for solvents that enter through the lungs, and goggles for anything that is likely to hurt the eyes.

How can you tell if a solvent is dangerous, very flammable, or how much it takes to hit the LEL? I'm glad you asked. Every finish manufacturer is required to issue a Material Safety Data Sheet (MSDS) for every product, and most manufacturers will send you a copy if you request it. On it you will find a wealth of information about the material, including any hazardous substances in it, the suggested exposure limits, the flash point and LEL of any solvents, safe handling practices, protective gear needed, and even what to do in case of a spill. These data sheets are not always easy to decipher, but they are getting better. Some of the more obscure acronyms on the MSDS, like TLV (Threshold Limit Value), are explained in the Glossary on pp. 204-209.

Reading the Label

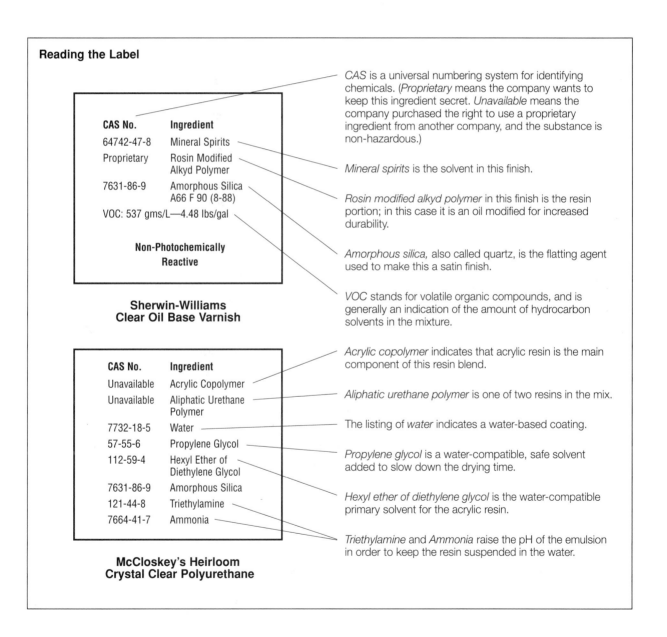

CAS No.   **Ingredient**
64742-47-8   Mineral Spirits
Proprietary   Rosin Modified Alkyd Polymer
7631-86-9   Amorphous Silica A66 F 90 (8-88)
VOC: 537 gms/L—4.48 lbs/gal

Non-Photochemically Reactive

Sherwin-Williams Clear Oil Base Varnish

CAS is a universal numbering system for identifying chemicals. (*Proprietary* means the company wants to keep this ingredient secret. *Unavailable* means the company purchased the right to use a proprietary ingredient from another company, and the substance is non-hazardous.)

Mineral spirits is the solvent in this finish.

Rosin modified alkyd polymer in this finish is the resin portion; in this case it is an oil modified for increased durability.

Amorphous silica, also called quartz, is the flatting agent used to make this a satin finish.

VOC stands for volatile organic compounds, and is generally an indication of the amount of hydrocarbon solvents in the mixture.

CAS No.   **Ingredient**
Unavailable   Acrylic Copolymer
Unavailable   Aliphatic Urethane Polymer
7732-18-5   Water
57-55-6   Propylene Glycol
112-59-4   Hexyl Ether of Diethylene Glycol
7631-86-9   Amorphous Silica
121-44-8   Triethylamine
7664-41-7   Ammonia

McCloskey's Heirloom Crystal Clear Polyurethane

Acrylic copolymer indicates that acrylic resin is the main component of this resin blend.

Aliphatic urethane polymer is one of two resins in the mix.

The listing of *water* indicates a water-based coating.

Propylene glycol is a water-compatible, safe solvent added to slow down the drying time.

Hexyl ether of diethylene glycol is the water-compatible primary solvent for the acrylic resin.

Triethylamine and *Ammonia* raise the pH of the emulsion in order to keep the resin suspended in the water.

CHOOSING A FINISH:
Brushables and Wipe-Ons

Brushable finishes

	Shellac	Lacquer	Oil varnish	Polyurethane varnish	Enamel	Spar varnish (oil/phenolic)
Type of film former E = evaporative, R = reactive	E	E	R	R		R
Thinning solvent A = denatured alcohol, L = lacquer thinner M = mineral spirits or naphtha, T = toluene, W = deionized water	A	L	M	M		M
Dry/cure time	30 min.	20 min.	2-6 hrs.	2-6 hrs.		4-8 hrs.
Brittleness/flexibility 1 = brittle ◀▶ 5 = very flexible	2	2	4	4		5
Durability 1 = poor ◀▶ 5 = excellent	2	3	3	4		3
Stain resistance 1 = poor ◀▶ 5 = excellent	4	4	3	4		3
Heat resistance 1 = poor ◀▶ 5 = excellent	1	1	2	3		3
Moisture resistance 1 = poor ◀▶ 5 = excellent	3 (dewaxed)	3	4	5		5
Solvent resistance 1 = poor ◀▶ 5 = excellent	1	1	3	4		4
Adhesion 1 = poor ◀▶ 5 = excellent	5	5	4	4		4
Ease of use 1 = poor ◀▶ 5 = excellent	4	4	3	3		3
Compatibility 1 = poor ◀▶ 5 = excellent	5	3	3	3		3
Clarity 1 = poor ◀▶ 5 = excellent	5	5	5	3		3
Color	amber	amber	amber	amber		lt. brown
Best applicator	fitch	fitch	china	china		china
Flammability F = flammable, NF = nonflammable	F	F	NF	NF		NF
Safety NH = nonhazardous, H = hazardous, VH = very hazardous	NH	H	NH	NH		NH
Protective equipment	gloves	gloves, mask	goggles	goggles		goggles
Page references Finish characteristics, application tips	9, 148	10, 148	10, 147	10, 147	10	10

The term "enamel" is widely used to define almost any type of coating, and hence has no specific meaning. For coating characteristics, refer to the modifier, for example, "latex" enamel or "oil" enamel.

| Water-based varnishes | | Wipe-on finishes | | | | Gel finishes | | | | |
Acrylic	Polyurethane	Shellac	Danish oil	Linseed oil (raw and boiled)	Tung oil	Oil	Oil/ polyurethane	Wax	Water-based polyurethane	Moisture-cured polyurethane
E	E	E	R	R	R	R	R	E	E	R
W	W	A	M	M	M			M		
30 min./ 30 days	30 min./ 30 days	10 min.	4-6 hrs.	24 hrs./ 3 days	6 hrs.	2 hrs.	2 hrs.	15 min.	15 min.	4 hrs.
3	4	2	4	4	4	4	4		4	1
3	4	1	1	1	1	1	1	1	2	5
3	2	2	1	1	2	3	3	1	2	4
2	3	1	1	1	1	2	2	1	2	3
4	4	1	1	1	1	2	2	3	3	5
2	2	1	1	1	1	1	1	1	2	5
3	2	5	5	5	5	5	5	5	4	5+
3	3	5	5	5	5	5	5	5	5	5
1	1	5	5	5	5	5	5	5	3	1
2	2	5	5	5	5	5	5	3	2	5
clear	bluish	amber	amber	amber	amber	amber	amber	tan	bluish	clear
nylon or pad	nylon or pad	rag	rag	rag	rag	rag	rag	rag	rag	rag
NF	NF	F	NF	NF	NF	NF	NF	NF	NF	F
NH	NH	NH	NH	NH	NH	NH	NH	NH	NH	VH
goggles	goggles	gloves	goggles	goggles	goggles	goggles	goggles	goggles	goggles	cartridge mask, gloves
13, 148	13, 148	14, 153	15, 151	15, 151	16, 151	16, 153	16, 153	16, 153	16, 153	16

CHOOSING A FINISH:
Sprayables

	Shellac	Nitro-cellulose	Acrylic	CAB
Sprayable finishes				
		Lacquers		
Type of film former E = evaporative, R = reactive	E	E	E	E
Thinning solvent A = denatured alcohol, L = lacquer thinner, M = mineral spirits or naphtha, T = toluene, W = deionized water	A	L	L	L
Dry/cure time	10 min.	10 min.	10 min.	10 min.
Brittleness/flexibility 1 = brittle ◄► 5 = very flexible	2	1	2	3
Durability 1 = poor ◄► 5 = excellent	2	3	3	4
Stain resistance 1 = poor ◄► 5 = excellent	4	4	4	4
Heat resistance 1 = poor ◄► 5 = excellent	1	1	1	1
Moisture resistance 1 = poor ◄► 5 = excellent	3 (dewaxed)	3	3	4
Solvent resistance 1 = poor ◄► 5 = excellent	1	1	1	2
Adhesion 1 = poor ◄► 5 = excellent	5	5	5	5
Ease of use 1 = poor ◄► 5 = excellent	4	4	4	4
Compatibility 1 = poor ◄► 5 = excellent	5	3	3	3
Clarity 1 = poor ◄► 5 = excellent	5	5	5	4
Color	amber	amber	clear	bluish
Best applicator SS = stainless-steel fluid passages *do not use aluminum	steel or SS*	any gun	any gun	any gun
Flammability F = flammable, NF = nonflammable	F	F	F	F
Safety NH = nonhazardous, H = hazardous, VH = very hazardous	NH	H	H	H
Protective equipment	vapor mask	vapor mask	vapor mask	vapor mask
Page references Finish characteristics, application tips	17, 155	17, 157	17, 157	17, 157

		Water-based lacquers				Crosslinked finishes			Water-based crosslinked finishes	
Vinyl	Urethane lacquer	Acrylic	Polyurethane	Polyacrylo-nitrile	Nitro-cellulose	Catalyzed lacquer, vinyl, CAB	Conversion varnish	Polyester	Aziridine	Carbo-diimide
E	E	E	E	E	E	R	R	R	R	R
T	L	W	W	W	W					
10 min.	10 min.	15 min.	15 min.	15 min.	15 min.	10 min./ 24 hrs.	10 min./ 24 hrs.	30 min./ 8 hrs.	15 min./ 2 days	15 min./ 5 days
4	4	2	4	2	1	4	4	1	4	4
1	4	2	3	3	3	5	5	5	5	5
2	4	3	2	2	4	5	5	5	5	5
1	2	1	3	4	1	5	5	5	3	3
5	4	2	2	2	3	5	5	5	5	5
2	2	2	2	3	1	5	5	5	3	3
5	5	3	2	2	3	4	4	3	2	2
4	4	1	1	1	1	2	2	2	1	1
5	3	1	1	1	1	1	1	1	1	1
3	4	2	1	2	3	3	3	4	2	2
clear	amber	clear	bluish	amber	amber	clear	amber	clear	clear	clear
any gun	any gun	SS	SS	SS	SS	SS	SS	SS	SS	SS
F	F	NF	NF	NF	NF	F	F	F	NF	NF
H	H	NH	NH	NH	NH	H	H	VH	VH	NH
vapor mask	vapor mask	vapor mask	vapor mask	vapor mask	vapor mask	vapor mask	vapor mask	vapor mask	vapor mask	vapor mask
18, 157	18, 157	18, 159	18, 159	19, 159	19, 159	19, 161	20, 161	20, 161	20	20

CHAPTER 2
Tools of the Trade

Once you've decided on the perfect finish for your project, you have to choose the proper application tools. An inappropriate rag, brush or pad can turn a simple, pleasant operation into a nightmare, whereas selecting the right applicator at least portends good results. In some cases, the finish limits your options. For example, wipe-on finishes are formulated to go on easily with a rag and do not require brushes or spray guns. In other instances, there is enough latitude so that you can base your decision on your personal preference, finishing style or budget. In this chapter we will go over some of the applicator choices available to you and talk about their strengths and weaknesses, as well as how to get the most out of each one.

Brushes

Mention finishing to most people, and the image of a brush comes to mind. Brushes are not the only tools finishers use to get material onto wood, but they are certainly one of the most common, and they have been around for a long time. Brushes are handy, cost effective and versatile. They can coat any size, shape or configuration of piece with just about any material and do it without waste. Properly cared for, they can be used for years, and even the best-quality brushes are a bargain when compared to other applicators (such as spray systems) or when viewed against the value of work they do.

Finishing tools can range from the mundane to the exotic. Some of Dresdner's include foam pads, kitchen utensils and credit cards, as well as badger, horse and sable-hair brushes.

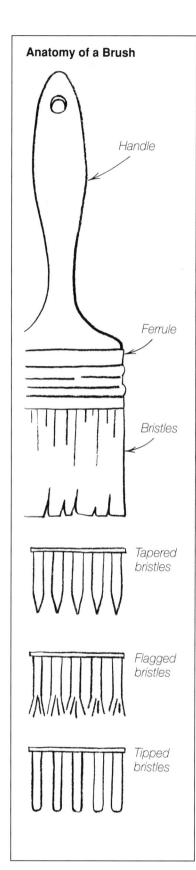

Anatomy of a Brush

Handle

Ferrule

Bristles

Tapered
bristles

Flagged
bristles

Tipped
bristles

Brushes used for finishing consist of three major parts: the handle at one end, the bristles at the other, and the ferrule, which joins the bristles to the handle. Buying a brush can be intimidating because, at first glance, there seems to be an almost endless variety. In reality, with just a few rules of thumb, you will be able to choose a brush that is right for both your style and the material you'll be applying.

Brushes can be divided into categories based on three sets of criteria: the structure of the bristle, the type of bristle and the structure of the brush. Understanding the major differences in these three categories will make it easy to choose the right brush for a particular job. Let's start from the tip and work back.

Structure of the bristle

If you look carefully at the very end of each of the hairs or bristles in a brush, you will notice that they come in three configurations. This is true whether the bristles are natural animal hair or synthetic fibers. Tapered bristles thin to a point from the ferrule to the end of the brush. Flagged bristles split into several smaller fibers at the end, and look like the split ends that hair commercials warn us about. Tipped bristles end abruptly, like the ends of the bristles in a toothbrush.

Usually, the tip style is far less important than the type of fiber, but there are cases when one type is best avoided. Because they tend to be a little softer at the very end, flagged or tapered bristles are usually better for varnishes that show brush marks easily. Classic oil varnishes, like spar varnish or alkyd urethane (polyurethane) varnish, lay out best if you "tip them off," and flagged or tapered ends are best for that operation. To tip off, you drag just the very tip of the brush lightly across the surface of the wet varnish in the direction of the grain. This gentle dragging of the soft ends will remove air bubbles and blend the streaked brush marks that sometimes show up as you apply the varnish. On the other hand, flagged tips can be a nightmare with some water-based coatings because they tend to cause foaming by creating more bubbles as the splayed tips drag through the thin material. Consequently, if you are using thin, water-based coatings, such as clear finishes, tapered or tipped ends are your best choice.

Type of bristle

Bristles may be either natural fibers or synthetic fibers. However, the single most important aspect of the brush fiber, whether synthetic or natural, is its degree of flexibility or stiffness. Thin, fast-drying finishes work best with soft, flexible brushes; thick, slow-drying materials demand a stiffer bristle.

Before water-based coatings and latex paints, natural bristle brushes were viewed as undeniably superior. In fact, they are still preferred by most finishers for oil-based and solvent-based coatings, such as shel-

The brush on the left is splayed from water. Splaying is a common problem when natural-fiber bristles are used with water-based finishes.

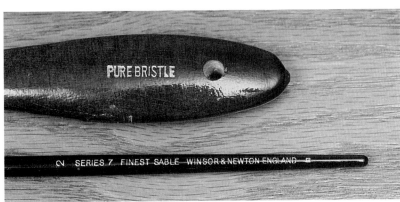

The type of bristle is usually identified on the handle of the brush.

lac, traditional varnish, brushing lacquer and alkyd urethane (polyurethane) varnish. Natural-fiber brushes hold these materials well and release them evenly. However, most natural hair splays when put into water and becomes uncontrollable in short order. If you are using a water-based (latex) finish, stay with a synthetic-fiber bristle.

Synthetic-fiber bristles, like leisure suits, are offered in nylon, polyester and nylon/polyester blends. Assuming that the diameter of the fiber is the same, nylon is the softest of the three. A nylon brush is best for very thin materials, especially thin, water-based varnishes. Polyester, the stiffest of the synthetics, is meant for heavy-bodied coatings that would overpower a nylon bristle. The nylon/polyester blends are good all-purpose brushes that fall somewhere in between on the stiffness scale. Some polyester blends have been specifically designed to work with solvent-based coatings as well as to offer the finisher one brush that can apply the widest variety of materials. A good-quality synthetic blend can often outperform a cheap, inferior bristle brush, even with solvent-based finishes. However, if you can afford it, it is still best to get the brush that is ideal for the job at hand.

Natural-bristle brushes have been made using the hair of almost every animal that grows it, including squirrels, badgers, hogs, sables, polecats, horses, oxen and even humans. Natural hair is the first choice for solvent-based coatings and paint removers because, unlike synthetics, hair is unaffected by even the harshest hydrocarbon solvents that show up in lacquers and paint strippers. Variations in the thickness, length, and stiffness of the hair result in brushes that behave differently, and make possible a vast array of specialty brushes.

Although there are many more varieties of natural hair than synthetic fibers used in brushes, the critical variable is still the same: the flexibility or stiffness of the bristle. Very flexible bristles are used for thin materials, and stiffer types of hair are best for thicker, more viscous coatings. But when it comes to natural fibers, the enormous disparity in price will also affect your choice. For example, camel hair behaves much like squirrel hair, but is quite a bit cheaper. Similarly, ox hair is a close match for badger, which is more expensive.

China bristle   The most common natural fibers for garden-variety paintbrushes are either white or black China bristle. Most brushes you will find on the paint-store or hardware-store rack will be of this widely used fiber. China or Chinese bristle is the generic name for hog hair, whether or not it actually comes from China. Both colors are excellent for oil and solvent-based finishes, stains and fillers. Although most brushes designed for applying marine (boat) coatings are made with white rather than black China bristle, the reason behind this is more traditional than practical. In fact, when black China bristle is scarce, white and grey bristles are often dyed black.

Specialty brushes   Other natural hair is used for a wide range of specialty brushes. The choice of hair is based on the length a particular type of hair grows, along with its relative stiffness or flexibility. In most cases, the name is descriptive of the animal that it comes from (e.g., sable, fitch, ox). One curious exception is camel hair, which, as you've probably guessed, does not come from a camel. Camel-hair brushes have very soft, flexible bristles, and are good blending or touch-up brushes. Legend has it that an Englishman named Camle is credited with developing this style of brush using squirrel hair, and a corruption of the spelling of his name became associated with this excellent applicator. Because of the present scarcity and cost of English squirrel hair, most camel brushes are now made from pony hair.

Fitch is another name for polecat or skunk, and the hair is exceptionally thin, soft and pliable. Relatively short bristles ares set in an oversized ferrule, making a brush that is excellent for applying shellac.

The sable, a weasel-like relative of the marten, provides one of the most expensive of the natural hairs. Red sable is unusually resilient and will shape to a fine, controllable point, making it ideal for touch-up brushes. A good red sable brush will allow you to lay down an extremely thin grain line with its well-defined point.

Brushes come in various bristle types, shapes and sizes. This array includes (left to right) a rectangular-format, natural China bristle brush; a round-format, natural China bristle brush; a fitch brush for shellac; a nylon brush for water-based coatings; and (top to bottom) a badger-hair brush; a lettering quill; a camel-hair touch-up brush; a red sable touch-up brush; a dagger striper; pin-striping quills.

Dagger stripers and quills are fine, long-haired brushes used primarily for pinstriping, and the best ones are still made from squirrel hair. As they are pulled across the surface, the paint tensions the hairs so that they maintain a uniform width, and their long length allows them to feed out paint for a considerable distance while maintaining a constant density of coating.

Badger brushes are distinctive two-toned, black and white haired brushes. They are moderately stiff and supple, and are favored for applying violin varnish and gold size. Badger hair is also used in shaving brushes.

Top or block grainers, flap grainers and pipe-stem grainers, which are designed for *faux bois* or fake wood grain, are fast becoming scarce. Flap grainers have extra long, stiff, springy bristles; top grainers are dense with turned-over ends; and pipe-stem grainers are like a row of touch-up brushes evenly spaced in one wide handle.

Gilder's tip, a brush without a handle, consists of a thin row of camel hair set into a cardboard ferrule. It never actually gets wet or touches finish. Its sole purpose is to pick up and place fine gold leaf. The tip is rubbed across a surface to generate a static charge just strong enough to hold the gold and release it without tearing.

Structure of the brush

Both natural-fiber and synthetic-fiber brushes are made the same way; the bristles are set into an epoxy plug inside the ferrule, which connects the handle to the hair. The key differences in a brush's structure all revolve around the size and shape of the bundle of fibers that constitutes the bristle portion. The handle is almost completely irrelevant since most finishers do not ever use it except perhaps when they are cleaning the brush.

Brush bristles are set into an epoxy plug inside the ferrule, which connects the handle to the hair.

Brushes can be round, rectangular, wide and flat, or squarish. Picking a shape is largely a matter of what appeals to your hand and temperament. As for size, a bigger brush will hold more finish and cover a wider area on each pass, but it is more important to get a brush that feels comfortable and controllable to you. After all, even a small brush will cover a large area, given enough time. That leaves the two factors that are somewhat controlled by the finish material: bristle length and end shape.

In addition to holding more paint, longer bristles are floppier; shortening the bristles stiffens them up. Many specialty brushes take advantage of these traits, like extra long pinstriping quills and short fitch brushes for shellac. Brush manufacturers take into account the firmness of the bristle when they decide on the brush's length, and they usually come up with an appropriate combination. Still, it is not unusual to spot cheap brushes sporting bristles that are way too short for their relatively high rigidity.

The ends of the bristle bundle are either square or chisel trimmed. A square trim means that the fibers are lopped off so that they are all the same length. A chisel trim is what we woodworkers would call a knife edge if it appeared on a cutting tool; the sides of the brush taper to a central ridge, like an A-frame roof. The chisel trim is better for tipping off, or for coatings that want a soft trailing edge. For the vast majority of furniture finishes, both solvent and water-based, a chisel-trim end is a better choice.

Buying a brush

Once you've decided on the type of brush you need, you'll be faced with the question of cost. Is a more expensive brush really better? Usually, yes! In what way? Will it save time, last longer, leave a better surface? All of the above. Will a cheaper brush lose its hair as quickly as some of us are losing ours? Yes, indeed.

When it comes to brushes, there is a fairly direct relationship between cost and quality. Better brushes are more expensive, and cheaper brushes are almost always worse. A good brush will carry and deliver more paint, will lay the coating out better, smoother and more evenly, and will last longer than its cheaper counterpart. It is almost impossible to get a really good finish surface using a junky brush. When you consider how much you can do with a brush, and the amount of time, finish and aggravation you can save by buying quality, it is surprising how inexpensive a really top-notch brush can be.

Most attributes of a good brush are obvious. Look at the length of the hair, the evenness of the trim whether it is chisel or square, and the straightness and uniformity of the bristles. Flex the bristles against your hand. They should feel soft and have good springback in accordance with the brush's function. With synthetic-bristle brushes especially, there are times when the differences are subtle. Occasionally you will run across two synthetic bristle brushes that look and feel the same, and are both made of the same material in the same diameter, but have very different prices. To save money, brush makers often produce brushes from hollow bristles instead of solid. Hollow bristles will perform comparably initially, but they tend to flag and break more easily than solid bristles. When in doubt, buy the more expensive brush.

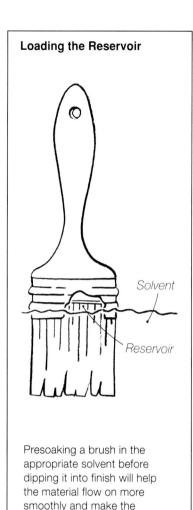

Solvent

Reservoir

Presoaking a brush in the appropriate solvent before dipping it into finish will help the material flow on more smoothly and make the brush easier to clean.

Is there a place in the workshop for bargain-bin brushes? Yes, but it is limited. Use bargain synthetics for applying bleach (bleach destroys natural hair) and cheap natural hair for applying paint remover (which may melt some synthetics). But when it comes to applying finish, if you consider the cost of wood, finishes and your time, a cheap brush is no bargain.

Foam brushes are another story altogether. They are not really brushes, but rather foam sponges on sticks. A few types of material respond well to these applicators—mostly those that are designed to be applied by rag or sponge. However, at best, they should be considered to be firmly in a class with the cheap, throwaway brushes. The most likely use for these hybrids is with materials that don't demand much surface control but are very problematic to clean up, such as stains and bleaches. Don't try to use them with lacquer or stripper, though. You're likely to end up with a melted sponge on a stick.

Caring for your brushes

The first step in the proper care of a brush occurs before you use it, the first time and every time thereafter. Both natural-bristle and synthetic-bristle brushes should be soaked in the appropriate solvent before the brush is dipped into paint. The correct solvent is whatever is used to thin and clean up the particular coating—water for latexes, paint thinner for oil varnishes, lacquer thinner for brushing lacquer, and so on. Immerse the brush into the solvent all the way up to the ferrule, and leave it there for a few minutes. When you are ready to paint, shake hard or wipe off any excess before dipping the brush into the coating material.

There are several reasons for presoaking the brush. The first is that it loads the reservoir. This is the area inside the bundle of bristles just below the ferrule. Although the reservoir is technically not part of the working brush—only one-third to one-half of the brush end gets dipped in paint and touches the wood surface—it nevertheless plays an important role in how the brush works. This reservoir of solvent acts as a buffer to keep the top edge of the paint on the brush liquid and flowing. Without it, the upper line of the paint would dry while the brush was in use. A dried crust of paint will effectively shorten the flexible length of the bristle, changing its character, and may also drop flakes of dried finish onto your wet coating.

In addition, presoaking makes cleanup much easier because it prevents paint from drying inside that hard-to-reach area just below the ferrule. When nylon brushes are used with water-based coatings, there is a further reason for presoaking. Although nylon will not splay or deform in water, it will absorb a certain amount. Presoaking in water loads not only the reservoir, but also the bristles themselves, thereby preventing them from absorbing paint that would be very difficult to remove after the job was done.

Once you have finished painting, the cleaning sequence is straightforward. Remove the bulk of the paint in the brush by wiping it across the edge of the container, or by brushing out the excess onto scrap wood or cardboard. Then clean off all remaining paint by massaging the bristles in the appropriate solvent. Merely soaking is not enough. Make sure you get all the way up toward the ferrule, but be gentle — the hair is held in only with glue. Squeeze out the excess solvent, then remove as much as possible by shaking it out hard, or by spinning the brush between your hands. The brush should now look and feel clean, and only slightly damp.

Next, wash the entire length of the bristles in warm water and a sudsy soap (I prefer shaving soap) and rinse until all of the soap is removed. Once again, shake or spin off as much water as possible.

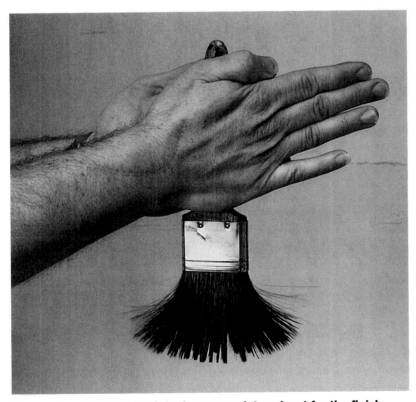

Clean a brush by soaking it in the appropriate solvent for the finish. Squeeze out the excess, and then spin the brush between your hands to remove most of the rest.

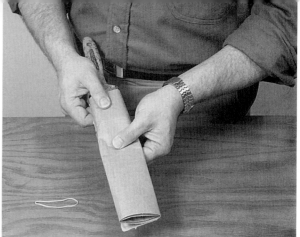

After spinning out the water, wrap the brush with absorbent brown paper (above), locate the tips of the bristles (above right) and fold the paper over on itself about 2 in. past the ends of the bristles (right). Secure the wrap with a bit of tape or a rubber band.

Finally, wrap up the brush in paper. Lay the brush onto unprinted absorbent paper (brown paper bags are perfect) that is at least twice as long and four times as wide as the bristles. The paper should extend from the top of the ferrule past the end of the bristles, and well off to one side. Roll the paper tightly around the ferrule, allowing it to form an absorbent, protective sheath around the bristles. Fold the paper over on itself about 2 in. past the end of the bristles, with the crease parallel to the widest direction of the ferrule (any direction for a round brush) and secure it with a bit of tape, rubber band, or just the weight of the brush itself. This paper shroud will wick off all the excess water while it is forcing the ends of the bristles to remold themselves into their original shape. Leave the paper on until you are ready to use the brush again—it also acts as a protector. When you unwrap the brush, it will look and feel as it did when it was new—pliable, clean and correctly shaped.

This procedure seems like a lot of work when compared to the concept of the throwaway brush, but there are serious benefits to good habits. I have some China, squirrel and sable brushes that are in new condition after more than ten years of intermittent service. I have had the pleasure and performance advantages of using the best brushes made. I waste no time on repeated panic trips to the hardware store looking for the right brush. And, over the long haul, I have spent less money. Good habits allow you to afford good equipment, and good equipment encourages good habits.

How to use a brush

Like any woodworking tool, brushes are merely an extension of your hand, and so any technique that works for you is just dandy. I've seen finishers achieve remarkable results with unorthodox techniques, and if your grip falls into that category, don't be swayed by what others tell you. The rules of brush handling are like rules of etiquette: they are there as guidelines when you are feeling unsure of how to proceed.

The best way to control a brush is to wrap your fingers and thumb around opposite sides of the ferrule, leaving the base of the handle resting in the crook of your hand. If you think of the brush bristles as extensions of your fingers, this grip makes a lot of sense. It positions the brush comfortably and aligns bristles with your hand, virtually forcing you to move the brush efficiently, whether you are coating vertically or horizontally. This grip also gives you a lot of control over the bristles, since you are so close to their ends, and lets you feel their resistance on the wood surface.

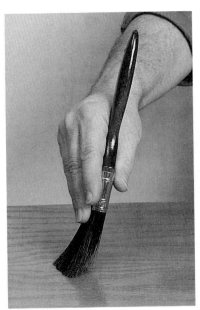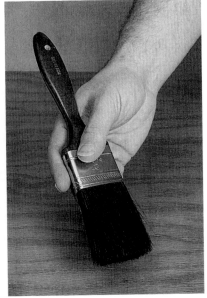

The ideal brush position is as an extension of your fingers. Wrap your fingers and thumb around opposite sides of the ferrule, in whatever grip feels comfortable.

Dip the end of the brush into the finish about one-third to one-half of the way up toward the ferrule, then touch the tip to the side of the container to prevent drips. Wiping it off will simply unload it again. Move the brush from your arm, not your wrist. Hold it at a comfortable angle—anywhere between 45° and 90° to the surface of the wood—and apply enough pressure so that the ends deflect slightly. If the finish requires tipping off (see p. 30), do it lightly with the brush at 90° and just the tips dragging the surface.

To load a brush with finish, dip about one-third of the bristles into the finish, then touch the tips against the side of the container to prevent drips.

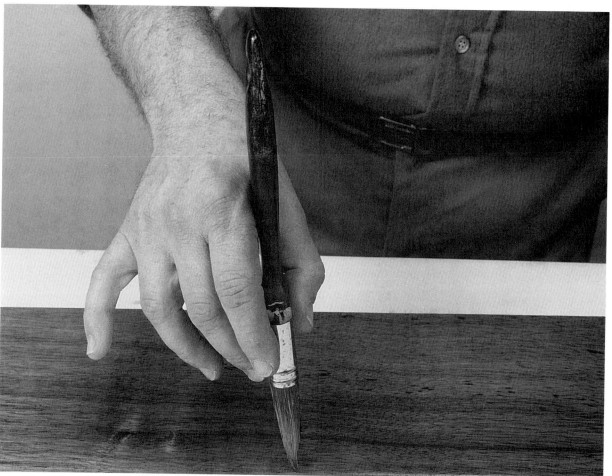

When tipping off, drag just the tips of the bristles very lightly across the wet varnish. Tipping off removes air bubbles and blends in brush marks.

Paint rollers and pads

Paint rollers are the darlings of the drywall set because they cover huge areas very quickly with little wasted paint. They are less popular among woodworkers, because they are hard to control in tight or small spaces and they don't leave a very good finish surface. They are sometimes used for floor finishing, where there are large areas to cover that no one will be looking at too closely. Short-nap rollers will offer a smoother layout, and because of the texturing effect of the nap, they are best on slow-drying finishes that have plenty of time to flow out and hide roughness.

Paint pads, on the other hand, are quickly gaining a following with woodworkers, in part because of the increased use of water-based finishes. Essentially short-nap polyester brushes with a huge tip area, paint pads will move a lot of paint very quickly with almost no waste. They work especially well with clear water-based coatings. The ultra-short hair length all but eliminates the foaming that is common to these touchy finishes, and the large surface area holds a good bit of material without dripping. Unlike a brush, though, it is easy to overload a

Paint pads come in a variety of styles for versatility and ease of handling. They work very well with clear, water-based coatings.

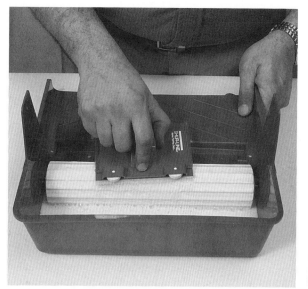 

Load the paint pad from a roller (above), or dip it, then scrape off the excess (above right).

paint pad. It is best to load it from a hard-roller device, or dip it, then lightly scrape it on a straight edge. While you may be tempted to manipulate a brush back and forth several times, the best paint-pad technique is to lay the material down on the first stroke, then repeat the stroke once more in the same direction to smooth it out.

*R*evenge of the Luddites

It was about midday when my boss and I called the shop to check on things. We were on an installation, and had left two men back at the shop with a particularly odious finishing task. One of them was a new employee, so it was only prudent to call. When Katie, the woman who staffed our office, answered the phone, what she had to report struck fear into our hearts.

One of our house accounts was finishing large wooden frames that held glass doors. The specs called for a water-based finish, and we had been having a world of problems. Neither the finish nor the frames were cooperating with our spray equipment, in spite of several upgrades that turned out to be a waste of money. The frames were too big for the spray booth, and their simple four-sided design and open interior caused us to waste lots of lacquer on overspray in spite of the flat wood surfaces. Even with new equipment, the layout was poor, and the final coat looked like orange peel.

To top it all off, the frames were so unwieldy that it took two people to muscle each one in and out of the spray-booth area. So when Katie told us that one of the men had called in sick, leaving Drew, the new employee, alone, we started to sweat.

"Drew says he'll be finished with these door frames today," Katie informed us. "He asked for $5 early this morning, made a trip to the hardware store, and has been at work ever since. He says the frames look great."

The best paint-pad technique is to lay the finish down on the first stroke, then repeat the stroke in the same direction to smooth it out.

It seemed impossible. One person could barely get one of those frames in the booth alone, and certainly could not have removed it once it was covered in wet lacquer. We hurried back to the shop, fully expecting some sort of disaster and wondering what kind of $5 hardware-store item could adequately replace a whole employee.

Drew was just cleaning up when we arrived. All the frames were laid out on sawhorses exactly as they had been the night before, except that they each had two coats of lacquer. The finish was smooth and free of orange peel, and had been done in less time by one man than was normal for two. On top of that, Drew had used about half the normal amount of the water-based lacquer, and there wasn't so much as a hint of overspray in the air.

"How did you do it?" we asked in amazement. Drew held up a cheap, $3 paint pad with a white nylon nap on a bright red plastic holder. Rather than move the frames to the finish, he had brought the finish to the frames. "Paint pads work great with this water-based stuff," Drew pointed out. "After all, isn't that what latex paint is?" "Besides," he went on, "the pad costs only $3, so you can throw it out if you don't feel like cleaning the thing."

Drew had his coat on and was halfway out the door before my boss shook off his stupor enough to call after him. "What was the other $2 for?" he asked. Drew shrugged slightly as he calmly turned to answer. "Coffee and doughnuts. I woke up late and didn't have time for breakfast."

Cloth rags and paper towels

There are times when the least sophisticated applicator is best. When it comes to staining a piece of wood, I can think of nothing simpler or more satisfying than grabbing an absorbent rag and flooding the surface of the wood with color, then wiping it all off with another cloth. The same goes for thin, penetrating-oil finishes, such as linseed oil or premixed Danish oil, and even the newer, thicker wipe-on varnishes. A bit unorthodox, but very effective, is the concept of applying the first coat of a film-forming sealer, such as shellac, by rag. No matter how evenly you brush or spray a coat of sealer onto wood, you will end up with an uneven coat because wood does not absorb finish evenly. End grain takes in more, close flat grain takes in less. Thus, an evenly applied sealer coat will be heavier in some areas than others. If, on the other hand, you apply it by flooding it on and wiping off the excess while it is still wet, each area will be allowed to absorb as much as it can, but any excess still on the surface will be removed. For many years, I've been letting very thin shellac perform as a self-regulating sealer with this low-tech method. All it takes is a lint-free applicator and a cavalier attitude.

With low-tech applicators, anything goes. I like to use washed, bleached cotton cheesecloth, especially if it's been washed enough to remove the lint, but any material that absorbs is fair game. Sponges, cotton wadding, paper towels, and old diapers are all useful in the finishing room. For thicker materials, I lean toward 3M brand ultra-fine Scotch-Brite nylon pads; they hold a remarkable amount of material, stay wet indefinitely, and, because they contain a mild abrasive, even smooth the wood surface as you work.

Oily rags left in the shop are a fire hazard. Let them dry by hanging them out one layer thick, then dispose of them.

One word of warning: If you are using an absorbent applicator, such as a rag or paper towel, with anything that contains oil, dispose of it carefully and properly. Oily rags are subject to spontaneous combustion. If they are left alone, they can ignite at room temperature even with no outside spark or flame. If possible, incinerate the wipers immediately after using them. If that is not practical, hang them out to dry on a line or table edge one layer thick. When they are completely dry, they can be added to your trash or burned at a later date. Rinsing or wetting them will not make them safe. Once the water dries, you are back at square one.

Just recently, newspapers carried the story of a very serious fire in an urban high-rise. The fire raged for 19 hours, killing three firefighters and doing millions of dollars in damage. The cause of the fire was traced to a work crew that had been refinishing the wood paneling. They had left some linseed-oil-soaked rags in the building at the end of their first day on the job. It took the rags less than five hours to start the blaze.

Goggles, gloves and respirators

As woodworking goes, finishing is one of the safer parts of the job. There are, however, some inherent dangers involved, and safety equipment is as important as good brushes. The charts on pp. 24-27 recommend safety equipment for specific finish categories.

If you are likely to get chemicals splashed in your eyes, wear goggles. This problem is most common when stripping old finish off wood, or when you are mixing solvents into coatings. If you wear glasses anyway, you're probably protected from occasional spatters, but goggles provide more complete protection, particularly from the side.

Some solvents, such as alcohol and dichloromethane, have the ability to enter the human body through the skin. Others may be skin sensitizers, causing rashes or other reactions. If you are putting your hands in solvents, choose gloves that will block them. Neoprene is impervious to virtually all chemicals, and is the first choice for those using paint remover. For applying a finish, you can usually graduate to vinyl or latex gloves, which are thinner and less clumsy. I keep a box of inexpensive disposable vinyl gloves by the bench. They are thin, comfortable and sensitive, and even when they aren't essential for protection, they keep my hands clean.

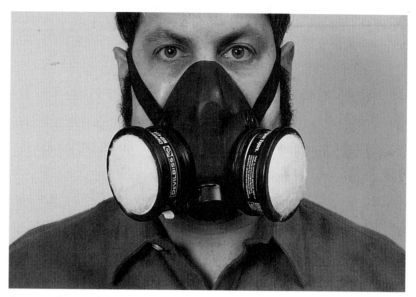

An organic cartridge mask will block many solvent vapors.

Most people who use spray equipment are aware of the importance of an organic vapor respirator to block solvent inhalation, but the same amount of solvent comes off a finish applied by brush. Many hydrocarbon solvents used in finishes can cause long-term health problems to those who are overexposed. An organic cartridge mask will block the bulk of these fumes. Remember that the life of the cartridge is based on its exposure to air, whether or not you are wearing it. When you take it off, seal it in a plastic bag immediately. Most cartridges are good for only about eight hours of use. If you can smell the solvent while wearing the mask, it is time to replace the cartridge.

Spray guns

For many amateur woodworkers, the spray gun has become finishing's version of the Holy Grail. Everybody seems to want one, but few know what to do with it. Still, as the name "gun" implies, there is something inherently powerful about pulling a trigger and releasing a blast of air and lacquer toward the target. But before you succumb to ego over reason, you should know that there are some drawbacks to the glamorous world of spray finishing that may offset any advantage to you.

On the positive side, spraying offers some serious advantages to the high-volume finisher, and there are good reasons why most production shops boast spray booths and compressors. The primary one is speed. A spray gun can coat vast surfaces uniformly in very little time, even if they are intricate with carving, turning, or raised panels. By atomizing the finish material, guns can use fast-drying finishes, like lacquer, and deliver them smoothly and evenly with no brush marks, drips or sags. And a finish gently laid on by gravity and air will not smudge or move glazes and stains layered between coats of finish. This combination of versatility, speedy application and fast drying means that furniture can go out the door much sooner. Consequently, when the combination of fast-drying lacquer and spray guns entered the scene around 1920, it was quickly adopted by the larger finish users.

But spray technology brought with it a loss in transfer efficiency (the measure in percentage of the amount of finish that makes it to the wood surface). A typical compressed-air gun has a transfer efficiency of between 20% and 35%; at best, only about one-third of what goes through the gun lands on the wood. The rest ends up floating in the air, through bounce-back off the surface or overspray that misses the wood entirely. (By way of contrast, a brush has a transfer efficiency of almost 100%.)

In addition, the sprayed finish material has to be fairly thin so that it can be atomized. This means adding more solvent, causing the finish that does get deposited on the wood to shrink more as the solvent evaporates. Consequently, more solvent is released into the air, and thinner layers of finish are deposited per coat.

In the quest for speed there is a lot of waste. As a result, the shop is going to be laden with airborne finish and solvents. To clear the air and isolate the contamination, you need a spray booth with a strong fan to evacuate the contaminants. Because many of these solvents are flammable, the fan motor, lights, and switches in the booth must be explosion proof. Not surprisingly, a proper setup can get expensive.

Over the years, America has had to pay the price for its love of speed and wastefulness. High-solvent spray finishes, along with extensive fossil-fuel use, contribute to the condition we call smog. Solvents release hydrocarbons into the air, which, in the presence of sunlight, create ozone, the dangerous component of smog. These photochemically reactive (light-reacting) hydrocarbons are called volatile organic compounds (VOCs). Since 1978, the Environmental Protection Agency (EPA) has been encouraging finishers, along with other polluters, to cut back on the amount of VOCs emitted into the air. For finishers, they are requesting a two-pronged approach: reduce the amount of solvent in each gallon of finish, and increase the transfer efficiency of the application method.

Q&A: Limiting overspray

Q: I just bought a 2-hp, 20-gal. compressor for spraying finishes and for sandblasting wood and glass. However, when I started to spray water-based polyurethane, I created a fog bank in my basement. What can I do to limit the overspray? I have a standard 1-qt. spray gun, but I'm not sure of the needle size or nozzle size.

A: Standard compressed-air siphon guns typically have at best around a 35% transfer efficiency; hence, only 35% of the finish material you buy ever makes it on to the wood. The rest forms a "fog bank" of waste.

Here are some ways you can mitigate the overspray problem by tweaking your current spray gun. To avoid rust from the water, choose a stainless-steel fluid tip (and its attendant needle) with a fluid aperture of between 0.040 in. and 0.050 in. and an air cap that will draw less than 5 cfm at 30 psi. (Your spray-gun dealer will help you with this conversion, which should cost less than $60.) This combination will allow you to get an acceptable spray fan pattern at around 25 psi, and about as high a transfer efficiency as you can expect from a standard siphon gun. Since your water-based finish is nonflammable, you can most likely get away with a common window fan to evacuate what little overspray you create, but check with your local fire marshal or your insurance company just to make sure.

A spray gun is essentially a carburetor. It atomizes liquid finish (i.e., breaks it up into small droplets), mixes it with air, and directs it outward in a controlled pattern. In an airless gun, the second step is omitted. The liquid flow is adjusted by using a larger or smaller fluid tip, a fluid control valve, or by increasing or decreasing the amount of pressure used to move the fluid. The air volume and pattern are controlled by the size and placement of holes in the air cap, and by the amount of air pressure and volume delivered to the cap. This is true for all spray guns, from high-volume, low-pressure (HVLP) guns to low-volume, high-pressure guns (standard compressed-air guns). But there are differences in how each type of gun achieves its ends.

Both paint formulators and spray-equipment manufacturers are responding with new technology that strives to reduce VOCs while retaining the speed advantages of fast-dry spray finishes, and the results are encouraging. In the coatings field, formulators are offering new materials that match or exceed performance characteristics of lacquer with far less solvent, by using different resins and/or by replacing some of the solvents with non-polluting diluents (inactive thinning agents) like water and carbon dioxide. The spray-equipment field is doing its part as well, and as a result, we are seeing more and more high transfer-efficiency systems. Some, like the HVLP systems, claim to achieve transfer efficiencies as high as 90%. In reality, though, it is difficult to achieve transfer efficiencies that high with most practical applications, and transfer efficiencies of 65% are probably more common. Other systems, such as airless spray guns and the oxymoronic air-assisted airless spray guns, allow much thicker, ultra-low solvent materials to be sprayed at transfer efficiencies of up to 75%, which is still a great improvement. As we go on, you will notice an inverse correlation between transfer efficiency and air pressure at the tip of the gun. Higher air pressure means lower transfer efficiency.

Spray systems

Start a conversation about spray systems, and most people want to talk about spray guns. There is more to it than that. Spray guns are really quite similar. All guns have triggers, regulators and interchangeable tips that let you spray finishes with different viscosities. The real differences occur in the spray system. The key to choosing the right spray system is first determining the finish you want to spray, then finding out the ideal kind of gun for that finish and finally selecting the compressor, filters, regulators and other gear appropriate for that spray gun. The following overview of the various spray systems should give you an idea of which, if any, is right for you.

Siphon-feed systems A siphon-feed system employs relatively low volumes (up to 20 cubic feet per minute [cfm]) of compressed air at relatively high pressures (25 to 100 pounds per square inch [psi]) to move liquid. In a typical siphon-feed spray gun, the air blows across a tube, creating a partial vacuum, which in turn draws the fluid up from the cup. As the fluid is pulled up, the space in the cup must be replaced with air. Siphon cups therefore have an air-intake hole in the cap that must be kept open at all times. The fluid is then atomized through the tip, where it mixes with air that fans out in a controlled pattern.

Regulators at the back of the gun body adjust air and fluid flow respectively. The air-flow regulator cuts back both the volume of air delivered and the width of the pattern. The fluid pin is controlled by the trigger, and its regulator is just a governor. In fact, it should always be full open when the trigger is pulled. The main purpose of the fluid-

Typical Spray Gun

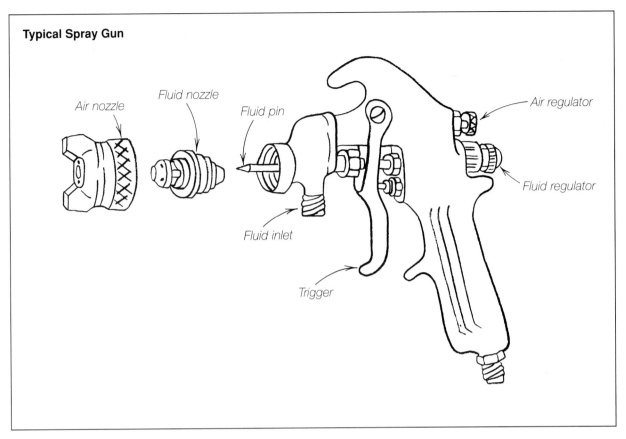

Air nozzle

Fluid nozzle

Fluid pin

Air regulator

Fluid regulator

Fluid inlet

Trigger

Siphon-Feed Hookup

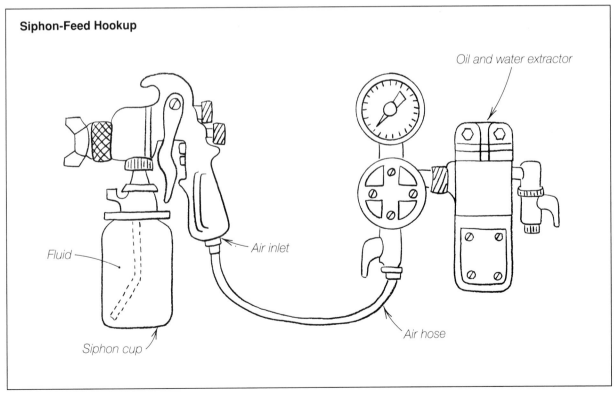

Oil and water extractor

Air inlet

Fluid

Air hose

Siphon cup

regulator knob is to tension the spring behind it so that it shuts off the fluid flow when the trigger is released. To set this spring, unscrew the knob (counterclockwise) almost all the way out, pull the trigger until it stops, and while holding the trigger, screw the knob in (clockwise) until it meets resistance. The correct way to control fluid feed is by changing the size of the fluid tip or by altering the fluid's viscosity.

Pressure-feed systems (pressure pots) A pressure-feed system differs from a standard compressed-air model in how it moves the fluid. Rather than a siphon that draws fluid up, it uses a sealed, pressurized container called a pressure tank, or pressure pot. Instead of an access hole in the lid, it has an intake port through which compressed air is fed. The air, which must be cleaned and regulated by an extractor/regulator, creates pressure in the cup or pot that forces the fluid out. Instead of being drawn into the air flow, it is pushed into it.

A pressure-feed system is both more efficient and more controllable than a siphon-feed system. With it, you can move thicker materials, or separately manipulate the fluid flow with a variable valve that changes the pressure in the pot without altering the air feed. Because the pressurized system does not rely on the rather weak pulling power of a vacuum, it is not limited in distance. The fluid container need not be attached to the gun, but can be far away, connected only by a hose. This in turn means that the size of the fluid container is no longer limited by what you can carry. A pressure pot can be any size from a quart

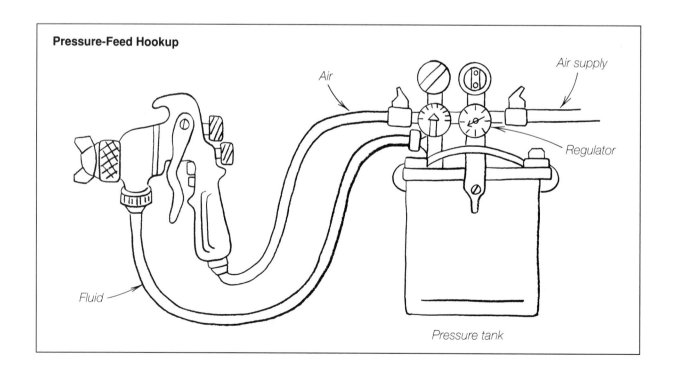

Pressure-Feed Hookup

Air

Air supply

Regulator

Fluid

Pressure tank

In a compressed-air system, the air is cleaned and controlled by an extractor/regulator combination.

A remote pressure pot allows you to spray a large volume of finish without refilling the spray gun.

that is attached to the gun, up to a "tote" (350 gallons) that sits in another part of the building. The most common sizes for pressure pots are 1 qt., 1 gal., 2½ gal., 5 gal. and 10 gal.

High-volume, low-pressure (HVLP) and compressed-air (CAS) systems An HVLP gun works on very low pressures (3 to 10 psi) at high volumes (65 cfm and above). These low pressures will not create a vacuum strong enough to siphon finish material, so all HVLP guns require pressure pots. Rather than use an air compressor that generates cool, moist air at high pressure, an HVLP gun can be fed by a turbine that puts out large volumes of warm, dry air at low pressure. A compressed-air system (or conversion air system) allows an HVLP gun to run off a standard air compressor by readjusting the air with a converter. It is easy to reduce pressure, but creating a high volume is a bit tricky. As a consequence, compressed-air systems are rather inefficient, and demand a fairly large compressor (3 to 5 hp minimum) to run them.

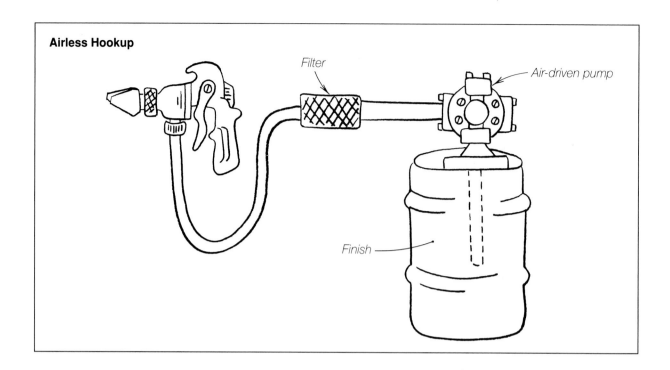

Airless Hookup

Filter

Air-driven pump

Finish

Airless systems Airless rigs do not mix air into the fluid, but merely propel the liquid at high pressure through a shaped tip to create a fan pattern. To generate the high fluid pressures needed, most airless guns rely on a liquid pump rather than a pressurized pot. Although airless systems deliver a large amount of fluid very quickly, they sacrifice quality for speed, and are generally not used in furniture finishing because of the poor quality of layout.

Air-assisted airless systems A newcomer to the scene, air-assisted airless systems use the fast, efficient liquid delivery of a pump, but mix in just enough air at the tip to give the fine atomization desired by wood finishers. The transfer efficiency is much higher than with a siphon system, but not as high as an HVLP, since the air-assisted airless gun generates air pressure at the tip of at least 10 psi.

Buying a spray gun

Just as with brushes, spray-gun quality is related to price, and in the long run, quality is by far the cheapest way to go. But although it is almost impossible to buy too good a brush, you can end up with a spray gun that will do a lot more than you'll ever require of it. The smartest consumer advice I can give is to anticipate the kinds of spraying you are going to do and shop accordingly, rather than buying a gun that does everything.

On the other hand, don't be afraid to buy and use more than one setup (a setup is the combination of the fluid tip, air cap and fluid needle). A gun with only one setup is like a radio that receives only one channel. A reputable company will offer a wide range of fluid tips and air caps for each gun so that it can comfortably handle many viscosities of finish at many different pressures and volumes of feed.

Look for a spray gun with versatility and a reputable name behind it. Ive used guns from Binks, DeVilbiss, Graco, Kremlin and Accuspray, and they meet my standards for reliability, versatility and availability of parts. Make sure that the gun you select comes from a company that will be around when you need new tips, parts, gaskets and pin packing to spray different materials or do routine maintenance.

It might seem logical to buy a compressor first, then retrofit the spray gun to the compressor. From a finisher's perspective, that's completely backwards. You must determine the kinds of finishes you want to spray first, then select a gun and finally get a compressor to power it. Curiously, it is the air cap that controls the size of the compressor needed. The size and hole pattern of an air cap determines the volume of air necessary to feed it, which in turn determines the size of compressor you'll need. The rule of thumb to convert volumetric (cfm) requirements of the cap into horsepower (most compressors are sold by horsepower) is that 1 hp will generate about 4 cfm. Hence, a 5-hp unit should put out 20 cfm.

Buying the gun is easy; the hard part is choosing the setup. (The Binks model 2001, for example, will take hundreds of different available setups, allowing it to spray almost any material at almost any pressure. Its versatility is staggering.) Each air cap will usually work with several different fluid tips, and the setups used with pressure pots are frequently different from those for siphon cups. A larger air cap will need more cfm, but will move more material in a wider fan pattern. The fluid-tip aperture (hole) size will control both the flow rate and the droplet size of the finish. Most manufacturers offer charts that cross-reference setups with air cfm and psi requirements as well as fluid viscosities. At times, finish manufacturers will suggest that a certain size fluid aperture or pressure is most appropriate.

Many woodworkers already own compressors that they use to run power tools and fill bicycle tires, but few have turbines lying about. Therefore, most HVLP units are sold as complete systems consisting of a gun, hose, and a turbine. For this reason, the air cap is often chosen for you based on the output of the turbine; all that remains is to decide on fluid tips based on the range of materials you plan to spray. Still, the rules are the same as for compressed air guns.

How to spray finishes

It is absurd to think that anyone can master spraying by reading a chapter in a book, but at least we can cover some rudiments. Spraying is like playing the guitar. Almost anyone can quickly learn to hack through a three-chord song, but when it comes to developing real proficiency, there is no substitute for practice.

Begin by adjusting the air-control knob and pressure so that the fan pattern created by the emerging fluid is fairly wide and very uniform. You can check this either by viewing the pattern in the air while it is being sprayed at right angles to your line of sight, or by spraying a test blast on some scrap cardboard or wood. Move the gun before you pull the trigger, and release the trigger before you stop moving your arm. Make sure that the air cap is positioned so that the widest part of the fan is at 90° to the direction of gun travel. Move from your arm, not your wrist, and always keep the tip of the gun moving parallel to the wood surface. Avoid moving the gun closer to and farther from the wood at different points. Try to keep each pass of the gun at the same speed. If too much material is going on, speed up; if too little is going on, slow down.

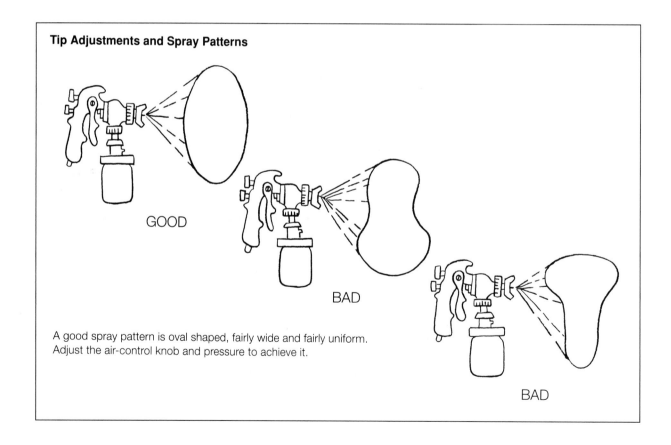

Tip Adjustments and Spray Patterns

GOOD

BAD

BAD

A good spray pattern is oval shaped, fairly wide and fairly uniform. Adjust the air-control knob and pressure to achieve it.

Spraying Technique and Spray Patterns

For even coverage, spray with the gun held at a constant distance from the wood; do not move it in and out in an arc pattern.

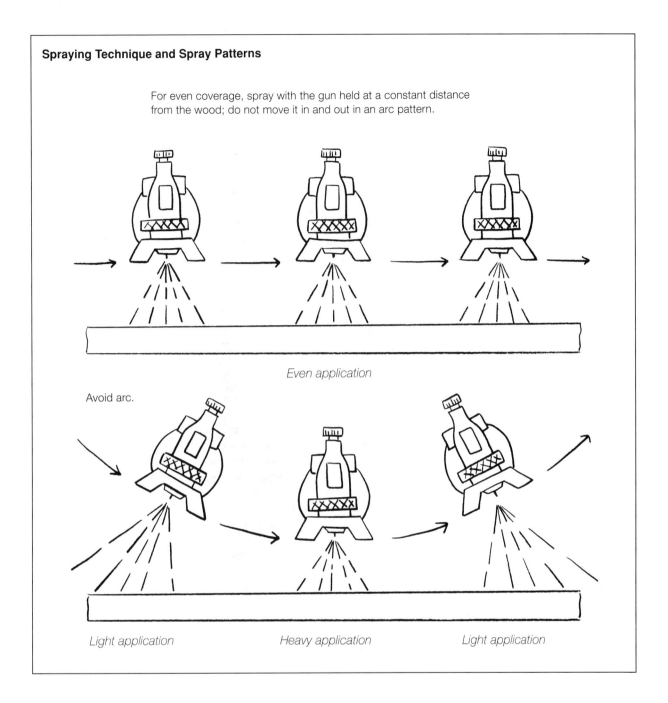

Even application

Avoid arc.

Light application   *Heavy application*   *Light application*

Start with a horizontal surface (it's easier) and above all, practice spraying on firewood, not furniture. You should be facing and spraying toward your exhaust fan, with the wood between you and the fan. Make your first pass across the edge closest to you and with the tip of the gun about 8 in. from the wood. This distance may change, depending on the air pressure and the material, but 8 in. is a good starting

Make your first pass across the edge closest to you and with the tip of the gun about 8 in. from the wood (top). Each successive pass brings you closer to your exhaust fan (above).

point. On each pass of the gun, overlap about one-half of the previous pass. For a more uniform coverage, I like to split each coat into two lighter half coats: the first across the grain and the second with the grain. To make it easier to apply the half-coats and still spray toward my exhaust fan, I use a revolving turntable to support the wood.

For vertical spraying, use the same approach—try to aim toward the fan and move the pattern away from yourself if possible. If you are moving the gun up and down, you may want to turn the air cap so that the fan is horizontal instead of vertical. If you are spraying with a siphon-feed cup, remember that there is a hole in the cap, and if you turn the gun upside-down it will stop spraying and finish will drip out the air hole. If you're not using a remote pressure pot, you may have to stop and reposition the piece that is being sprayed in order to avoid this problem.

When you are finished spraying, clean out the gun. Occasionally, you will have to dismantle it to clean it thoroughly (use the exploded parts drawing that came with the gun as a disassembly guide), but you can often get away with just spraying the appropriate solvent through it. If the solvent is hydrocarbon based, like lacquer thinner, spray it back into a container and re-use it; there are already enough hydrocarbons in the atmosphere, thank you. Try to avoid immersing a gun completely in lacquer thinner because it is liable to destroy the graphite packing around the fluid needle. If that happens, replace the packing. Your gun manufacturer will offer replacement packing as well as the other less sensitive gaskets. I like to put one drop of machine oil in the packing every now and then, just to keep it supple, especially if I am forced to immerse the gun in thinner.

As with brushes, a little bit of care will result in years of service. I have several guns that I've been using regularly for more than ten years, and one that has been with me for almost twice that long. They are all still in mint condition, and will certainly outlast me.

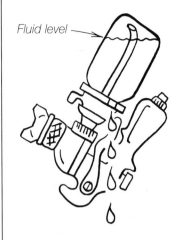

Gun Position and Spraying

Fluid level

A siphon-feed gun won't work upside-down—and finish will drip out the air hole.

CHAPTER 3
If You Must Refinish

Refinishing has developed a bad reputation over the years, and most people view it as a troublesome and messy task. There's a good bit of truth to this. But it is much less daunting if you just remember that refinishing consists of only two simple steps; stripping an old finish and putting on a new one. Once the old finish is off, you are merely at the first step of the finishing process, and it is no harder to finish old wood than it is to work on new wood. In fact, it is often easier, since the sanding has already been done for you by the first person who finished the wood.

You may be tempted to remove a finish either by sanding it off or by scraping it off with a cabinet scraper or even (heaven forbid!) a piece of glass. Please resist this temptation. Using glass is dangerous, and sanding or scraping makes hard work of a simple operation. In addition, sandpaper and scrapers don't know when to stop and usually remove wood along with the offending finish. The nice thing about chemical paint removers is that they affect only the finish and not the wood. Most commercial strippers make it almost impossible to harm even old veneered wood.

After the stripper has soaked in, scrape the wrinkled paint with a putty knife or scraper.

There are some situations where abrading or scraping off a finish is the best choice, but they are few. One example that comes to mind is refinishing a guitar or other musical instrument. Guitars are frequently edged and inlaid with plastic binding, which will dissolve if they come in contact with chemical strippers. But even in cases like this, I would first scrape only the areas that hold plastic, then use chemical removers on the other wood areas.

The other stripping method that I find less than appealing is using a propane torch or heat gun. Using heat to remove paint, especially finishes of unknown composition, is likely to release very harmful vapors, and should be done only by someone wearing adequate breathing gear, or better yet, not at all. In addition, heat, like sandpaper, is sadly non-selective, and will cheerfully burn wood along with the finish. If you have to remove a polyester finish that will simply not budge under any chemical removers, heat may be your only resort. If so, wear an organic vapor mask, goggles, and heat-resistant welder's gloves, and work outdoors or with the windows open and a fan blowing. And keep a fire extinguisher handy.

Chemical strippers

Removing finish chemically is both the simplest and most controllable method. Let's take a look at the different types of chemical removers, what they are best at doing, and what precautions need to be taken when using them.

It used to be almost impossible to tell what was inside a can of finish or paint remover. With the upgraded labeling laws that came into effect in 1991, it is getting somewhat easier, but deciphering contents still takes a bit of detective work. A good example of this comes in drawing the line between refinishers and paint removers. This is a fairly important distinction, since refinishers will work only on evaporative finishes like shellac and lacquer, while paint removers ostensibly work on most reactive finishes as well. Let's look at some typical contents to see what clues the label gives.

Refinishers generally consist of some mixture of common finish solvents, such as acetone, toluene and methanol (wood alcohol), and are therefore poisonous and flammable. To boost their effectiveness, some refinishers are formulated with a small amount of methylene chloride (CH_2Cl_2) also known as dichloromethane. If a large amount of methylene chloride is added to this same mix, you have the makings of a full-blown paint remover. The key to distinguishing a refinisher from a paint remover is the methylene chloride, which is a nonflammable material. If enough of it is added to a flammable mixture, it will raise the flash point of the mix and make it nonflammable. Hence, if a questionable can lists methylene chloride on the label and also says that the contents are flammable, you can be certain there is very little methylene chloride in that can, and that the product is a refinisher.

Wood refinishers

Refinishers are usually thin, watery mixtures that will dissolve shellac, lacquer and some varnishes, but will have little effect on most paints and polyurethanes. If you're not sure what finish you are removing, try some refinisher on a small obscure spot and see if it melts the finish. Once the refinisher has turned the old finish back into a liquid, you can move it around to "re-knit" an old checked or cracked surface, remove most of it and leave only the barest sealer coat, or keep washing down the wood until the old finish is completely gone. Admittedly, leaving only a partial finish that still looks good will take some practice. Because refinishers contain only solvents and no waxes, they leave the wood surface clean and ready to refinish. On the down side, refinishers are very flammable, create lots of solvent fumes, evaporate quickly and generally smell awful. It is best to use them outdoors away from any source of sparks or flame, and to wear neoprene gloves.

Paint and varnish removers

Paint and varnish removers contain a variety of strong solvent mixtures designed to remove a wide range of finishes, and are a good choice if you don't know what the old finish is. Some of them are flammable, some are not. Most smell and produce annoying and harmful fumes, are poisonous if swallowed, and most contain solvents that you should avoid getting on your skin. Paint and varnish removers are sold both as thin liquids and heavier-bodied semi-pastes; the latter can cling to vertical surfaces and stay wet longer.

Most paint and varnish removers contain methylene chloride, a very fast and effective solvent. One curious aspect of methylene chloride is that it works as a "bottom up" rather than a "top down" stripper. This means that once the remover is put onto the surface, it drops down through the coating and softens it at the wood line, allowing most finishes to peel off in sheets rather than turning into sticky gunk. That can translate into less material waste and easier disposal. With all methylene-chloride-based removers, wear neoprene gloves, eye goggles and long sleeves, and stay outdoors or in a decent cross-draft.

Flash point and flammability

The flash point of a solvent is the legal basis for designating a product as flammable or nonflammable. The flash point is determined by heating a vial of solvent while passing a spark above it to find out at what temperature the fumes above the liquid will ignite. Simply stated, a solvent whose flash point is below 100°F is called flammable. A solvent whose flash point is above 100°F may legally be called nonflammable, in spite of the fact that it will ignite. A combustible solvent is one that will ignite (hence, has a flash point) at some temperature, no matter how high; a noncombustible solvent will not ignite at any temperature. Thus a solvent like mineral spirits, which has a flash point of 120°F, may legally be labeled both nonflammable and combustible. Alcohol, on the other hand, is a flammable solvent with a flash point of only 51°F. Water is both nonflammable and noncombustible; you can heat water until it evaporates completely, and the fumes (steam) will still not ignite. When solvents are added together, the flash point usually ends up between the respective flash points of the two components. For example, if you add flammable alcohol to noncombustible water, you can get a mixture that is nonflammable, but still combustible.

Hazards of methylene chloride   Methylene-chloride-based removers are the largest group of strippers, because they work fast on most finishes. Recently, the Environmental Protection Agency (EPA) lowered the amount of methylene chloride that could be measured in the air in the work environment from 300 parts per million (ppm) to 25 ppm. That may limit the availability of methylene-chloride-based strippers.

Lately, the splash "contains no methylene chloride" on paint-remover labels has led people to ask what, if anything, is so bad about the stuff. Like other chlorinated hydrocarbons, such as carbon tetrachloride and 1,1,2 trichloroethane, methylene chloride is being looked at very carefully for possible health hazards.

Ironically, when methylene chloride was introduced, it was hailed as a miracle for the level of safety it provided to the field of paint removers, all of which were either highly caustic or highly flammable. To this day, fires from flammable remover mixtures continue to cause vastly more documented damage than methylene chloride. Methylene chloride is also cheap, effective, biodegradable, recoverable and reusable, and does not contribute to the smog-creating ozone problem like many other hydrocarbons. (It was once used to decaffeinate coffee.)

There are, however, some very real hazards connected with methylene chloride. When it is inhaled, the body metabolizes it, creating carbon monoxide. Excess carbon monoxide in the body causes dizziness and difficulty in breathing, and may trigger a heart attack in people with a history of heart problems. (People with heart conditions should

*E*vil twins

There are several solvents that appear very similar either in their activity or chemical structure, but are vastly different when it comes to their relative safety to humans. It is important to be very careful with these distinctions. The most common example is alcohol.

Ethanol/methanol
Ethanol (grain alcohol) is the potable spirit that many of us consume in beer, wine and "hard stuff." Methanol (wood alcohol) will cause blindness, insanity and even death if taken internally in sufficient quantity either by mouth or through the skin.

Propylene glycol/ethylene glycol
Propylene glycol is a safe solvent used in soda, pancake syrup and vanilla extract. Ethylene glycol is the poisonous component of antifreeze.

1,1,1 trichloroethane/1,1,2 trichloroethane
The chemicals 1,1,1 trichloroethane and 1,1,2 trichloroethane have the same chemical formula and differ only in their physical structure. Although 1,1,2 trichloroethane is regarded as very dangerous, its sister solvent 1,1,1 trichloroethane is, at least for now, still considered a safe degreaser. In fact, 1,1,1 trichloroethane is generally offered as a safer alternative to carbon tetrachloride, a material that used to be widely sold, and is now as scarce as hen's teeth.

avoid methylene-chloride strippers entirely.) It is therefore essential to work with it in a well-ventilated area. Methylene chloride also has the unfortunate ability to enter the human body through the skin. In addition to that, it is a chelating molecule. This means that as it passes through old paint and varnish, it has the ability to grab onto heavy metals, such as lead and cobalt, used in paint and varnish as colorants and driers. When the methylene chloride crosses the skin barrier into the body, it can take with it these dangerous heavy metals that would otherwise be unable to enter through that avenue. That is the reason that you should always wear neoprene gloves when handling it.

These risks of carbon monoxide and heavy metals are immediate, and therefore very controllable. What about the insidious label of suspected carcinogen? High-dosage studies with rats and mice indicate that methylene chloride may be a carcinogen, though the studies have been inconsistent enough to be regarded as inconclusive. So far there is no strong evidence that low-level exposure to methylene chloride causes cancer in humans. In fact, a 20-year study of a group of factory workers being exposed to moderately low levels of methylene chloride fumes eight hours a day for long periods, some for 10 years or more, showed that the incidence of cancer and heart disease in the group as a whole was statistically lower than in the general populace.

Does all this imply that low-level exposure to methylene chloride is safe? No, but it certainly suggests that rejecting a material out of hand due to small-rodent overdose studies may be overreacting. More important, it suggests that occasional users, like the home owner who strips two or three pieces of furniture a year, have little to worry about so long as they work with adequate ventilation and good gloves.

Using strippers safely Every brand of paint remover suggests good ventilation, but few explain what that means. The ideal situation is to work in a shady area outside in 75°F weather with a light breeze, but ordering up good weather is as difficult as finding good advice. If you can't strip outdoors, open the windows and turn on a fan, but in any case, get some fresh air moving in and old air moving out. Unless you've chosen one of the new safer paint removers, stripping furniture is not a wintertime activity. Ventilation is particularly important around methylene chloride. When you inhale the fumes, your body metabolizes them to carbon monoxide. This can be particularly dangerous to heart patients, but is not too good for anyone.

Goggles are a must for protecting your eyes from splashes, and decent neoprene gloves and long sleeves are essential for protecting your skin. Both alcohol and methylene chloride can be absorbed through the skin, and methylene chloride in particular will carry with it heavy metals, such as lead, that it may have picked up from the old paint being stripped. Buy extra-long gloves and turn the ends up into a cuff

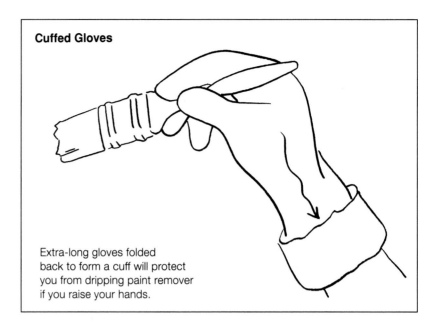

Cuffed Gloves

Extra-long gloves folded back to form a cuff will protect you from dripping paint remover if you raise your hands.

when you put them on. That way, when you lift your hands, the paint remover will run into the cuff and not down your arm. Temperature notwithstanding, I'd suggest closed shoes (not sandals), long pants, long sleeves and a plastic apron if you have one handy. Finally, use your common sense. If the smell of the stripper sickens you or makes you dizzy, stop, get out into the fresh air and revise your game plan.

If all these warnings have you wondering whether using strippers is worth the trouble, you have one other alternative. Look in the Yellow Pages and find a commercial furniture stripper. That way you can let somebody else take the risk, and you can skip to the next chapter. Just make sure you find a company that specializes in wood stripping. Outfits that work mostly with metal stripping often use caustic strippers, and these may loosen glue joints and play havoc with the wood grain.

"Safe" strippers

Like other paint and varnish removers, the so-called "safe" strippers are designed to remove most common finishes. The difference is that the "safe" strippers try to use solvents that are much safer in every respect. They don't always succeed. Some manufacturers specify that their material works with only some classes of finish, such as oil-based materials, while others offer two or more different "safe" formulations to cover all the bases. Generally, these strippers are thick, slow drying, non-flammable, have very little odor, and won't burn or harm bare skin. (One company offers a product so gentle to skin that it can be used as a hand cleaner.)

What fumes do come off are regarded as safe, so that work can be done indoors. The trade-off is that these strippers work more slowly than methylene chloride or harsh solvent mixtures, and frequently cost more. But they are the ideal choice for people who are particularly sensitive to hard solvents, must work indoors, or are willing to trade time and money for safety.

What makes the new "safer" strippers safer? Formulators of these materials are shunning toxic and flammable solvents like toluene and methanol, as well as methylene chloride, the workhorse of the paint-remover world. Instead, they are turning to an emerging batch of tongue-twisting solvents: dibasic esters (DBE), n-methyl-2-pyrrolidone (NMP) and gamma butyrolactone (BLO). These strippers frequently have little or no fumes or odor, are often not flammable, and are at worst only very mild skin irritants.

The epitome of this class is undoubtedly 3M's patented Safest Stripper, a DBE-based material so benign that it can be used with no gloves and no ventilation, and in the presence of children and pets. However, it works very slowly and is designed to remove primarily oil-based paints and varnishes. But to its credit, it will lift paint right out of the wood's pores, something traditional strippers do only with a large amount of manual assistance. NMP- and BLO-based strippers are not quite as benign (they may sensitize the skin on some people), but they are faster acting and are decidedly safer than their traditional solvent counterparts. For those who find stripper solvents particularly annoying, and many people do on a number of levels, these new products are worth looking into.

Caustics

Certain types of paint, such as milk paint, won't respond to solvent mixes, but will soften in the presence of strong acids or alkalies. Caustic strippers were the most common type before the advent of methylene chloride, but have virtually died out along with the milk paints that necessitated them. Some folks still like the idea of using lye to remove paint, and it does work on many coatings. Unfortunately, it also burns and discolors wood if it is left on too long, softens some glues, and seriously raises the grain of old wood. More important, it will seriously burn skin and eyes. Since the bulk of the liquid is water, caustics are nonflammable, but the fumes can be antagonistic to the nose, throat and eyes. Work with good ventilation, old clothes with long sleeves, good gloves, goggles and synthetic-bristle brushes (caustics will destroy natural bristles and fibers). Above all, keep your wits about you and watch where you splash. Better yet, see if you can find a suitable "safe" alternative.

It's a good idea to assemble all of your stripping gear before you get started.

Getting started

A stripping project is the perfect chance to use up those big, old splayed brushes you've been saving without quite knowing why. It doesn't really matter if they are clean or crusty; using them to apply paint remover will be just the ticket for getting off hardened varnish. You'll also need some sort of scraper or putty knife for scooping off the goo. I like to round the corners so they don't dig into the wood. Gather up some wood shavings from the planer or jointer, a wooden dowel sharpened to a point in a pencil sharpener, and a few stiff, nylon-bristle scrub brushes. You'll also need some coarse (0 or 1) steel wool, or better yet, some nylon abrasive pads, a handful of rags or paper towels, and a few containers (old steel or porcelain bowls, or even oversize tin cans). Then grab a stack of old newspapers and put a drop cloth over the floor, or anything else you want to keep clean.

If you are stripping a piece of furniture, remove the shelves and all the hardware first, and take it apart as far as you can. It is easier to work on horizontal surfaces. If there are unfinished areas, like the insides and sides of drawers, mask them off. Where there were drawer handles, cover the holes from the inside with masking tape to prevent the goo from dripping through.

Removing an old finish is fairly easy if you remember to let the paint re-mover do the heavy work. The object of the game is to keep the finish wet with stripper until the old finish is completely off. If you've cho-sen a liquid stripper, that means immersing the piece of wood, or con-tinually rewashing it to keep it wet. Unless the piece is small, in most cases a semi-paste formula will lighten your workload. Shake the can a few times, lay a rag over the cap to stop any spurts, and open the cap slowly to release the pressure gradually. Pour some remover out into one of your cans or bowls, and using the biggest, floppiest brush you have, daub it all over the finish. When you've got a nice thick coat on, leave it alone. Semi-paste removers contain either waxes or clays, and for a good reason. Once the remover is applied, these additives rise to the top and form a crust that slows down the evaporation of the active solvents, thereby keeping the remover wet and active longer. If you keep going back to rebrush the remover, you will break up the crust and defeat its purpose. Make sure the entire surface is wet; if you see any dry spots go back and daub on some more.

Q&A:
Stripping a fake-grain finish

Q: I purchased four painted chairs to strip, refinish and cane (the seats). After stripping them, I found all the chairs to have "wood graining" beneath the paint. The graining has many faded and worn off areas.

When did the art of wood graining first become popular? Would the value of my chairs be greater if the graining were left as it is, but covered by a couple of coats of polyurethane, or should the graining be removed?

What methods and/or materials would you recommend to remove the "wood graining"?

A: I'm more than a bit surprised that the stripper you used to remove the paint did not take the graining off as well. If you do choose to remove it, any good paint remover will take it off. Just make certain that you leave the remover on long enough to do its work.

Fake wood graining, or *faux bois* after the French for "false wood," has been going in and out of popularity for quite a long time, so its presence cannot by itself be used to determine the age of your chairs. Before you make the decision to remove it completely, you might want to investigate the age and value of the chairs. It is hard to imagine a case in which removing an original finish, if indeed the graining is original, would not diminish the resale value of a collectible.

Putting a coat of polyurethane over the top of the graining may make the chairs more practical for your own use, but once again, it would hurt their value as collectibles. Conservators prefer to add protective coatings only when absolutely necessary, and then using only reversible materials—those that can be removed without affecting the original finish. It would be almost impossible to remove polyurethane selectively.

Now sit down and take a rest for at least 10 or 15 minutes, but keep an eye on the stripper. If you see any dry spots develop, re-wet them. If you let the mixture of finish and remover dry completely before taking it off, the resulting crust will be far more difficult to remove than the original finish. After 15 minutes, scrape a small area to see if the finish will come off all the way to the bare wood. If it doesn't, but the remover is still wet, leave it alone for a little while longer.

When your test area shows bare wood (or when your patience is exhausted), carefully scoop the goo off the wood and onto some of those old newspapers. If the wood is not completely clean in all areas—and don't be surprised if it isn't—re-wet the area with more remover immediately so that it doesn't get a chance to dry completely. In areas with carving or fluting, grab a handful of wood shavings and scrub them into the softened finish to help absorb and dislodge it. Then take a stiff bristle brush and scrub out the loaded shavings.

In very tight corners, use the pointed dowel to clean out the recesses. Stringed abrasives or just lengths of coarse cord are good for turned work. If paint refuses to come out of the pores of large-pore wood, like ash or oak, use the stiff bristle brush to scrub the pores while the remover is still wet. In severe cases you may have to resort to a fine brass-

A handful of wood shavings helps remove the finish in hard-to-reach areas (left). You can use a stiff bristle brush to clean out the soaked shavings (right).

Coarse cord works great for cleaning old finish from the grooves on turned legs.

If the wood is not completely clean, scrub it with fresh remover on a nylon abrasive pad.

bristle brush to clean the pores. Re-apply the remover as often as necessary to make sure everything is dislodged, and finish up with a final scrub using a remover-soaked nylon abrasive pad, just to be sure. Then wipe off the surface with rags or paper towels.

At this point the wood should look clean, but may actually contain wax, silicone or other oils that may impede the finishing process. The wood may also contain old filler and stains that you'd be better off without. The best way to remove these contaminants is with a series of solvent washes. Using a clean abrasive pad, scrub down the wood with a liberal amount of lacquer thinner. Then repeat the scrub using alcohol for the second wash, and mineral spirits or naphtha for the third. It is not necessary to wipe the wood off in between. If flammables are out of the question, scrub the surface with a solution of trisodium phosphate (TSP) in water. TSP is a degreaser found in most paint and hardware stores; just mix it according to the directions on the box. It is not as good as the solvent sequence, but it is better than nothing. Finally, scrub the wood down with a solution of ammonia in warm water (about 2 oz. of ammonia per qt. of water), then wipe off any excess liquid. Take a good look at the wood during this final wash. It should look clean, and the color should be somewhat uniform. If the water wets the wood unevenly or leaves splotchy areas, it means that all of the residue has not been removed. Go back to the paint remover and repeat the sequence.

Let's assume that the wood is now as clean as a whistle and ready to refinish. It needs to dry overnight, so we'll turn our attention to cleaning up the mess.

We often talk about a bleach removing a stain, and in the visual sense it does just that. But there is value in understanding more about this action. The bleach does not actually remove the stain; instead it changes its color. The original components of the stain remain in the wood. A good example is the iron stain that occurs on oak. Tannin in the wood reacts with iron to create ferric tannate, which shows up as a bluish-black stain. When oxalic acid is applied, it reacts with the ferric tannate, converting it to colorless ferrous oxalate. But both the iron and the tannin are still present in that oak, and under different conditions, the vanished stain could mysteriously reappear.

Cleaning up

The sludge you've collected on the newspapers, rags, steel wool and paper towels is viewed as toxic by most communities, and they will be less than ecstatic to see it showing up with your weekly trash. Some areas have collection sites for used oil and unused paint and solvents. If so, this sludge may come under that heading. It is best to check your local area's regulations. If it is going to end up in a landfill, let the residue dry completely on the newspapers before you dispose of it. It will become hard and crusty, and this dried material is less damaging than the solvent-laden sludge. Provided you catch them before the residue on them hardens, your brushes, putty knives and even the abrasive pads will clean up in lacquer thinner. It should come as no surprise that this dirty lacquer thinner falls into the same disposal category as the sludge.

Removing stains

Just because the wood is free of finish does not mean that it is completely clean. It may be graced with both intentional and accidental stains, and you may want to remove them. By intentional stains I mean whatever dyes or pigments the first finisher applied to the wood; by accidental I mean water rings, ink spills, uneven sun fading and other marks of age and use. Many people feel that accidental stains add character and history to furniture, and should remain under the new finish, but for the most part, these are the same people who believe that old furniture should not be refinished in the first place. Though not all stains and discolorations can be removed, there are ways of dealing with at least some of them. First, let's talk about the intentional stains.

Wood stains are either pigments or dyes (see pp. 92-97). Most, if not all, of the pigments should have been removed during the various solvent scrubs; whatever is left now is likely to remain forever. But dyes are an entirely different story. Most aniline dyes can be denatured by using either commercial decolorant solutions or chlorine bleach. Chlorine bleach is sold in grocery stores as laundry bleach under trade names such as Clorox and Purex, generally in a rather weak concentration (usually a 5% solution). In this concentration, the bleach will work slowly and take several applications to remove the dye. The alternative is to make a stronger bleach by mixing swimming-pool chlorine into water to make a saturated solution. Chlorine for pools is sold under various trade names including Shock Treatment, and the label will indicate the percentage of active ingredient (usually 65% to 85%) in the form of either calcium hypochlorite or sodium hypochlorite. Get the highest percentage available. Add the white crystals to a glass jar of hot water; let them sit a few minutes and stir occasionally. Keep adding crystals until no more will dissolve, and a layer of white residue settles to the bottom of the jar. With gloves on your hands, use a synthetic sponge to flood the surface of the wood with the warm mixture, and let it dry overnight. In the morning, there will be a layer of dried crystals on the wood. Wash the surface with plenty of clean water, then wipe off the excess water. You can repeat the process if all of the dye has not been removed, but one application of a strong solution will usually do the job. Too many washes of chlorine bleach will start to pull some color out of the wood in addition to removing the dye.

Removing accidental stains is not as straightforward as taking out aniline dyes. To be certain of removing a stain, it is best to know exactly what caused it, and that is impossible with old furniture. Therefore, the best course of action is to use a stain remover that works on a wide variety of stains without altering the natural color of the wood. The best choice in this category is oxalic acid. It is sold in most hardware stores in 1-lb. boxes, and looks like a white crystalline powder. In this form, it is both toxic and irritating to mucous membranes in the nose, throat and eyes, so treat it with care and wear a dust mask while handling the powder. Oxalic acid is safer to handle once it is in liquid form since it is not particularly irritating to skin, but gloves and goggles are always appropriate. Mix 2 oz. of oxalic acid (about ¼ cup of dry powder) to 1 qt. of very warm water, and stir the mixture once or twice. The powder should dissolve. After you flood the liquid onto the wood, let it dry overnight. There will be a crystalline residue on the wood surface once it dries completely; wash it off with several rinses of clean water, wipe off the excess water, and let the wood dry. Occasionally this treatment will lighten but not completely remove a stain, and a second wash will be even more effective.

Oxalic acid is often (but not always) effective on water rings and ink stains and on silvered weathered wood. (It is sometimes sold as deck brightener in liquid form.) But its true call to glory is in removing the bluish-black iron stains that often show up when woods with a high tannin content, such as oak, have come in contact with iron hardware or nails. Oxalic acid will remove these stains quickly and completely. However, it is important to remove the hardware beforehand, or it may create new stains as the wood dries. It is always wise to check for hidden nails near these stains, and if they can't be removed, countersink them and putty over the holes before you apply the oxalic acid.

Both chlorine-bleach and oxalic-acid treatments introduce a lot of water to the wood surface, and it is not uncommon for some grain raising to occur. Although it is usually not necessary to sand wood when refinishing, it will probably be necessary after stain removers are used. Use a very fine sandpaper (220 grit or finer) and scuff sand quickly and lightly. For turnings and carvings, use general-purpose nylon abrasive pads instead of sandpaper.

Q&A:
Bleaching walnut

Q: I recently experienced less than spectacular results bleaching a walnut tabletop. I used a two-part system and bleached the wood three times, but the results were poor. What is the best way to apply wood bleach, and is the two-part or one-part system better?

A: I'll assume that by "poor results" you mean the bleach did not lighten the wood sufficiently. A two-part bleach should make walnut as light as butternut. If it did not, check to make sure that the surface of the wood was free of materials that can block the bleach, such as finish, oil or wax, and that the bleach used was fresh and strong. Stale bleach loses its effectiveness. Flood the wood with the first solution, and apply the second heavily while the first one is still very wet. There should be some foaming or bubbling in the pores of the wood, indicating that the bleach is strong and working. Allow the wood to dry overnight, and repeat the process if necessary. However, with walnut, one application should do it.

CHAPTER 4
Preparing the Wood

One of the maxims of woodworking is, "A finish is only as good as the surface it covers." Finishes are designed to be revealing. In some cases, they actually intensify what appears at the raw-wood stage to be extremely minor defects and scratches. A finish acts like a lens, drawing the eye to any minor imperfections that the stain has delineated. They say the three most important considerations when buying real estate are: location, location, location. The finisher's version is: preparation, preparation, preparation.

Degreasing and dewaxing

If you are machining your own wood, you can skip this section, but if you are inclined to use preformed turnings or millwork, listen up. To compensate for less than perfectly sharp blades, or just to keep blades resin-free, some production millwork houses lubricate their cutters with wax or a non-drying oil like silicone. I'm glad to report that with the development of finish-compatible lubricants, these practices are quickly becoming a bad memory. Nevertheless, it is still possible to run into wood that has been contaminated with oil or wax during machining, and this residue can play havoc with certain finishes. Naturally, I have every confidence that you won't scuttle your own work with such bad habits.

**A surface should be as smooth as possible before finish is applied.
Dents can be steamed out with an iron.**

Silicone oils on the raw wood announce their presence as fish-eye when lacquer finish is applied.

It is usually not obvious when wood is contaminated in this way, and moderate sanding only moves the wax or oil around to new areas. However, wax or oil is easy to remove once you discover it, and neither affects most oil-based finishes. Lacquers and water-based finishes, however, are quite sensitive. You generally discover the problem upon spraying or brushing the first coat of water or solvent-based lacquer. Silicone oil announces its presence with fish-eye, a pattern of uneven flowout caused by variances in the surface tension of the liquid. Lacquer applied over wax will simply stay wet in the waxed areas. If this happens, immediately remove the finish with its solvent (one coat of partially dried finish will come off easily). This will usually remove any wax; remove silicone with the method described below.

If you suspect contamination

You may suspect that the raw wood has been inundated with wax or silicone before you find out the hard way. If one piece of millwork from a batch goes haywire under the first coat of lacquer, it is reasonable to assume that more of that group will do the same. It is hard to spot wax on raw wood, but a quick scrub with a nylon pad soaked in naphtha will generally remove it. Silicone will often show its presence by causing a wash of naphtha or water to "walk," that is, to display the same fish-eye pattern that will occur with lacquer. If this happens, scrub the wood with mineral spirits, mop up the liquid, then scrub with an ammonia solution (1 cup of ammonia in 1 gal. of warm water). Wipe the wood dry before resuming the finishing process. Mineral spirits is the solvent for silicone, but merely dissolving it just gets it in solution and moves it around on the wood. By mopping up the solution rather than just letting it dry, you remove some of the silicone by absorption. However, not all of it will come out. That's where the ammonia comes in. Ammonia is a surfactant; one end of the molecule will grab onto the silicone oil, and the other end will grab onto the water. If the surfactant is strong enough, and ammonia is, it will make the silicone let go of the wood and stay with the water as it is mopped up.

If after all this, the wood still shows silicone fish-eye when lacquered, you have two fail-safe alternatives. Either seal the wood with a light coat of shellac, the best silicone seal I know of, or fight fire with fire by adding more silicone (called smoothie or fish-eye eliminator) to the lacquer. (The latter technique works only with solvent-based lacquers, not water-based ones. Water-based fish-eye eliminator is a different type of surface-tension reducer.) The extra silicone reduces the surface tension of the entire mix so that it is no longer so different from those areas of silicone contamination. In a sense, instead of having many fish-eyes, you have one huge one so big that it is the same size as the entire surface, hence, it is invisible. If you add silicone to one coat of lacquer, you must add it to each successive coat. In addition, overspray from the mix will contaminate any other wood that it lands on, sealed or raw. Silicone in the finish will change the gloss and feel of the final coat. For these reasons, I prefer removing and sealing in this contaminant rather than bringing more of it into the finishing area.

Dents and gouges

Although they look similar at first glance, dents are quite distinct from gouges, and may be handled differently as well. A dent is an indentation in the wood surface where the grain of the wood has not been torn or broken, only crushed or deflected. A gouge is an indentation where the grain is torn or removed. Whereas gouges must be filled with wood or putty, dents can be repaired by "steaming up."

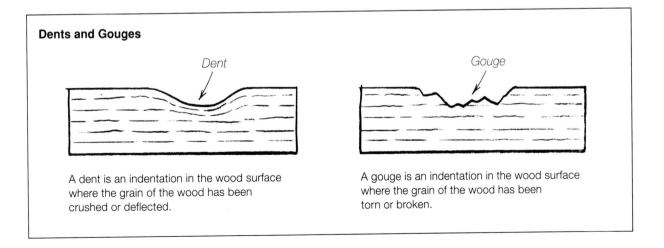

Dents and Gouges

Dent

A dent is an indentation in the wood surface where the grain of the wood has been crushed or deflected.

Gouge

A gouge is an indentation in the wood surface where the grain of the wood has been torn or broken.

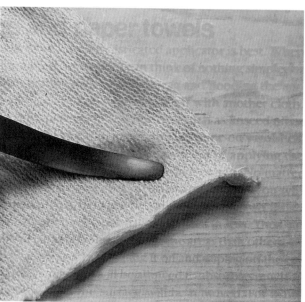

To steam out a dent, place a drop of water in the depression (left), then cover the spot with a damp cloth and apply a hot knife (right) or an iron (facing page).

Dents should be steamed up before sanding, which could cut wood grain. Steaming up can be done only on raw wood. Position the wood so that the dent is on a horizontal surface. Place a drop or two of water into the dent and allow it to sit for a minute. Cover the spot with a damp cloth and apply a hot iron, soldering iron or burn-in knife directly over the spot for several seconds. The hot metal should cause steam to rise from the spot immediately. The damp cloth is to prevent the hot metal from burning the surrounding dry wood; if you omit the cloth, be a bit more careful. You can use either a regular iron (see the photo on p. 73) or a steam iron (see the drawing on the facing page). The dent should be level after just one or two applications of water and heat. If it isn't, it is probably a gouge.

How does steaming up work? A dent consists of crushed wood fibers that look like a bundle of partially flattened straws. They absorb some of the drop of water placed in the dent. As the hot iron is applied, the water turns to steam, expanding rapidly and pushing the crushed wood fiber walls out as it expands. Because the water is on the wood such a short time, it rarely if ever creates water marks, but if you find you must repeat the process and keep the area wet for very long, it is a good idea to wipe the entire area down with water.

If you are exceptionally impatient, you can also steam up dents using alcohol. If you decide to go this route, be very careful; alcohol is quite flammable and can burn the wood if too much is applied. With a fine touch-up brush, place one drop of alcohol into the dent. Make sure it

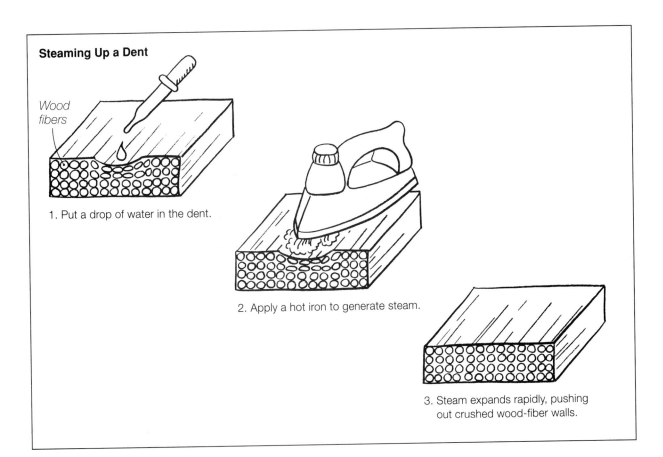

Steaming Up a Dent

Wood fibers

1. Put a drop of water in the dent.

2. Apply a hot iron to generate steam.

3. Steam expands rapidly, pushing out crushed wood-fiber walls.

*R*ain, rain, go away

I had been working for several weeks in a large shop that did no woodworking, only finishing. That morning, a shipment of unfinished Louis XIV chairs was delivered in the rain. Although the truck got close to the loading dock, the 3-ft. gap was enough to dot the chairs with a few raindrops as they were carried over the threshold. Someone called out, "Rain delivery," and by the time the freight elevator got to our third-floor shop, the entire crew was grabbing buckets of water and lots of rags. To the trucker's (and my) utter amazement, as each chair was brought off the elevator it was frantically washed from top to toe with water, then passed into the workroom, where the water was leisurely wiped off with a dry rag. The evenly damp chairs were then left to dry, as everyone returned to his work.

What appeared to the casual observer to be a rehearsal for a Mack Sennett slapstick routine was actually a vitally important precaution. Water spots are the finisher's nemesis, causing one of the most difficult stains to remove. However, an even wash of water over the entire surface of wood leaves no marks at all. The marks occur primarily at the edge of puddles or single drops; if the wet wood dries evenly, there will be no stains. In order to prevent the raindrops from becoming a problem, the finishers had simply incorporated them into the washdown, where the worst they could do was contribute to a small amount of grain raising. Since the chairs were to be sanded anyway, the grain raising was more of a help than a problem, but water marks would have been a disaster under a clear finish, even if a fairly dark wood stain was used.

does not run down the wood or spread out beyond the dent area. If you put too much on, just wait a few minutes for the alcohol to evaporate. Remove the alcohol and brush from the immediate area and make certain no alcohol is on your hands. While the alcohol is still wet, touch the drop with the tip of a lit match. It will immediately burn with an almost invisible blue flame, which should go out before it has a chance to burn the surrounding wood. (That's why you should use only one drop.) If the flame is not out in a few seconds, snuff it with a water-dampened rag. As the alcohol burns, it changes to a gas, expanding rapidly and acting on the wood in the same way as the steam. However, steaming up a dent with water takes several minutes, but using alcohol takes several seconds.

If some wood has been removed from an indentation, you are dealing with a gouge, and it must be filled to make it level with the surrounding wood. If the gouge is not too large or deep, you can fill it with putty; otherwise, patch it with a piece of wood. I would use a wood patch for anything wider than ½ in. (12 mm) or deeper than ¼ in. (6 mm).

There are many different wood putties on the market, but they all have several things in common. They combine some type of filling or bodying solids (wood dust, talc, clay or silica) with a binder and a solvent. The binder will form a matrix that holds the filler material in place once the solvent evaporates. The binder can be oil, latex, lacquer or any other film-forming material, and the solvent will be whatever the binder requires to make it thin enough to be manageable (mineral spirits, water or lacquer thinner). The combination of filler, binder and solvent will affect how quickly the putty dries, how much it shrinks, its brittleness or flexibility, its color and odor, how easily it will sand, and how it will absorb stains. With this many variables, there is an almost endless range of possible formulations, yet most putties are more alike than not. The reason is that most manufacturers are trying to achieve the same general results: a putty that handles smoothly, dries quickly, doesn't shrink much, and sands, looks and stains like the surrounding wood.

Not all putties come in ready-to-use form. Some are sold with the solvent missing, like a cake mix. Water putty, for example, is a powder consisting of the filler and water-soluble binder. It becomes a paste when water is added. The finisher can control the consistency by adding more or less solvent (water). Of course, if you know the appropriate solvent, you can also modify the consistency of ready-mix putty as well. A clue to the solvent will usually be on the label. The warning, "Contains toluene, xylene or MEK (methyl ethyl ketone)," for example, indicates that the putty will thin with lacquer thinner. "Petroleum distillates" is usually a euphemism for mineral spirits; "methanol" and "ethanol" are alcohols. Sometimes the label lists

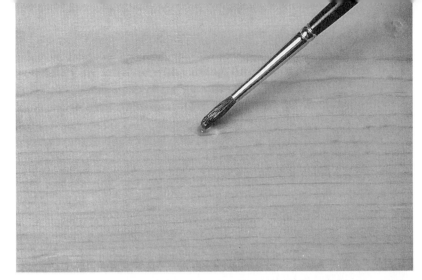

To raise a dent with alcohol, place one drop of alcohol into the depression with a fine touch-up brush (left) and touch the drop with tip of a lit match (middle left). The alcohol will burn with an almost invisible blue flame (bottom left), causing the surrounding wood to swell.

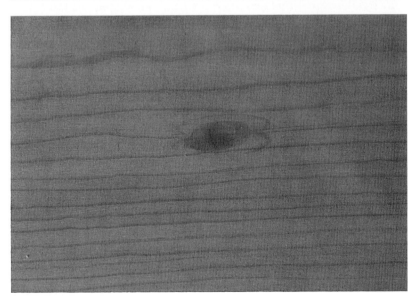

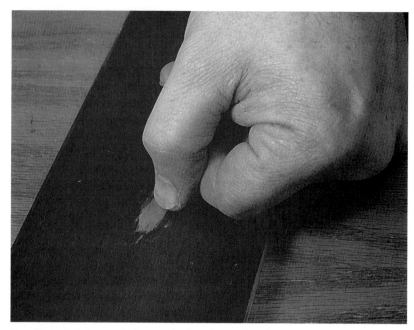

A putty patch is ready to sand when it won't take an impression from your thumbnail.

cleanup solvents, or even tells you what to use to thin the material. If all else fails, you can often rely on your nose to identify the solvent. For more on putty see pp. 123-126.

Using putty

To fill a gouge, take a small amount of the putty out of the can and press it into the defect using a putty knife or palette knife. Leave it a bit high to allow for shrinkage. Close the can immediately; its fast-drying nature means that it will harden if left open. When the patch is dry and will not take an impression from your thumbnail, sand the area so the patch is flush. You might prefer to use a sanding block to make sure the surface stays flat.

You will probably want to try several brands of putty to find one that is best for your style of work, the woods you use, and most important, the stain you prefer. You'll find that some types of putty sand more like hard woods than soft, and some types respond better to one sort of stain than another.

Coloring putty

In spite of the wide range of available colors, you will rarely find a putty that is precisely the color you need. But don't despair, you can color the putty you have. In my own shop, we buy only "natural" color putty, a sort of neutral pine color, and use it as a base to make any color we need, from holly to purpleheart.

To change the color of putty, mix it with powdered earth or fresco pigments (the same powders you use for touch-up). If you must add a lot of powder to get the color, add a few drops of solvent as well. Take a blob out of the can and mix it on a piece of glass, cutting the powdered pigment into the mix with a palette knife. Remember that by adding white or yellow you can go lighter as well as darker. On large jobs, we often mix a batch of color to match the wood and keep it in a baby-food jar, adding a few more drops of solvent as needed. If the putty you are using absorbs less stain than the surrounding wood, take that into account when you mix the color. After some experimentation, you will get used to how your favorite putty responds to your favorite stains. If the wood is figured (like walnut) or has contrasting grain color (like oak), mix the putty to the lightest background color and add the grain lines with a touch-up brush after the first coat of finish has been applied (for more on this technique, see pp. 171-172).

Sanding

If there is any activity germane to finishing that can truly be deemed a necessary evil, it is sanding. For most woodworkers, sanding rivals mowing the lawn as one of life's most tedious tasks. But if we must sand, it makes sense to learn how to do it as efficiently as possible.

The medium

Sandpaper, or more accurately "coated abrasive medium," is the catch-all term for any material made of tiny pieces of grit glued onto a backing. How a particular type of sandpaper behaves is controlled by the type of grit, glue and backing material chosen by the manufacturer. The type of grit determines how fast and easily a paper sands, while the backing and binder have a large influence on how the medium holds up and resists solvents.

Sandpaper as a manufactured product is only about 100 years old, but long before that woodworkers were using hide glue to stick flint (white quartzite sand) and other minerals to paper and parchment. Most abrasives today employ synthetic rather than naturally occurring minerals, and a wide range of backings including, paper, various types of cloth and even polyester film. Choosing the right coated abrasive for a given job involves picking the one with the most appropriate grit, adhesive and backing. Grits, glues and backings are designated by a variety of descriptive names and number or letter sizes, which, in theory, allow the consumer to make an informed choice. In some cases, though, manufacturers indicate the type of grit and adhesive only in code, if at all. Instead, they try to offer common names, like the term "production paper," to help consumers make the right choice. For more on the grits, backings and bonds, see the sidebar below; grits in various grading systems are compared in the chart on p. 85.

The method

The principle behind sanding is very straightforward. The abrasive is designed to remove machine and tool marks, and enables you to shape wood into smooth contours. In the process, the sandpaper leaves grooves in the wood relative to the grit size. By moving up to the next appropriate grit size, you remove the last set of grooves and replace those grooves with a smaller set. Each grit progression leaves a denser but shallower scratch pattern (see the drawings on p. 84). Ideally you should use a grit that is just coarse enough to remove the previous

Grit, backings and bonds

In simple terms, sandpaper is made by gluing some sort of sand (grit) to paper (backing). The various combinations of grit, glue and backing translate into a considerable number of possible abrasives. Relatively few of these are useful in woodworking.

The terms *closed coat* and *open coat* refer to the amount of grit applied to the backing. Closed coat means that 100% of the surface area of the backing is covered with mineral. Open coat means that only 40% to 70% of the area is covered. On exceptionally fine papers, this is a fairly insignificant distinction, but with medium grits, an open-coat paper will clog less and generate less heat.

Grit

Abrasive grit may be either natural or synthetic. Natural grit includes emery, diamonds, flint (quartzite) and garnet. *Emery* is a dull, black mineral (aluminum oxide) with a round, blocky structure. It is not generally used in woodworking, and since the advent of synthetic aluminum oxide, it has been largely abandoned. *Diamonds* are used to cut stone, ceramics and the tungsten carbide so essential to our favorite saw blades and router bits. Due to their high cost, they are not considered appropriate for wood or finish sanding. *Flint* is a soft mineral that looks like white sand. It was sold primarily for home use, but disappeared a number of years ago in favor of other minerals. Production of flint grit in America was abandoned mainly because the dust produced during its manufacture (grinding) is a suspected carcinogen. *Garnet* is a reddish-brown mineral familiar to many as a gemstone. It is only moderately hard, but has good cutting edges. Garnet is friable, meaning it has a tendency to

fracture before it dulls. As it breaks, it presents a new, sharp edge, allowing it to sand quickly and easily. Although it wears faster than some other grits, it is still excellent for woodwork. Like other natural minerals, garnet sandpaper is becoming scarce.

Synthetic grit includes aluminum oxide, silicon carbide, alumina-zirconia and ceramic aluminum oxide. *Aluminum oxide,* a tough, durable brown or white mineral, is probably the most widely used grit for coated abrasives, and is excellent for both wood and finish sanding. Unlike natural minerals, which are usually identified by their proper names, aluminum oxide is marketed under a variety of trademarked names, including Production, Three-M-ite, Imperial, Cutrite, Aloxite, Metalite, and Adalox. *Silicon carbide* is a shiny, black mineral that is both sharp and hard. It is excellent for wood, and especially effective for sanding finishes. Tri-M-ite and Durite are two of the trademarked names it takes.

scratches and replace them with smaller ones . Too heavy a grit size will cause you to repeat your work with no advantage; too light a grit will not completely remove the deepest marks from the last paper. The rule of thumb for grit progression is to jump under 100 points with coarse papers, 100 or more with medium papers, and 200 or more with very fine papers. For example, either 80/120/220/400 or 100/180/280/400 would be appropriate grit progressions. If you are not sure, it is better to have too many steps than too few. Too small a jump may waste a little time, but too large a jump will leave visible scratches that may show up only after the finish is on. Although most sandpaper is marked by grit size, some companies use only descriptive names, such as medium, fine or extra fine; refer to the chart on p. 85 for number/name equivalents.

Alumina-zirconia is not quite as hard as aluminum oxide or silicone carbide. This alloy of aluminum and zirconium oxide is used for coarse removal of wood stock. It is sold under the trademarked names Cubicut and NorZon. *Ceramic aluminum oxide,* a white, synthetic mineral, is two to three times tougher than conventional aluminum oxide. The trade name of the mineral itself is Cubitron, and coated abrasives manufactured with it include Regal, Regalite, Vulcan SG and Medalist.

Stearated (self-lubricating) abrasives are preloaded with a dry lubricant to eliminate clogging and heating. Various stearates (dry, powdery soaps) are used, including stearates of zinc, aluminum, magnesium and calcium. Stearated papers are especially helpful when sanding between coats of finish, which tends to gum up regular sandpaper. Stearated sandpaper is easily distinguished by its greyish-white color.

Backings

Backings for sandpaper include paper, cloth, vulcanized fiber and polyester film. *Paper* backings are designated by a letter, according to thickness: going from lightest to heaviest, A, C, D, E or F. Most standard sheets are either A or C, depending on the grit size. Cotton, rayon and polyester *cloth* in a variety of weights is used for abrasive belts and discs, and occasionally for sheets. The weight classes, from lightest to heaviest, are J, X, Y, T and M. *Vulcanized fiber* is a tough material made from rags; it is used mostly for disc and drum sanders. *Polyester film* is especially prized for use with fine grit. Durable and extremely uniform in thickness, polyester film is coated with many types of mineral. As a rule, abrasives with micron-graded mineral grit are backed with film (see the sidebar on p. 86).

Some abrasives come with a sticky backing, called *pressure-sensitive adhesive* (PSA), for quick application and removal with hand-held sanders.

Bonds

Two coats of adhesive are used to hold the grit to the backing: the make coat and the size coat. Some typical combinations are glue and glue, glue and filler, resin over glue and resin over resin. The simplest bond uses hide glue for both coats. Hide glue can also be combined with a heat-resistant inert filler, as in the trademarked product Gritlok.

A resin over glue heat-resistant bond is composed of a size coat of resin over a make coat of glue. Resin over resin, usually referred to as resin bond, is both heat and moisture resistant. When used with a waterproof backing, it makes *wet/dry sandpaper,* which, as the name implies, can be used wet or dry.

For most woods, it is not necessary to sand finer than 180 grit, and in some cases, 120 grit is adequate. But there are situations in which finer sanding is needed. Some very hard woods, like ebony and boxwood, show even fine scratches, and you may have to sand the raw wood to 400 or even 600 grit. If you can see the scratches, go to a finer grit. Some light woods, like maple, show scratches with certain types of stains, and may have to be sanded to 220 grit. It is also a good idea to sand woods to 220 grit if they are going under a water-based finish; finer sanding in these cases reduces grain raising.

When sanding on raw wood, use either aluminum oxide "production" paper, garnet paper or stearated paper. Both garnet and stearated papers will sand faster than production paper, but the latter will last longer. Production paper heats and clogs too easily for finish sanding, so between coats of finish it is best to use a paper with lubricant, in grits no coarser than 200. The stearated papers have a soft, powdery soap already on them, and therefore are self-lubricating. The other alternative is wet/dry sandpaper, made with silicon carbide grit on a waterproof backing that makes it compatible with a liquid lubricant such as naphtha or soapy water.

Appropriate Grit Sequence

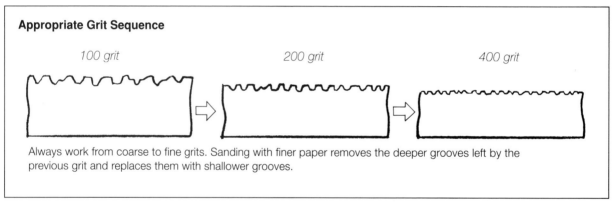

Always work from coarse to fine grits. Sanding with finer paper removes the deeper grooves left by the previous grit and replaces them with shallower grooves.

Skipping a Grit

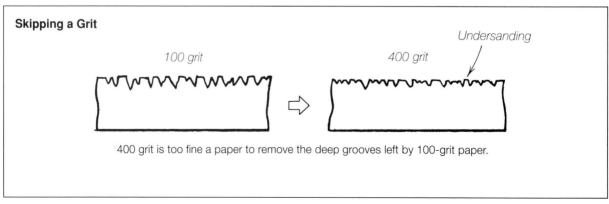

400 grit is too fine a paper to remove the deep grooves left by 100-grit paper.

Grit Grading Systems Compared

Micron grade	U.S.A. CAMI grade	European "P" grade	Coarseness rating
½			
1	2,000		
3	1,500		Micro fine
6	1,200		
9	1,000		
	800		Ultra fine
12	600	P1200	
15			
18	500	P1000	
20		P800	
22	400	P600	Super fine
30	360	P500	
35	320	P400	Extra fine
		P360	
40	280	P320	
	240	P280	Very fine
		P240	
	220	P220	
60	180	P180	
80	150	P150	
100	120	P120	Fine
	100	P100	
	80	P80	Medium
	60	P60	
	50	P50	Coarse
	40	P40	
	36	P36	Extra coarse
	30	P30	
	24	P24	
	20	P20	
	16	P16	
	12	P12	

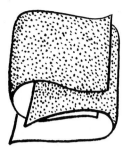
I'm sure you've heard the dictum, "Sand with the grain, not against it." The reason behind it is to avoid cutting across the grain with scratches that might show under the finish. If the scratches are in the same direction as the grain, they will be hidden in the grain pattern. This philosophy presupposes that you will be leaving visible scratches in the wood, and it has some validity if you are sanding only to 120 grit. But if you plan to sand wood any finer, it doesn't much matter which direction you sand, since you will be removing virtually all visible scratches. That is why it is possible to do all your sanding with orbital vibrating sanders, known in the trade as jitterbugs. Once you start sanding the finish, it is completely irrelevant which direction you sand. Not only are you using paper that is too fine to leave marks, but more important, you are not touching the wood at all. You should be abrading only the coating, and finish does not have grain.

Sandpaper grading systems

Sandpaper is graded in various ways, and because the scales are different, it may be difficult to evaluate the coarseness or fineness of a product relative to others. Grading systems are discussed below; the chart on p. 85 compares various sandpaper grit scales.

Screen grading

The common process for sorting and grading mineral for use on sandpaper is to run it through a screen with a certain number of holes per inch. Anything that will fall through an 80-mesh screen, for example, but will not go through a 100-mesh screen will be suitable for 80-grit paper. (This explains why higher numbers equal finer grit.) Screen grading is used for most papers coarser than 240 grit. Above 240 a different separation method is used.

The problem with screen sizing is that it can allow oversize grit with a particular aspect ratio through (aspect ratio is the ratio of width to height). These renegade grit particles will cause sporadic scratches that are obvious with very fine papers on some surfaces, such as 600-grit wet/dry on anything black.

In the U. S. and Canada, screen-graded grit is rated on the CAMI (Coated Abrasives Manufacturing Institute) scale; in Europe, the "P" scale is commonly used ("P" stands for PHEPA, the acronym for the French association for coated abrasives).

Micron grading

One of the newest entries in the field of coated abrasives consists of a polyester film (Mylar) backing loaded with a very accurately sized grit, sorted by micron grading. Micron grading does not use screens, but rather separates the particles more accurately by size, shape and weight, so the range of particle variation is greatly reduced. Micron grading of grit is based on the actual size of the particle in microns (millionths of a meter). Hence, in contrast to the screen grading system, as the grit gets coarser, the numbers get bigger.

Micron-graded grit is applied to a film backing that is itself of a completely uniform thickness. (The thickness of paper and cloth backing in conventional sandpaper varies from spot to spot.) Also, under pressure, the grit can "embed," or push into the relatively soft paper or cloth. Film is much harder, and resists the tendency to embed.

Micron-graded particles on a Mylar backing yield a coated abrasive that starts with a completely uniform grit and prevents pressure from changing that status. The film itself is water and solvent resistant, the grit is applied in an open-coat pattern, and waterproof resin is used for both adhesive coats. For these reasons, film abrasive can be used wet or dry.

Sanding paraphernalia comes in different shapes, sizes and configurations to fit almost any job.

Other details are a matter of personal taste. Some woodworkers feel more comfortable with a sanding block to guarantee flatness; others like to fold the paper double or triple to gain stiffness and friction against their hands. The same is true of the choice between light and heavy backings; thin backings are more flexible, but may tear more easily. There are a myriad of configurations of sanding media — in addition to flat sheets of paper, there are tapes, strings, flexible sponge blocks, sticks, flap wheels and drums, all with grit attached. You can even use woven synthetic hand pads with abrasive grit embedded in the mesh, such as 3M's Scotch-Brite pads. Anything that works for you is the right choice.

Hand-held sanding machines

Hand-held or pad sanders are viewed as a great laborsaving device for finishers and woodworkers, and indeed they are. But there is a misconception that they speed up the work, and more often than not, this belief results in the problems attributed to them.

Q&A:
Steel wool leaves cherry grey

Q: I am building a table made from cherry. To smooth the wood I am using steel wool, which leaves a grey color on the wood. How do I remove this grey color?

A: It sounds like the residual bits of steel wool that are left on the wood's surface are reacting with the tannin in the cherry. You can avoid this problem in the future by switching to 3M brand Scotch-Brite hand pads. These nylon abrasive pads contain no steel and will work as well as (or better than) steel wool without staining the wood.

For the pieces that are already stained, first remove any metal residue by abrading with hand pads or sandpaper, then brushing or vacuuming the surface. It is important that all the metal be removed before treatment. Then liberally wash the wood with a 4% solution (by weight) of oxalic acid in water. Allow it to dry overnight, and remove any white crystals remaining on the surface by flooding the wood with several washes of clean water. If you remove the residue dry, be certain to wear a dust mask and goggles (dry oxalic acid is an irritant to eyes and mucous membranes). Once the oxalic-acid residue is removed and the wood is dry, you can go ahead with the finish of your choice.

The truth is that sanding with a pad sander is less tiring than doing it by hand, but it is no faster. Sanders are designed to be moved at a certain speed, depending on the oscillation speed of the sanding pad. For example, a sander that oscillates at 10,000 revolutions per minute (rpm), a respectably fast rate as sanders go, should be moved only about one inch per second. Try moving your hand over a 10-in. span (about the length of this page) and take a full ten seconds to do it. Pretty slow, isn't it? Most people move sanders faster than they should, and the result is those characteristic swirl marks that embarrass us later by showing up under the finish. When a sander is moved at the correct speed, it won't leave swirl marks. If you are curious as to the correct travel speed for your sander—and I know this will be viewed as a radical suggestion—read the directions that came with it.

Raising the grain

Much has been made of water raising the grain of wood—too much, in fact. I frequently hear of woodworkers avoiding certain stains and finishes because they contain water and will "raise the grain." This last phrase is generally uttered in a tone of reverential horror, as if raising the wood's grain is something to be avoided at all cost. The truth of the matter is that many, if not most, finishes and sealers raise the grain of wood, and frankly, it's no big deal. It simply means that after the first coat of sealer, you will lightly scuff-sand the surface with 220-grit or 280-grit stearated sandpaper, or in the case of turnings and carvings, with nylon abrasive pads. This scuffing will remove the light fuzz caused by the now stiffened grain fibers. Once removed, they will not come up again.

There are some good reasons for raising the grain of wood before applying stain or finish. One reason is to avoid cutting through the finish and stain during scuffing, a mishap that would create the need for annoying touch-up work later. (Wood whose grain was previously raised requires markedly less sanding after the first coat of finish.) Another is that wetting the wood tends to pop out subtle dents, and cause other hard-to-see defects to become more obvious. This can translate into better preparation of the wood and a smoother surface before finish is applied. As with most areas of finishing, though, there are right and wrong ways to raise the grain.

Let's say that you are planning to sand with 120-grit paper, then follow that with 220 grit. After the first sanding, wet the wood thoroughly with water, and wipe off any excess to avoid sitting puddles. Let the wood dry thoroughly (overnight is best), then sand lightly with the 220-grit sandpaper. The water will raise the grain of the wood, and the 220-grit paper will de-fur it by cutting back the raised fibers. Notice that this process does not add any more sanding; the only added work is wetting down the wood between two sanding steps that were already planned. What is important is to avoid sanding too much, or with too heavy a grit, after the water has been applied. If, after the wood has been soaked, you were to sand with a paper that is too coarse — 120 grit, for example — you would cut through and expose new wood fibers in addition to removing the raised ones. These newly exposed fibers will fur up if more water is added. If you scuff off only the raised fibers, you will not have any more significant furring at subsequent steps.

One friend likens the grain-raising process to shaving. The water or sanding sealer does the job of shaving cream; it makes the hair stand up. The fine sandpaper is the razor, shaving off the raised fibers. Once the hair is off, you stop shaving. Going any deeper would be counterproductive, and, in the case of shaving, rather painful. For that reason, I never use anything coarser than 220-grit stearated paper after wetting the wood, and I keep my sanding to a minimum. If the 120- grit sanding was done carefully and completely, it should take only a few minutes of very quick, gentle scuffing with the 220-grit paper to have the surface ready to stain or coat.

Clearly, the whole process of raising the grain is relevant only if you are planning to sand to 220-grit level before applying any finish. If your finish and wood are such that sanding to 120 grit is adequate, then don't concern yourself with wetting the wood. A good example of this is a solid-colored coating over a white primer. Another case is if you are going to fill the grain with pore filler; forget the water and save the 220-grit paper until after the filler is on and dry (for more on filling wood, see pp. 126-136).

Scraping vs. sanding

Many devoted woodworkers feel that scraping or planing wood leaves a surface that is smoother than a sanded one. Smoothness depends on many things: the grit of sandpaper, the sharpness of the scraper, the operator skill level, etc. I'm not so sure that talking about that level of smoothness means anything when you are discussing a material like wood, which, when viewed under a magnifying lens, appears to be more empty spaces than solid material. Nevertheless, it is true that scraped or planed surfaces are different from sanded surfaces, at least in how they accept stain. If you take a piece of wood and scrape half of it and sand the other half, you will find that most (not all) stains will "take" differently on the two sides. Usually, the scraped surface will absorb less stain and remain lighter. Therefore, if you are going to sand part of a surface, sand all of it, and to the same grit.

CHAPTER 5
Coloring Wood

There is a hierarchy in the larger finishing shops of New York City, a class system that affords some jobs more status than others. At the top of the finisher's pyramid is the color man, that fortunate soul entrusted with the task of adding color to wood. For those of us who were not born composers, dancers or poets, this may be one of our finest avenues for artistic expression.

Over the years, I've heard a large number of woodworkers preach against the idea of coloring wood. "Doesn't need it," they snap grumpily. "I tried it, and the wood looked better before I stained it." But I often wonder if behind their aversion to color lurks the fear of not doing the wood justice. To be sure, it is as easy to deflate wood with stain as it is to enhance it. Coloring wood is an art—and a joyful one at that—and like all such endeavors, contains for the artist the constant fear that in the end, the canvas would have looked better untouched.

But it doesn't have to be that way. With just a few basic rules and an understanding of the raw materials involved, staining wood can open the door to controlling, changing, upgrading and creating on wood with nothing more intrusive than a bit of dye.

The right dye or stain can make subtle or muted grain leap out.

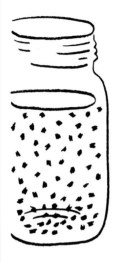

In a pigmented stain, the pigmented particles are suspended in a liquid medium; they do not dissolve.

Pigments vs. dyes

Much of the confusion about whether stains make wood deeper or muddier has to do with the type of coloring material used. Wood stains are made with either pigments, dyes or a combination of the two. Pigments are opaque and sit on top of the wood; dyes are translucent and penetrate into the wood.

Pigments and pigmented stains

Pigments are solid, colored, inert particles of mineral. These particles clump together into small lumps of color that are visible to the naked eye. The particles are not soluble, but rather are suspended in a liquid medium to make them easy to apply. In other words, a pigmented stain is like a glass of water with small specks of dirt floating in it. Theoretically, if you were to force a pigmented stain through a fine enough strainer, it would filter out the pigment and leave you with a clear liquid. When pigmented stains are allowed to sit for some time, the particles (which are usually heavier than the liquid medium) tend to settle to the bottom, so these stains must be stirred before being used.

If you were to put some pigmented stain onto glass and hold it up to the light, it would appear more or less opaque, like paint. In fact, paint is made by putting white or other colored pigments into a clear base. Now, if you were to take a colored paint and thin it out by adding a lot of extra solvent, you would end up with a somewhat opaque liquid that had a relatively small amount of binder and colorant; in other words, you would have made a pigmented wood stain. Many finishers do just that; when they need a particular color of pigmented stain, they buy paint and thin it out with its proper solvent. This is perfectly valid, but it will yield a fairly weak stain; commercial stains generally have a higher ratio of pigment to binder than paints.

Pigmented stains consist of solvent, binder and pigment. The solvent makes the material an easy-to-handle liquid, and the pigment imparts color. What, then, does the binder do? That will become clear when you understand how pigmented stains color wood. Wood is a very porous material whose surface, even when very smooth, is actually full of minuscule nooks and crannies that can trap pigment particles the way an English muffin traps butter. When stain is applied, the pigment settles in these spaces as the solvent evaporates. If the stain sitting in these recesses is only colored dust, you should be able to blow it off the wood once the solvent evaporates, right? That's where the binder comes in—like a glue, it holds the pigment in place once the stain is dry. Without it, you would be able to get most of the pigment back off the wood with a scrub brush and an air gun once the stain was dry. As it is, you can remove most of a pigmented stain by scrubbing the wood with solvent before the binder dries.

**A dye stain (top) is transparent;
a pigmented stain (bottom)
is opaque.**

Pigmented stains are likely to act differently depending on the pore structure of the wood being stained. The more nooks and crannies the pigment can find to settle in, the more the wood will take the stain. If those nooks and crannies are in a particular pattern, the pigment will enhance the pattern. For example, a pigmented stain on ash, a ring-porous wood with very large pores in a cathedral grain pattern, will color the grain much more than the areas between. A wood that is diffuse porous, such as poplar, will take the stain much more evenly. Maple, which is also diffuse porous but has smaller, tighter pores than poplar, will take less stain but will take it evenly. Mahogany has large, medium and small pores in a semi-ring-porous pattern, so it takes some stain in the areas between the grain lines, but even more in the large grain itself.

Too much pigment left on (left) will completely obscure the wood.

The wood is not the only element that contributes to how much stain is imparted to the surface; the other part of the equation is the finisher. You can wipe off all of the stain that will come up while it is wet, leaving only what is grabbed by the pores, or you can leave some extra on the wood to make the color deeper. Allowing more stain to remain on the surface will impart more color, but it will also result in less clarity as it hides more of the wood. If you leave too much pigment on, it will completely block all of the wood below it, and you will have what looks like, and in fact is, a coat of paint instead of a stain.

Dyes

Dyes differ from pigments in that the colorant is in solution rather than in suspension. Remember the suspension made by floating some dirt in a glass of water? Imagine putting salt in the water instead of dirt. Rather than floating around making the water look cloudy, the salt would disappear, leaving the mixture transparent, but a quick taste would confirm its presence. The salt would dissolve, and its large crystalline structure would break up into very small charged particles called ions. Dyes work in exactly the same way; they are crystals that break up into tiny ions when dissolved. Because the dye ions are so small compared to pigment particles, dyes appear more transparent than pigments, and are able to color wood without hiding its figure or rendering the surface muddy.

The charged dye ions are polar; that is, they are like magnets, with a positive charge at one end and a negative charge at the other. And like magnets, they are attracted to anything else that is polar. Because wood fibers are also polar, they attract the dye ions. The smaller particle size, combined with a polar attraction, allows a dye to penetrate more deeply into wood and impart a color that will not scrub off. In contrast to pigments, which tend to sit on the surface, dyes will penetrate more deeply.

The polar attraction of dye to wood also means that the dye will bind to the wood with no outside help. Unlike pigments, dye stains do not require a binder and can be made of just colorant and solvent. Once the solvent evaporates, the wood has nothing but color in it, so binderfree dyes are always employed under (or in) a finish and must be topcoated. Since binders are generally polymers of some sort, these stains can be thought of as non-polymeric. Lacking a binder, a non-polymeric stain will go under virtually any finish with no compatibility or adhesion problems. If you are not sure whether the stain you're considering will cause problems with your favorite finish, one way to avoid the issue is to opt for a non-polymeric dye stain. However, some dye stains

*T*he secret of Stradivarius: a pigment that acts like a dye?

I can't tell you how many musical-instrument repair shops have ultraviolet black lights as part of their equipment, but I can tell you why. They are used to detect fake Stradivarius violins.

It all goes to show how easy it is to fool the human eye. Allow me to explain. We normally see pigments as opaque, largely because of their size. But a pigment with a small enough particle size may appear transparent in normal white light, yet become cloudy when viewed under ultraviolet light.

The light we are able to see (the visible spectrum) is made up of light waves ranging in size from 400 to 750 nanometers (nm). (A nanometer equals .000000001 meter, or billionth of a meter.) A particle will appear translucent if it is smaller than one-half the size of the wave length of light under which it is viewed. For example, let's consider a pigment stain with an average particle size of 300 nm. If you look at the finish under light with a 700 nm wavelength (more than twice the size of the pigment particle), the pigment stain will appear translucent, just like a dye. But if you look at the same finish under a black light, it will appear cloudy and opaque. Ultraviolet black lights generate light in the low 400-nm range;

viewed under this light, the same 300-nm particle is now larger than one-half the wavelength.

What does this have to do with a violin? It is widely believed that Stradivarius used a pigmented stain on his violins, but the particles are so small that the finish appears translucent. But, the story goes, the particle size is just large enough so that if you shine an ultraviolet light on it, the golden red finish turns a cloudy pink. Hence, the proliferation of black lights in instrument-repair workshops.

Can you really detect a Strad by shining ultraviolet light on it? No. But I'll bet the rumor doesn't hurt the black-light business any.

do contain a binder. They are usually referred to as self-sealing stains. Binders are a must with pigments, but they hold no real advantage when it comes to dyes, and in fact, limit their use.

The transparency and particle size of dyes will result in a totally different appearance on wood. A dark brown pigmented stain applied to ash would yield a high contrast of dark brown pores and rather light areas between the grain lines. The same color in a dye would render the entire surface an even brown, with only slightly darker grain lines. On woods with subtle grain effects, such as curly or quilted maple, dyes enhance the figure in the wood where pigments might easily overrun it. On very porous woods that lack a prominent grain or figure pattern (poplar, for example), the difference between pigments and dyes will be less noticeable. However, woods that tend to take stain in a splotchy or uneven way, such as cherry, will usually color more evenly with a dye. The same is true of end grain; spindles and raised panels that have both flat and end grain showing will stain much more evenly with a dye.

Unlike pigments, some of which are quite lightfast, all dyes fade in sunlight; some faster than others. For that reason, dyes are usually not suggested for exterior work unless the clear top coat over the dye is well buffered with ultraviolet (UV) absorbers (see pp. 20-21); these clear compounds, when added to a clear finish, protect the substrates from UV degrade.

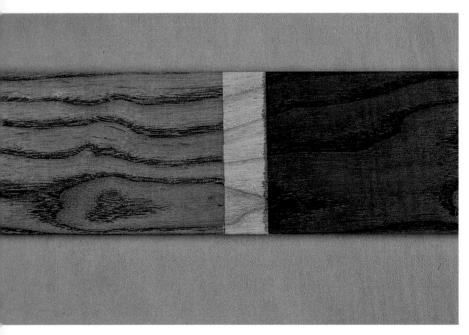

A pigmented stain (left) colors mainly the pores of ring-porous woods; a dye (right) colors wood more evenly.

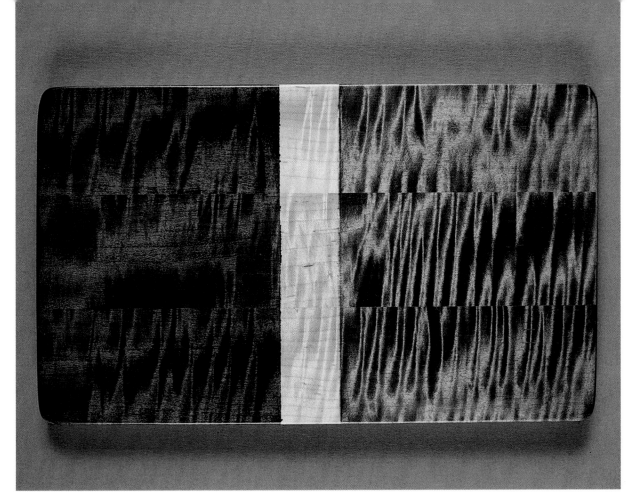

Pigments (left) mute subtle figure; dyes (right) enhance it.

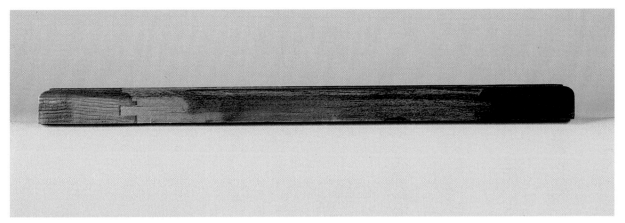

On the edge of a panel frame, the pigment (right) takes much more heavily on the open-pored end grain than does a dye (left).

Stain solvents and binders

Dyes are colorants dissolved in some liquid that penetrate and color wood without obscuring it; pigments are mineral particles suspended in a vehicle, consisting of solvent and a binder, that allows the stain to sit on top and in the pores of wood. But what of the vehicle itself? How does the solvent or solvent/binder combination affect the action of the stain?

Because pigments do not react chemically with their solvent, the vehicle makes little difference in terms of how they color. The vehicle is important only in that it must be compatible with whatever top coat is going over it. By that I mean that it should allow the top coat to adhere without adverse reactions, and that it should not completely dissolve under a brushed finish. If the top coat does not adhere adequately, it is likely to peel later. If the top coat redissolves the binder, the color may get unintentionally pushed around when the top coat is brushed on.

In the past, the most common vehicle for pigment has been a drying oil such as linseed oil, thinned, if necessary, with mineral spirits. Oil is a particularly good binder because it will not redissolve itself once it has cured and will work under most lacquers and varnishes—almost everything, in fact, except water-based coatings. By varying the ratio of pigment to binder to solvent, you get the wide range of oil-based stains currently on the market. Artist's oil colors contain lots of pigment in oil with no thinners. Add Japan driers—heavy metal salts used to speed up the drying time of the oil—and you get Japan colors. Dilute with mineral spirits and you get commercial, ready-to-use oil-based wood stains. Incorporate a thickening agent, and you can turn the mixture into a wiping stain or gel stain. To reduce the amount of

Are anilines dangerous?

A good percentage of the stains based on aniline dyes, as well as the powders themselves, are sold as nontoxic. Yet if you look up "aniline" in a chemical dictionary, it is listed as quite toxic. How is this inconsistency possible?

Just as there is no sin in sincere and no good in goodbye, there is no aniline in an aniline dye. The dye is so named because aniline is used as an intermediate in manufacturing, but none remains in the final product. (An intermediate is a material that is part of a process, but does not become part of the product; at least not in its original form.) Similar examples can be found in white bread and decaffeinated coffee. White flour is bleached, but no bleach remains in the bread. Methylene chloride is often used to decaffeinate coffee, but is removed long before the dark brew visits your morning cup.

solvent needed, the oil/pigment mix can also be added to water to create a water-based emulsion. Although the various additives offer a wide range of handling characteristics, the resulting mixes are quite similar in how they stain.

Dyes are an entirely different story because they are actually dissolved in a liquid. Therefore, the solvent is quite important; attempting to dissolve an aniline dye in the wrong solvent may fail completely or may result in a different color solution. Dyes come in three solvencies: oil soluble, alcohol soluble and water soluble. All three types are available both premixed in an appropriate medium or in powder form.

Oil-soluble dyes can be dissolved in oil or any of a wide range of petroleum and coal-tar distillates, such as naphtha, mineral spirits, toluene, xylene, acetone or lacquer thinner. The drying speed and depth of penetration depend on the particular solvent.

Alcohol-soluble dyes use any common alcohol (ethanol, methanol, isopropynol). They dry very fast (a situation that can cause lap marks) and are quite flammable. Alcohol dyes penetrate deeply and offer a rich range of colors. There is a subcategory of these dyes that will dissolve in both alcohol and water. Alcohol dyes will also tolerate the addition of water and/or glycols and glycol ethers after they have been predissolved in alcohol.

Water-soluble dyes penetrate the deepest of all anilines, and tend to be the most lightfast and richest of all colors. They are also the most user friendly, in that they do not leave lap marks and are completely self regulating, as well as being nontoxic, odorless and nonflammable. Non-polymeric water dyes will not only go on evenly, but can also invisibly repair "holidays"—those annoying missed spots that you generally find only after the stain has dried. Water dyes will also tolerate alcohol, glycols and glycol ethers after they have been dissolved.

Some common types of stains

Unfortunately, there are no laws governing what terminology manufacturers may use to define their products, so an explanation of terminology will always have some exceptions. The discussion that follows should make the translation from the label a little easier by defining categories. Where a material's description differs from the common name, go with the description. After all, what's in a name?

Q: I've been trying to dye a maple table, but I can't get the color as dark as I'd like. What can I do?

A: Wood accepts dye to varying degrees, depending on the wood species, type of dye and its solvent (water, oil, alcohol). Maple is one wood that is reluctant to accept dye—especially oil-soluble dye. You will get the deepest and darkest color on maple with a water-soluble aniline dye. Make sure that the wood is clean of any oil or wax and that the stained areas are resanded. Control the intensity of the color by increasing the ratio of dye powder to hot water.

Penetrating oil stains

Although penetrating oil stains can contain pigments, in most cases this term indicates an oil-soluble dye in a mixture of oil and thinner. Penetrating oils are usually thin liquids that color with a good bit of depth and clarity, but may become splotchy and uneven on certain woods, like cherry or pine.

Penetrating dyes (oil-free)

Predissolved dyes in solvent, most often free of any binder, offer deep, rich, even coloring, fast drying and compatibility under virtually any finish. They are often mixed as liquid, but can be thickened to almost any consistency. One company has already started offering a very forgiving water-soluble dye in an easy-to-control gel. Look for this category to expand—especially water-soluble versions—as the Environmental Protection Agency (EPA) further restricts the use of solvents.

Wiping stains

Named for their handling properties rather than their content, wiping stains are thicker pastes, rather than liquids. As a rule, they are made with pigments, and as such, retain pigment's characteristic ability to be applied lighter or darker, depending solely on how much is wiped off or left on. The vehicle can be either oil based or water based; both have wide but not unlimited compatibility under various top coats.

Pigmented oil stains

Pigmented oil stains are oil-based liquid versions of wiping stains. They contain only pigment, no dye. All the options and restrictions of pigments apply.

Water-based pigmented stains

If you add extra water and a binder to universal tinting colors (see p. 102, you end up with water-based pigmented stains, a low-solvent alternative to pigmented oil or wiping stain. They handle the same, smell better and will go under almost any finish.

Pickling stains

Offered in either water-based or oil-based formulations, pickling stain is nothing more than a fancy name for pigmented stains that are either white or light pastel in color. Incidentally, there is no such thing as white dye. White only exists as a pigment. Therefore, any stain that is pastel, or has white in it, is pigmented.

Water-based oil stains

Although the term "water-based oil stains" sounds like an oxymoron, these relative newcomers are actually hybrids designed to reduce organic solvents. They consists of an oil-based stain in an aqueous emulsion (droplets of oil stain suspended in water). Treat them as you would any oil stain; they can be made with dye, pigment or both.

Stain colorants

Even with all of the various brands and types of stains on the market, you can't always find precisely the color you need in the vehicle you want. To gain an extra measure of flexibility, most professional finishers routinely stock a few raw materials that can be made into custom stains and glazes. These are essentially the same building blocks that manufacturers use to create their materials. With the right solvent and a dollop of courage, you'll find yourself mixing the perfect stain instead of settling for the hardware-store "catch of the day."

Artist's oil colors

Artist's oil colors are more a raw material than a stain. These pastes (sold in toothpaste tubes or cans) are pigments ground in oil, usually linseed or soya. Add some mineral spirits or naphtha, and you have a pigmented oil stain. Some finishers mix them to create colors that are not usually available as wood stains. You can also add them to pigmented oil stains when you need that hard-to-find shot of, say, bright purple to get just the shade you want.

Japan colors

Japan colors are artist's oil colors to which Japan driers have been added. Also sold separately as an oil-stain additive, Japan driers contain metallic salts or soaps that speed up the drying time of certain drying oils (they work great with linseed or soya oil, but not at all with tung oil). Japan colors are almost always made with linseed oil, and like the slower-drying artist's oil colors, are perfect for mixing or adding to oil-based stains, glazes and pore fillers.

Universal tinting colors (UTCs)

Universal tinting colors are thick colored pastes that look and handle very much like artist's oil colors and Japan colors, but with one primary difference: UTCs are designed to go with coatings that might react badly to the presence of oil. Rather than having oil as their base, UTCs are dispersed in a solvent that is compatible with a wide range of other solvents and binders. As a result, UTCs are compatible with both water-based and oil-based vehicles. When dispensed from a paint-store carousel, UTCs are used to custom color water-based latex paints, but will also work with most lacquers. Add some distilled water and some clear (or colored) latex paint for body and you'll have a water-based wiping stain. When they are thinned out and some binder—usually acrylic resin—is added, UTCs become water-based pigmented stains. Cut with a bit of lacquer thinner and linseed oil, these versatile colorants will be ready to mix with oil or Japan colors, varnishes and solvent lacquers, too.

Pigment powders

Less common, but still frequently available are pigment powders. These are pure pigment with no solvent or binder added. Sold primarily for touch-up work, they are usually called fresco colors or earth colors. They are handy for making stains from scratch (an endeavor that few finishers indulge in) or for formulating specialized putties, fillers, stains and glazes.

Asphaltum

Although asphaltum is not easy to find in art-supply stores, it is too good a material to pass up. The base of this tar-like gunk can be either petroleum or bitumen (coal), but the colorant responsible for its beau-

Characteristics of Pigment Stains and Dye Stains		
	Pigments	Dyes
Lightfastness	*Very Good*	*Poor*
Ease of application	*Good*	*Excellent*
Solubility/miscibility	*Non-Soluble*	*Soluble*
Evenness	*Fair*	*Excellent*
Compatibility	*Fair*	*Excellent*
Clarity	*Fair*	*Excellent*

ty is a natural mineral called gilsonite. Use it as a stain on raw wood and you have a deep brown/black color perfect for dark Jacobean or mission oak; but use it as a thin glaze between coats of finish and it breaks out into a rich brown with overtones of both green and red, reminiscent of the iridescent rainbows on the oil-slick tainted puddles that show up on your driveway after a hard rain.

Trade secrets

By the fall of 1973, I had completed my apprenticeship and had graduated to a real job in a good-sized finishing shop in south Florida. I landed the job by convincing the owner that I knew virtually all there was to know about finishing; at the time, I probably believed that myself. No matter, within a few days we both knew the truth.

In spite of the rocky start, I ingratiated myself with the boss, a transplanted New York finisher, by working hard and being more than eager to learn. Soon I was allowed to order materials for the shop, and I began to learn the sources for all our finish supplies—all but one, that is.

You see, we had a secret finish called Golden Oak, and it was popular enough that the shop had developed a local reputation for it. We'd stain oak with a pigmented French ochre wiping stain on the raw wood, then seal it with a coat or two of lacquer. When that was dry, we'd glaze the wood with "special glaze," a dark, thick, oily concoction that was secured in the front office in unmarked cans.

One day the boss, Wade, called me into the office to reveal the formula for our special glaze. But first, I was sworn to secrecy; after all, no one outside of the shop was privy to the key to this near magical glaze. I was elated; here was my chance to learn one of the coveted trade secrets that separate professional finishers from the hoi polloi.

Special glaze was asphaltum (roofing tar), purchased from a local contractor and cut with mineral spirits to a liquid consistency. It was easy to understand the secrecy. Our high-class customers would be less than ecstatic to learn their oak antiques were being smeared with tar, even though the end result was rather alluring. Still, it was now my secret to protect, and I kept it to myself in spite of numerous onslaughts of curiosity by fellow workers. "What is this stuff?" they'd ask, sniffing the can. "It smells like tar." I'd just shrug and look foolish, ever mindful of my position as keeper of the flame.

A few years later, I found myself working in one of the top finishing houses in New York. My first day on the job, I was checking out the familiar cans of finish on the shelf when, to my shock, I came across one labeled "asphaltum," and sure enough, it contained the old familiar glaze.

Clearly, some cad had stolen Wade's secret formula and brought it up north. I quizzed one of the older employees about the can, and he looked at me as if I had just fallen off the turnip truck. It seems that asphaltum was a staple in every New York finishing shop, not only for glazing a variety of finishes, but as a raw-wood stain as well. The local finishing-supply company had been selling asphaltum to shops for longer than my former boss had been alive. I smelled a rat.

It didn't take too long to figure out that Wade, who had been only a mediocre finisher in the competitive arena of New York, must have found himself as a big fish in the smaller pond of the Deep South. He parlayed his knowledge of asphaltum, a common material that had not yet arrived on the local Florida scene, into a finish based on a trade secret. Such is the stuff that myth is made of.

As for me, I would never again be conned out of sharing information. I learned early on that in finishing, there are no trade secrets.

Mixing colors

The folks who devote their time to working with how we see different hues estimate that the average person can differentiate among approximately four million shades of color, and trained colorists can often see twice that many. This should help to explain why even if you buy every color of stain that every company offers, you still won't have found the exact color you want to stain that ash end table you made for cousin Martha.

Don't despair. You can mix your own colors of stain, and it is surprisingly simple. Stay with one type of stain, and you won't have any problems. For example, if you are using a penetrating oil (dye) stain, you can mix it with another penetrating oil (dye) stain — or four others if you like. It is not a good idea to mix pigments with dyes, or oil with water, or one solvent/resin pair with another. But you can usually mix any color of one type of stain with any other color of the same type.

Surprise — metamerism!

"Biedermeier cherry," she announced with conviction. "That's the color I want. Biedermeier cherry."

Although she was one of the most exacting decorators we had to work with, Suzette was quick with a compliment when we did what she asked. Besides, she always knew what she was looking for, so I rather enjoyed it when she brought us finishing jobs. At the time, I was the foreman of a four-man "daylight" shop; a cavernous cinder-block garage whose huge door let in copious amounts of bright South

Florida sun. As finishers, we were especially boastful of how our "natural" light let us hit colors so well. On that day, though, it wasn't much help.

"But Biedermeier is a style of furniture, not a color," I complained. The truth was, I had no idea what she wanted.

The next morning, she was back; this time, with a sample. The small wood block had a rich, warm brown finish, and I quickly promised to match it perfectly.

Three weeks later, the large sideboard gleamed in its finished glory, and I proudly called on Suzette to grant her approval of the work. We positioned the piece by the big open door, partly to show it in its best light, and partly because it was to be delivered the next morning; once it was approved, we could quickly load it onto the waiting

truck. Suzette breezed in at quarter to five, and held the sample block next to our finish.

"Perfect!" she announced. "Send it." In ten minutes we had it wrapped in paper and inside the waiting delivery van. In another five, we were on our way home, pleased with ourselves for a job well done.

The pleasure was short-lived. By ten the next morning, the sideboard had made its way back into the shop, with a furious Suzette close behind.

"What did you do to my sideboard?" she demanded. "Why did you change the color?" I was dumbstruck. No one in the shop had even seen the piece of furniture since the night before. We couldn't have altered its color if we had wanted to. We all gathered around as she plopped

How do you know if two stain colors are in the same mixable category? The easiest way is to stick with one company's line for each combination. That is not to say that you shouldn't use stains from many manufacturers. You should. But, if you are not certain what is in the can, the safe bet is to mix it only with other stains in the same line.

You can also read the labels. If two stains have the same basic ingredients and the same descriptive title, odds are they'll go together well. I wouldn't hesitate to mix the hypothetical Diddlebach's Pigmented Oil Stain with Farnswoggle's Pigmented Oil Stain, especially if both labels say "contains linseed oil and mineral spirits." As a general rule, you can mix Japan colors with artist's oil colors, water-soluble dyes with other water-soluble dyes, alcohol-soluble with alcohol-soluble, and so on.

How do you know when the stain is the right color? After all, it looks different in the jar than on the wood. Try it first on a piece of scrap wood. Please don't use the top of that beautiful quilted maple table

the sample angrily on top of the buffet. For half a minute, there was dead silence. "It looks fine to me," I said quietly, and when I turned and saw Suzette's startled face, I realized that it looked fine to her, too. In embarrassed silence, we once again loaded the piece onto the truck.

Half an hour passed before someone from the front office walked into the finishing shop and, handing me a slip of paper, said, "Suzette wants you to come to this address right away."

As I strode into the room I saw the problem immediately. Sitting beneath a bank of incandescent spotlights, that sideboard stood out like a sore thumb; not the rich hue of the sample, but an almost garish orange. Sitting

atop the piece was the sample block, its soft brown color giving mute testimony to the disaster.

Without ever having heard the word, we had our first run-in with metamerism, the strange property that causes colored objects that look identical under one set of lighting conditions to appear different under a different light source. When viewed in daylight, the sample and the sideboard were a match; but under the yellow glare of the spotlights, they weren't even close. Apparently, whoever had made that sample had used a different set of coloring media, and the result was a metameric mismatch.

The incident reminded me of the make-up mirror in my cousin's dressing room. Around its frame sat three rows of lights, each

slightly different. She had once explained to me that by changing the lighting tint, she could make sure the eye shadow that perfectly complemented her dress in the daylight would still look good under indoor lighting come evening. Whoever designed her dressing-room vanity must have had a good understanding of both fashion-conscious women and metamerism.

And what of the sideboard? We refinished it, of course. But this time, we closed the big garage door and worked under a set of spotlights set up just for the occasion.

you just made as a sample board! If you really want to become proficient mixing and matching stains, do most of your learning by finishing scrapwood.

Assuming you've arrived at a mix that is wrong, how do you know which color to add to make it right? Ah, there's the rub. There is a lot of trial and error in mixing stains, and bypassing that requires a good understanding of how we see color, a whole field of study unto itself. As a jumping-off place, you can use the fact that complimentary colors will often disable one another. The pairs to remember are blue/orange, purple/yellow, and red/green. If your brown stain is too red, add a little green; if you need to soften the orange cast, try a bit of blue. The same is true of the earth tones. A greenish raw umber will somewhat counteract the reddish cast of a burnt sienna, and vice versa. If you want to go further with this, the best book on the subject that I have found is Michael Wilcox's *Blue and Yellow Don't Make Green*, available for $24.95 from North Light Books, 1507 Dana Ave., Cincinnati, OH 45207; (800) 666-0963.

Why are dye powders a different color than the liquid they form?

If you've used powdered aniline dyes, you have probably noticed that many of the powders are a very different color than the liquid dye they produce. They are usually quite a bit darker; yellows and oranges are often brown, for example. Pigment powders, on the other hand, are the same color in powder as in liquid. You may have wondered why.

It is tempting to make up some fable about how the fox and the rabbit fooled the dye gods, but the truth is that is has to do with the crystalline structure of dyes. The large dye crystals absorb and reflect light differently than the small ions that are formed in solution, and we see those differences as color alterations. If the dye solutions are allowed to dry, they will once again reform the darker large crystals.

Why, then, don't dyes get darker when they dry after you've put them on the wood? The polar wood fibers act like magnets to hold onto the polar dye ions, preventing them from rejoining into crystals. Thus, the dyed wood retains its true dyed color, and not the misleading color of the mound of dry dye powder. Just as you can't judge a book by its cover, you can't assess a dye in its powdered form.

Applying stains

What can you use to apply stain? Absolutely anything. If it works to get the stain to the wood, that is all that matters. You can grab a brush, rag, nylon scrub pad, spray gun or sponge. You can dip the part, or pour the stain over it. As long as the solvent in the stain does not melt the applicator (an unlikely eventuality), if it is comfortable for you, it is okay with me! For more on finishing equipment, see Chapter 2.

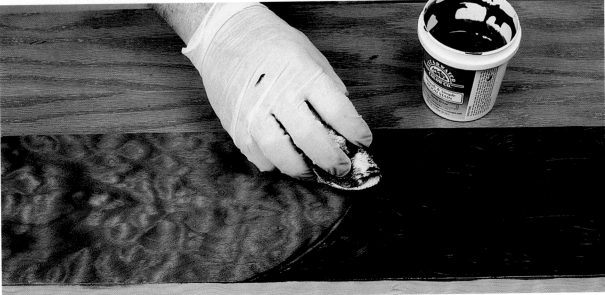

Flood the surface of the wood liberally with stain (top), then wipe off all the excess before it dries (above).

Considering all the various names and types of stains out there, I'm sure it will come as a relief to discover that the process of staining is quite simple, and is pretty much the same for all stains. In fact, there is really just one universal rule: Flood it on; wipe it off. This may sound simplistic, but to get the most out of your stain, use lots of it. Flood the surface of the wood, then wipe off all the excess before it dries. Trying to limit the amount of stain you use by putting it on sparingly is false economy, and will only result in an uneven stain job. Whether you are using pigmented or dye stains, let the wood swim in stain.

How much should you wipe off? You are always safe if you wipe it all off; however, you do have some other options depending upon whether the stain is polymeric (contains a binder), or non-polymeric (does not contain a binder).

Using polymeric stains

If a stain contains oil, says "self-sealing" or "pigmented" on the label or is a one-step stain/finish mixture, then it is a polymeric stain. The vast majority of commercial stains fit in this category. These stains contain binders, and will form a film when they dry.

Once you flood a polymeric stain onto the wood surface, how much should you wipe off? The easiest way to ensure an even stain is to wipe off all that you can. But you do have the option of wiping off only some, and leaving some. You can leave the stain on as uniformly as

You can control the color of a pigmented stain by wiping off more or less, as you choose.

possible, or you can wipe it off selectively, allowing it to remain heavier in certain areas and lighter in others, either for special effects or to compensate for the natural irregularities of wood coloring. How you control the color is an element of the art of staining.

Color changes can be made with polymeric stains after they are on the wood, but only while the stain is still wet. That is, you can create different staining effects by flooding on and wiping off any number of different colors of the same type (and brand) of polymeric stain, one after the other, as long as the stains you are working with have not yet begun to form a film.

Remember, when a polymeric stain dries, it forms a film barrier. If you wait for the stain to dry and then add another coat of the same mixture, it will darken the wood. However, the result will be another colored layer on top of the previous one, and this will look somewhat different than the stain on raw wood. It will have more of the appearance of a very thin layer of tinted varnish on top of the stained wood. Each subsequent layer will be more and more difficult to apply evenly. Any variation will result in lap marks—you will see darker areas where the stain rag overlapped unevenly. If the stain is pigmented, each layer will also obscure more and more of the wood below. Therefore, your best bet with polymeric stains is to apply the stain once, or work it before it dries.

Using non-polymeric dye stains

Non-polymeric dye stains are aniline dye mixtures that do not form a film when they dry; they contain no oils, resins, binders or pigments.

As with other stains, first flood the wood surface with stain, but with non-polymeric dye stains, always wipe all of the stain off. In other words, wipe off all that you can while it is still wet, and what remains will be exactly the amount that is supposed to be there. If you leave excess dye on a surface, it is likely to recrystallize and form a layer of powdery material that can prevent the clear top coat from adequately adhering to the wood.

In many cases, when non-polymeric dye stains dry, the dyed wood will appear to change color—it will get lighter and dusty looking. Don't let this disturb you; it is perfectly normal. The correct color—the way it appeared while it was wet—will return once you apply the finish over the dye. Remember that a dye is a coloring material, not a finish. Dyes will eventually require a finish on top, both to protect the wood and to help exhibit the dye's true colors.

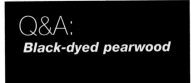

Q&A:
Black-dyed pearwood

Q: I am looking for a way to dye pearwood black, not just on the surface, but completely throughout its thickness (about .020 in.). So far, I have used alcohol-solvent dye (lightfast black). Even after soaking for four days, the wood is still not completely black.

A: The Italians seem to have the dyeing market wrapped up, and they are both successful and secretive with their methods. Word has it that they accomplish "through" dyeing by introducing the dye either under pressure or in a vacuum, and these methods would be impractical in a home shop. I suspect that they are using water-soluble dyes. You can also buy black-dyed pearwood. I have used black-dyed pearwood quite a lot, though, and to tell you the truth, the sample you sent was as good as any I ever bought.

If you are displeased with the color you get, there are three ways you can change the color of a non-polymeric dye stain even after you have stained the wood. They are:

• Restain with a more intense mixture of the same color (i.e., more dye per the same volume of solvent). Restaining with exactly the same stain mixture will not make the stain darker. To make it darker, you must add more dye to the mixture. When in doubt, start with a lighter shade. If the color is too light, you can reapply a darker mixture either immediately, while the first color is wet, or after the stain has dried.

• Restain with a different color dye, either immediately or after the first stain dries. If you feel the first stain was too weak (for example, a light brown), you can go over it with a different one (say, a black/brown). You can also lighten by restaining with a lighter color. For instance, you could put the light brown on after the dark brown to lighten it. You can even change the tint entirely by restaining with a totally different color dye. Each new color will add some of its character into the total look without completely replacing what is already there. In other words, if you start with brown, then restain with yellow, you will have a lighter yellowish-brown. And so

Repeated applications of the same dye will not change the color, but a more concentrated dye solution will.

With non-polymeric dyes, you can add a lighter color (yellow) to modify the original color (top), or go darker (brown) to change the color again (above). You can go back and forth through various tones indefinitely.

Let's recap
(pigment stains and
dye stains)

Pigment stains

Flood it on, wipe off as much as you want. Leave on more, and the color will be darker; wipe off more to lighten the effect of the stain. Mix colors before you apply; restain only after the first coat has dried—restaining while wet will often result in uneven results. Each successive coat of the same stain mixture will add more color, and hide more wood.

Dye stains

Flood it on, wipe it all off. Darken the color by adding more powder to the mix. Lighten the color by adding more solvent to the mix. Change colors by mixing dyes together, or by subsequent dyeing of the wood with a different color. Colors will average together, not replace one another entirely. With most dyes (especially water-soluble dyes), subsequent coats of the same mix and intensity will do nothing.

on. By wiping on various colors, you can go back and forth, lighter and darker, redder or greener, blacker or more yellow, almost indefinitely. You can't entirely replace the first dye you applied, but you can mitigate it.

• You can remove the dye entirely with a chlorine-type bleach, such as Clorox or Purex liquid laundry bleach. Bleaching is discussed on pp. 70-71.

If you don't want to change color, but merely need to restain to correct spots you missed the first time around, then simply restain with the same concentration of the same color. Even if you put this dye back onto areas that are already stained, it will not change the color.

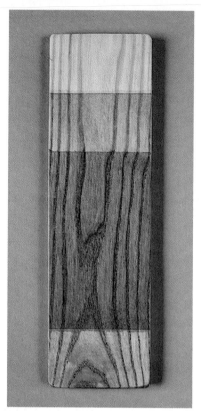

The effects of pigment and/or dye on an ash board. Top to bottom: raw wood, dyed wood, pigment over dye, and pigment only.

Shading, glazing, toning

There is more to coloring wood than just staining it. You can glaze, shade, tone, dry brush, and so on. In fact, the possibilities know no bounds—I couldn't cover them all if I filled up another book. Having control of dye and pigment stains will open up huge vistas for you when it comes to finishing variety. A few of the more esoteric techniques are discussed below.

Mixed doubles

One of the easiest ways to gain depth on a wood with deep grain patterns is to use a ground stain under a pore stain, i.e., a stain that colors the wood evenly under one that colors primarily the pores. By sealing between coats, you can use a dye over a dye, a dye over pigment, a pigment over dye, or a pigment over pigment, and each will have its own unique appearance. Try staining raw ash or oak with a warm, bright dye—perhaps the red/yellow of a honey amber—and then restain with a pigmented stain in a darker color. Wipe off all the pigment you can, so the dark pores contrast with the brighter background color.

Here's a recipe that is especially effective on mahogany, which often has an unsavory pinkish cast to it. Brighten up the background with a light yellow stain, then come back with a cordovan pigmented stain (or filler) to pick up the grain. To afford even more separation, seal the first dye with a light wash coat of finish before applying the pigment, and the pigment stain will stay only in the pores, where you want it. This particular combination yields a rich, dark mahogany with bright golden highlights.

The effects of various finishing techniques on a mahogany board. Narrow bands at left show raw wood, stained and filled wood, and a dry-brushed finish; the wide band at right shows a wet-glazed finish.

Glazing

Open-pore woods are not the only ones that benefit from multi-layer coloring. But on smooth surface woods, like maple, you will have to manipulate the second stain yourself if there are no pores to catch it. The most common technique, called glazing, employs pigmented stains on top of the first sealer coat of finish (you can also glaze with

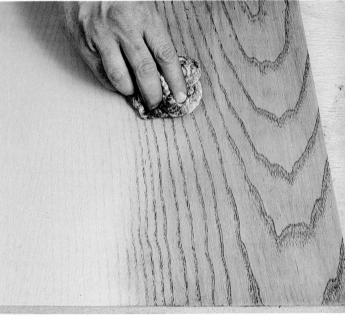

Glazing can impart depth and character to otherwise unexciting wood (above left), impart a woody appearance to solid colors (above), or even age paint (left).

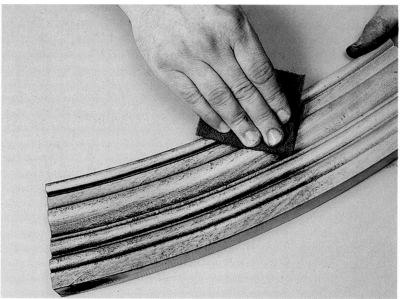

Glazes are applied wet (top left), then moved around with brushes, rags or nylon pads (top right and above) to create a variety of styles.

dyes). Glazing can impart depth and character to otherwise unexciting wood, or can even give a woody character to solid colors or age paint. Glazes are applied wet, then moved around with brushes, rags, steel wool or what have you to create a boundless variety of styles.

Shading can be applied with a small spray touch-up gun to create patterns in the finish.

Q&A:
Preserving the color of padauk

Q: I understand that sunlight may break down the natural color of padauk; further, that ozone or moisture may also have a chemical reaction, creating a duller or brown color. In order to keep or preserve the natural red color of the padauk, would sodium hydroxide, lye or possibly potassium permanganate stain be my best bet? A final finish of varnish or lacquer treated with UV-absorbing additives is also anticipated.

A: Woods with strong coloration and woods that have been dyed, either chemically or with anilines, are all susceptible to fading from UV radiation. Certain woods and dyes are more resistant than others, but generally reds and blues are the first to go, and woods like padauk and amaranth are notorious for losing their color under the sun's influence. Probably the best way to solve the problem is to add a UV absorber or blocker to the clear finish coat (see pp. 20-21).

Shading

The translucent properties of dyes lend themselves to shading: the selective application of tinted finish over wood. Shading is particularly popular with musical-instrument builders, who use small spray guns to apply colors in striking sunburst patterns. Another use of shading is to even up woods after the first coat of finish is applied. There are times when it is hard to spot tonal irregularities in raw wood, and by the time they show up under the finish, it is too late to stain.

Dry brushing

Wet glazing leaves color in low lying areas—pores, carvings, flutes, etc. Dry brushing does just the opposite. It darkens or highlights the raised edges. Pick up just enough color on a china bristle brush so that it is dirty but dry, then lightly glance it across a raw wood surface. The pigment can be controlled to darken carved edges, accentuate pores, or even create figure where nature left it out.

Top left: Wet glazing leaves color in low-lying areas (top of photo), while dry brushing (bottom of photo) highlights raised edges. Load the dry brush by lightly scrubbing its tips in a small puddle of stain (top right), then swipe the dirty brush across the raw wood surface (above left). Dry brushing can create figure where nature left it out (above right).

Pickling

Just as you can leave a dark pigmented stain heavy in the pores of wood or in inside corners for effect, you can do the same with white or pastel colors. The only difference is that when you put light pigmented stain over a darker wood, it is called pickling. If you can't locate pickling stains in the colors you want, buy latex or oil paint and thin it out.

Mixing your own dyes

Although there are premixed dye stains on the market, you can also mix your own by buying dye powders. Dye powders have an indefinite shelf life, and you can mix them to any concentration you like. However, because the concentration of the mix controls the color, if you want to be able to reproduce a color you make, you must weigh the ingredients accurately and keep good records. If you put too much dye in a mix, it can leave a residue on the surface that might prevent your finish from adhering. If you are willing to use an accurate scale and follow the manufacturer's limits for dye concentration, you shouldn't have any trouble.

Oil-soluble dyes will usually dissolve in a wide range of petroleum-derived solvents as well as oil. The manufacturer will usually list the likely candidates. Alcohol-soluble dyes will work in almost any alcohol. The cheapest and easiest to obtain is denatured ethanol, and it is an excellent choice. After measuring out the solvent and dye, put both into a lidded jar and allow the solution to sit overnight. Strain the mixture in the morning, and let it sit again for a few hours. If no precipitate settles out to the bottom, you are home free. (The precipitate will look like undissolved dye powder, and in fact, that is what it will be.)

Water-soluble dyes are somewhat easier to handle. Add the powder to the proper amount of very warm water, let the mixture sit a few minutes, and stir. In most cases, water-soluble dyes will dissolve completely. They will not need to be strained, and can be used almost immediately. (You might want to let them cool off first.)

Chemical stains

To me, chemical stains represent the epitome of finishing alchemy. There are various chemicals that alone or in combination react with chemicals in wood (and each other) to create color changes right on the wood itself. Some chemicals work alone, reacting solely with a component of the wood (usually tannin), while others react with or are fixed (set) by affiliated chemicals called mordants. (The word *mordant* derives from the Latin for bite; appropriately, some mordants help the stain bite into the wood.)

Because wood is not a particularly consistent material and because so many factors affect any chemical reaction, chemical stains are easily the least predictable method of coloring wood. You never know exactly what color you will end up with, and the vagaries of the wood's

*T*he wood-conditioner story

For those of us who have always believed we were buying wood that was already in good condition, the prospect of wood conditioner is unsettling. "What is it, and should I be using it?" we are apt to wonder. If you have to ask, you are probably doing fine without it. But there is a use for this material, and you may need it someday.

Wood conditioner is designed to solve a problem that is specific to oil-based stain on certain hardwoods, like cherry, and most softwoods, such as pine, fir, hemlock and spruce. Imagine a sponge and a block of wood side by side. If you pour water on them, both will get wet, but the sponge will absorb a lot more water than the block of wood. This is what happens with certain woods; they contain spongy areas that absorb significantly more stain than the

adjacent areas. Fir is a good example; the earlywood is vastly more spongy than the latewood. When stain is applied, it seems to bypass the latewood and grab the earlywood with a vengeance. For a variety of reasons, this characteristic is not prevalent with water-based dyes, but it is particularly problematic with oil-based stains—both pigment and dye.

To solve the problem, manufacturers of oil-based stains came up with wood conditioner. Let's go back to our composition often results in wide variances of color within the same piece of lumber. Many people find this lack of predictability exciting; but then, some people find bungee jumping exciting.

That alone would be enough to make me question the relative merits of chemical reactants, but there is more. Many (if not most) of the chemicals involved are poisonous, and some, like copper sulfate, are quite dangerous even in small amounts. Although I don't believe my young children are likely to eat something that has not been identified as food, I'm not so sure that I want to tempt them with a bottle of copper sulfate crystals that look surprisingly similar to blue menthol cough drops. Considering that I can match any chemical stain color with an aniline dye, I am rather at a loss to understand why I should keep unnecessary poisons in the same house with my children.

There is, however, one use of a chemical stain that is not easy to replace: the reaction of potassium disulfate on mahogany. Traditionally, this chemical was used to darken mahogany that was inlaid with holly. Potassium disulfate reacts with the tannin in mahogany to create a reddish-brown tone, but will not affect the tannin-free holly wood. Thus, the finisher was able to develop contrast in a piece of inlaid wood by darkening the background without affecting the light-colored inlay.

Incidentally, chemical stains are generally no more lightfast than aniline dyes, and in fact, most people can't tell the two types of colorant apart under a finish.

---

wood and sponge analogy. Once the sponge was saturated with water, any subsequent wetting would only sit on top. In fact, once the sponge was loaded, it would take in extra liquid at about the same rate as the block of wood. Hence, if the second coat of water in our example was stain, the two materials would take the stain pretty evenly.

Well, that is more or less how wood conditioner works. It is a clear oil that preloads the spongy parts of uneven woods while bypassing the harder sections. When the stain (the "second" coat) is applied, it takes more evenly than if you had put it on the raw wood. But remember, wood conditioner works only with uneven types of wood, and only with oil-based stain. Putting wood conditioner on under a water-soluble dye, for example, will have the opposite effect; the oil will block the naturally even absorption of the water and make the stain go on splotchy.

How do you know when you need to use wood conditioner? One way is to stain the wood, and if it comes out uneven, then you should have used conditioner. Of course, by then it is too late. You can rely on past experience; after your favorite stain goes onto pine unevenly nine times in a row, you can be fairly certain it will do that the tenth time too. Or you can test the stain first on a cutoff of the same wood you intend to stain.

CHAPTER 6
Putty, Filler, Primer and Sealer

Putty, filler, primer and sealer are four finishing materials that are almost as widely misunderstood as used. There seems to be enormous confusion as to which one does what job, and for that matter, if any (or all) of them are really necessary.

Part of the confusion stems from the fact that these foundations of the finishing world are much more alike than they are different. Putty, filler, primer and sealer are four variations of the same thing. From a paint formulator's point of view, they each consist of pigment, binder and solvent. Still, the distinctions are important.

Pigment is defined as any finely ground particle that is not soluble, but rather dispersed, in a liquid medium. Pigments can be natural or synthetic, organic or inorganic, and may or may not impart color to the mix. (That's right—some pigments are virtually transparent, and others add only a neutral cloudiness.)

Binder is the non-volatile portion (the part that does not evaporate) of the liquid vehicle of a coating. In other words, it is the part that forms a film or matrix once the solvent is gone, and not incidentally, the element that will lock the pigment in place so that it doesn't blow away

A credit card is perfect for removing excess wood filler.

like powder when the paint dries. The pigment and binder together form the material that will make up the dried putty, filler, primer or sealer so that it does the job it was intended to do.

The solvent is any liquid that will evaporate off, and is used simply to make the material thinner or easier to manipulate.

So far, it looks as if putty, filler, primer and sealer are all the same thing, right? Well, here's where they differ. Let's start with sealer, a fairly thin, somewhat transparent but milky coating that contains — you guessed it — some semi-transparent pigment along with binder and solvent. If you add some opaque pigment to that — say, some white titanium dioxide (TiO_2) — you have primer. If you take either the primer or the sealer and add a whole lot of extra pigment, either clear or colored, you get filler (sometimes called pore or grain filler). If you keep adding even more pigment until the filler is thick and dense, you end up with dent and gouge putty, or caulking compound. It's that simple.

Admittedly, there are types of binders that dry quickly or slowly, and types that work better with high levels of pigment than with low levels. Therefore, it is not wise to use one material for every job. These distinctions have more to do with convenience than flat-out inappropriateness. For example, you could fill a dent with sealer if you had to, although it would shrink more, require several applications and take a long time to dry. But it could be done.

Can you make your own putty or filler? You bet. Many gilders (gold-leaf finishers) routinely make their own gesso, a plaster-like intermediate layer between the wood and gold "size" (varnish), by mixing calcium carbonate (pigment) with water (solvent) and rabbit-skin glue (binder). One shop that I worked in used to deal with the problem of grain showing under solid colored finishes on ash by using a home-made pore filler. Gilder's whiting (calcium carbonate) was added to white primer to make a loose paste, which was then troweled into the large pores of ash or oak with a 6-in. wide putty knife. When this white mud was dry, it was sanded flush and covered with a coat of white primer. Once the surface was flat and pore-free, it was sprayed with its color coat. What we were making was a material quite similar to drywall joint compound, and had we known better, we would probably have saved a lot of effort by just buying that and using it.

Should you make your own putty or filler? Probably not. Although you can get away with it in a pinch, formulating effective materials, whether they are paints, lacquers or fillers, requires a good bit of knowledge about the raw materials involved. Pore fillers and putties, for example, are designed to be compatible with the top coat that will cover them. However, the top-coat solvents should not be able to dissolve the putty or filler. If the finish solvents were able to redissolve the filler or putty binder, it would cause the material in the pore or defect to swell up, dry more slowly, and leave a dent or wrinkle in the surface. This is a common problem when burn-in stick is used to to fill dents under a finish (see pp. 167-170). Other formulating considerations include how a pigment/binder combination will accept stain, drying time, shrinkage, adhesion, toxicity and flammability, as well as Critical Pigment Volume Concentration (CPVC)—the amount of pigment that can be added to a binder before the system becomes overloaded and crumbles when dry.

Just because it is unwise to dabble in formulating, that doesn't mean you can't substitute some unorthodox materials on occasion, provided you keep the basic rules in mind. There is a finishing tradition of using colored plaster of Paris, for example, to create contrasting colored effects in large-pored wood. By rubbing the dried plaster with some of the intended finish, you can check that it won't dissolve and swell the plaster, and by coating a sample board you can make certain the top coat won't peel, bubble or fish-eye over the filler. You will find that many common materials, such as spackle and joint compound, will pass these tests with most finishes.

Now let's get back to how and when to use the more traditional putties and fillers, since the methods are more or less the same for them and their less common substitutes. By discussing each material and its use, it will become clear what the differences are and how they work to our advantage.

Putty

Various wood putties make up the thickest category of pigmented binders. A quick survey of some of the brands on the market will indicate that they dry at different speeds, take stain differently and sand more or less easily than one another, but on the whole, are more similar than different. After all, they are all trying to achieve someone's interpretation of perfect working time, stain acceptance and sandability. The goal is to make the putty act as much as possible like the wood that will surround it. The problem is that all woods don't act the same. Any woodworker knows that rock maple doesn't take stain (or finish, for that matter) the same way that pine does. By trying out a number of brands and colors, you will find one or more putties that are right for your work and style. You may find that one brand is ideal for some woods, and a different brand works best with others. Likewise, you will find that some putties take water-based dye stain poorly, while others take it well, and the same will hold true for oil-based dye stains, solvent-based dye stains and various pigmented stains.

Choosing a putty color

If the wood is not going to be stained, pick a color that is close to the tone of the wet wood color. Wet the wood with naphtha or mineral spirits to get a representation of what it will look like with the finish on. Match the putty to the lightest background color, or, when an exact duplicate is not possible, go a tone lighter. It is always better to be too light than too dark; it is easy to touch up darker, but very tough to lighten a spot. Although the putty may lighten when it dries, its wet color will be close to its color under finish. Any grain or figure lines that go through the patch can be added later with a fine touch-up brush. If the wood is going to be stained, test the putty on a scrap to

Choose a putty color that is close to the tone of the wet wood.

see if it will take more or less stain than the surrounding wood once it is dry. In most cases, it will take less stain, but if you find it takes more or changes hue, make sure you compensate for that by choosing a different color putty.

Coloring putty

When putty is used to fill defects beneath a clear finish, the color becomes rather important. The immense variety of colors that show up in wood and stains makes it impossible for any manufacturer to make every color of putty, so at times it is up to you to adjust the color to what you need. Since putty is already opaque, there is no value in using dyes to color, so we'll just deal with using pigments, which are easier and more predictable, and present fewer compatibility problems than dyes. In addition, dyes tend to bleed; they leach out into the surrounding wood and/or finish.

In order to add color to a putty, you need to know what the solvent for that putty is. In some cases, the manufacturer makes it easy by offering a solvent for the putty. Otherwise, there are often clues on the label. For example, the warning "contains petroleum distillates" tells you that you can probably use mineral spirits or naphtha, and you can certainly use lacquer thinner, toluene (toluol) or xylene (xylol). If the putty is alcohol soluble, the label will say either that the putty contains alcohol or that it is flammable. These are the two most common putty types, but it is possible that you may run across a water-soluble one, in which case it will have no warnings, no smell, and be non-flammable. Latex putties are actually double solvent systems (emulsions of a solvent-soluble binder in water). To thin them either water or the appropriate solvent — usually lacquer thinner — will work.

The reason you need to know the solvent is that to change the color, you are going to add more pigment, and this will make the putty thicker. Use the solvent to thin it out again to make it more workable. In theory, you'd be better off adding more binder, but solvent is both easier to come by and easier to use. Because there are limits to how much pigment can be added to a binder, you have to avoid going overboard with the colorant. It is best to start with putty that is close to the color you want to achieve, so you have to add only a small amount of pigment. If you feel you may be exceeding the limit, let a small portion of the newly colored putty dry into a blob. If, when it is dry, you can easily crush it back to powder between two fingers, it has too much pigment. Otherwise, you are home free.

The pigments to use are finely ground colorant, either natural or synthetic. Coloring pigments are sold as earth colors, fresco colors or touch-up powders. Most mail-order companies that offer burn-in, touch-up and other finish repair materials will sell ground powders. Since pigments are not soluble, but only dispersible, they will work in all systems no matter what the binder or solvent.

Put a good-sized blob of putty into a small lidded glass jar (I like baby-food jars). Using an artist's palette knife, stir in a small amount of colored powder. Add whatever colors you need to get the look you want. Remember, you can add either lighter colors (like white) or darker colors. If the putty starts to get too thick, add a few drops of solvent.

Learning how to mix is a good bit easier than deciding what color to mix. For more on that, refer back to pp. 124-125.

Filler

Filler is used to create a level surface on wood by filling the small pores in the grain of open-pore woods, such as walnut, rosewood, koa, mahogany, and on rare occasions, ash and oak. Some other woods that can take filler are butternut, chestnut, elm, hickory, mulberry and pecan. When the pores are filled and level, the finish is referred to as a closed-pore finish. If the pores are not filled, the finish follows the indentations in the wood grain, creating an open-pore finish. Choosing between the two is a matter of personal taste and stylistic tradition. Some people prefer the look of one or the other. At various times, closed-pore finishes went in and out of style. Consequently, some types of period furniture are almost always done with filled pores. Although you could in theory fill the wood by adding finish and sanding it back until the surface is level, it is not a good idea. Over time, the finish will shrink, and the pores will show up again. By using a non-shrinking (high-pigment) material, the chance of shrinking pores is reduced considerably.

Why not just use putty to fill the pores? Because of the high pigment content, putty is so thick that it would be hard to push it down into the relatively tiny pore holes in wood. On top of that, it dries so fast that there would be no time to work on much more than a very small area. To make life easier, wood filler is thinner, so that it gets into pores better and dries more slowly, so there's enough time to manipulate it before it turns into a freeform rock sculpture. Outside of the homemade varieties, there are really just two types of filler currently on the market: oil based and water based. Although they look and act the same once they are dry, they handle differently enough that we should discuss them separately.

Oil-based filler

By far the oldest and most common filler is a mixture of pigment, linseed oil and petroleum-distillate solvents, usually naphtha and/or mineral spirits. In most cases, the bulk of the pigment is silex, or ground quartz, which imparts a small amount of translucence to uncolored neutral filler, but which refuses to be affected by dye stains. It comes in a variety of pigmented colors, most of them dark, as well as natural or neutral, which is a sickly shade of ecru. The neutral makes a nice base for mixing your own custom colors, but looks awful on any wood darker than oak, and it doesn't look any too good on that either. One exception is the "TV finish" that was popular during the 1950s and 1960s, which used neutral filler on ash to create subtle blue-grey grain patterns under a semi-transparent ivory top coat. It seemed like a good idea at the time.

Using filler on raw wood   The biggest advantage of oil-based filler is that it dries slowly, giving you plenty of time to work. The biggest disadvantage is that it dries slowly, making you wait in your finishing schedule. In spite of what most label directions say, I usually leave at least three days of drying time after the filler is on before I add a coat of finish. Otherwise, the uncured binder in the filler may create grey spots in the pores after the top coat is dry.

*T*hree men and a table

Working with filler involves timing—you need to catch the drying filler at just the right point, and still have time to get the mud off before it hardens. If the mud comes off too soon, you end up with partially filled pores; if you let it set too long, you inherit a disaster. Believe me, I know. Once when I was working for a finisher in New York, I was asked to fill a large mahogany conference table. It was only my second day on the job in a four-man shop, and I was not yet familiar with their mixtures. I started applying the filler with a large brush, and I paused after half of the top was covered. I didn't want to cover more than I could safely remove once it clouded, but I didn't want to look like I was just standing around doing nothing on a new job either. The filler still looked wet, so I kept applying more.

When the whole top was coated, I grabbed some burlap and started scrubbing off the now smoky filler. Within a minute I knew I was in trouble; the stuff was drying much faster than I could get it off, and there was a huge expanse of conference table stretched out before me. Visions of myself spending days trying to sand off dried filler flashed before my eyes, followed quickly by another vision of myself looking for a new job.

Just as panic was settling itself securely in the pit of my stomach, I looked up to see the other three finishers surrounding the table, armed with burlap. In minutes, the four of us had all of the filler mud removed, and the top was ready for the final wipe-down—an easy one-man job. The other three put down their burlap and went noiselessly back to their own benches. Not a single word had been spoken by anyone, and for all the time I worked at that shop, the incident was never mentioned. Nor was it ever forgotten—at least by me.

Brush the filler on in any direction (above), and let it dry until the top surface just begins to get hazy. In the photo at left, wet filler is on the right, hazy filler ready to remove is on the left. The filler should look and act like mud and will immediately clog the removal pad (below left).

Most filler comes a bit too thick to work easily, and I prefer to thin it out. Usually, it is about the consistency of custard in the can. I prefer it to be closer to the thickness of light cream. For a relatively slow drying filler to be used on large areas, I add mineral spirits. If I want it to dry faster, I add naphtha. Sometimes a mixture of both is just right.

Using any comfortable brush (natural or synthetic bristle), apply the filler on a surface of manageable size. Filler won't leave lap marks, so you don't have to worry about doing an entire surface or piece of furniture in one shot. Brush the mixture on any way you can; grain direction and brushing style don't mean a thing. Don't put it on too thick, and don't worry about getting it even because you are going to wipe it off soon anyway. Now let it dry until the top surface just begins to get hazy. Take some burlap, jute, wood shavings or coarse nylon abrasive pads and start removing the filler. It should look and act like mud, and will immediately clog the removal pad.

While the mud is still nice and wet, use the pad to pack the filler into the pores. I like to go in circles or at an angle. Going with the grain sometimes pulls the mud out instead of pushing it in. When the area is packed, or when the mud starts to dry to the point that it won't move easily anymore (whichever happens sooner), take a clean piece of burlap, jute, etc. (for this particular operation I prefer 3M-brand Scotch-Brite nylon abrasive pads), and remove the residue by going across the grain. By now, the pores are as packed as they are likely to get, and you just need to remove any residue on top. By cutting across the grain, you won't pull out what was already packed in. Flat surfaces

Remove the residue by rubbing across the grain with a clean pad, which should leave the surface clean enough for sanding later.

will be sanded later, so just get them moderately clean. In turnings, carvings, and areas that will be hard to sand later, get as much filler off as you can without undoing your previous work. It doesn't pay to be too aggressive when wiping off, or you are likely to wipe some of the filler out of the pore, leaving the material slightly concave instead of flat. Also, most wood fillers shrink somewhat as they dry.

When the filler is completely dry, scuff sand the flat surfaces with 220-grit stearated sandpaper (see the sidebar on pp. 82-83) to remove the excess residue, which should be visible as a haze on the surface. For turnings or areas that can't be sanded, go over them across the grain with medium (220-grit) nylon abrasive pads. Since it's hard to tell when the mud in those small pores is completely dry, I generally fill wood before the weekend and save the final scuff-sanding step until Monday.

When you first start to sand, the paper may clog with random shiny spots, but soon they will be replaced by an even dust pattern. When this happens, stop sanding lest you start cutting into the wood and expose new unfilled pores. If you are not quite sure if the dusty surface is residue or sanding swarf (sawdust), wipe down the wood with a rag that is just lightly dampened with mineral spirits or naphtha. Swarf will wipe off, but residue won't.

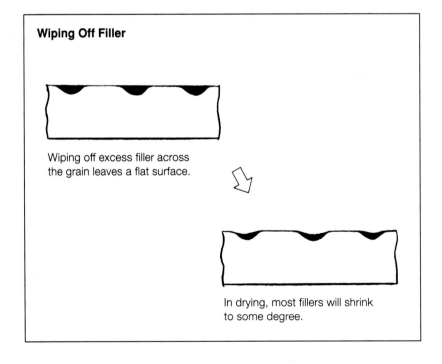

Wiping Off Filler

Wiping off excess filler across the grain leaves a flat surface.

In drying, most fillers will shrink to some degree.

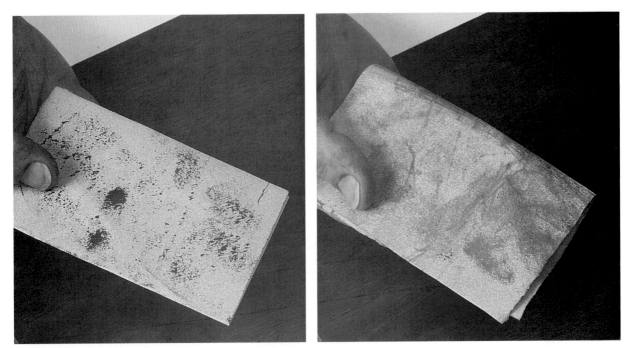

At first the sandpaper may clog with random shiny spots (left), but they'll soon be replaced with a regular dust pattern (right).

Dried filler before (right) and after (left) sanding.

Choosing a filler color   Choosing a filler color is strictly a matter of personal taste. Fillers that are close in color to the wood work well on dark woods like walnut and rosewood. (For information on custom coloring filler, see the next section.) On medium woods, like mahogany and koa, the prevailing opinion is that dark brown or reddish-brown filler provides a needed contrast of dark pores that adds depth and character. Because the coloring agent in the filler is pigment, putting colored filler on raw wood imparts a lot of color to the pores, but relatively little to the less porous wood between.

Which came first, the filler or the stain?

One of the most frequently asked questions regarding filler is: Should I stain the wood before or after I fill it? This always reminds me of Winnie the Pooh, who, when asked by his friend Rabbit whether he wanted honey or condensed milk with his bread, replied, "Both." The best time to stain wood that is to be filled is before—and after.

Although dark fillers contain colored pigment that will act like a stain, except for what remains in the pores, most of it will come off during the wipe-down and sanding after the filler is dry. In addition, the color you've chosen for the pores (the filler) is not necessarily the color you want on the rest of the background wood. A lighter, contrasting ground stain will brighten up even dark woods and add another dimension of depth. My favorite treatment for filled mahogany consists of a honey gold dye (yellow, amber and a touch of red) on the raw wood coupled with a dark

cordovan filler. The filler, being largely ground quartz, will not accept stain well, and the binder may prevent the stain from coloring the pores, even at the top of the pore "ramps," where there is very little pigment (see the drawing on the facing page). Therefore, to get the dye everywhere, it is important to stain before filling the pores.

But wait a minute. Won't you cut through the stain in areas during the sanding operation? Probably, no matter how careful you are, there will be edges or spots where you will cut through the stain. The solution is to use a

Staining the wood with a water-soluble dye both before and after filling and sanding ensures even coverage, as shown in this photo sequence. First, stain with a water-soluble dye (left). When the stain is dry, fill the pores (right).

If you want to isolate the background wood completely from the pore color, you can seal the wood first and get even more contrast. Use a very thin coat of low-solids (12%) lacquer (not sanding sealer) if you are spraying, or a hand-applied ½-lb. cut wash coat of shellac wiped on and off with a rag. When the shellac or lacquer is dry, fill the pores as usual. Be careful when you wipe off the filler, though, because the sealed pores make it easier for the filler to pull back out. When working on sealed wood, you will notice that the filler comes off much cleaner, and very little sanding will be needed after the filler has

water-soluble aniline dye. These dyes color deeply, so there is less likelihood of cutting through, and they are self-regulating. If you cut through, another application of the same concentration of dye will even up the spots where the stain was removed. The sequence goes like this: Wash the wood liberally with a water-soluble dye. When the stain is dry, fill the pores. When the surface is dry and sanded, go back over it with the same dye solution. Don't worry about grain raising. You are going to sand the filler soon anyway. It is important not to change the concentration of dye

powder, as that will change the color. One way of guaranteeing consistency is to buy premixed water-based dyes, but make sure they are resin free and oil free.

If you have chosen to use only the stain in the filler as your coloring agent, you can usually even up the sanded-through areas by restaining with the filler itself. Using a rag, wipe some thinned filler onto the wood and wipe it off immediately. There should be enough pigment in the mixture to get a passable job.

Staining with Filled Pores

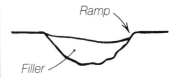

At the tops of the filled pores (ramps), dried binder can prevent the stain from penetrating. Therefore it's a good idea to stain both before and after applying the filler.

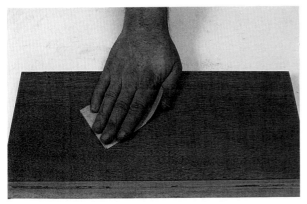

After sanding (left), restain with the original dye (right).

dried—so little that you are not likely to sand through and ruin the ground stain, if there is one. For safety's sake, use very fine 320-grit stearated paper when sanding.

There is one other advantage to sealing the wood before filling, and the best way to explain it is to recount an incident that occurred a few years ago. A very accomplished finisher asked me to look at a problem on a mahogany tabletop. It had been filled properly on the raw wood, with ample drying time before the lacquer top coat was applied, and the table looked beautiful when it was delivered. A few months later, the customer called to say that the top had developed a case of white spots. Sure enough, tiny pinhole-sized whitish spots had appeared at the mouth of quite a few of the pores, underneath the finish at the wood level. This condition is extremely rare, and I have never seen it on any wood other than mahogany. I suggested refinishing the table, but this time, sealing the wood prior to filling. The likely cause of the problem was that oil and/or solvent trapped deep in the pores had managed to migrate back up through the filler and cause the lacquer to separate in that small spot. Sealing the wood beforehand encloses the filler above and below in an envelope of finish. This envelope prevents the oil and solvent migration, and with it, the problem of white dots in the filler.

Coloring oil-based filler Although filler can be colored the same way as putty (with pigment powders) there are other options as well. Once again, you want to use pigments, but because pore filler is a slower drying system, you have the option of using several premixed pigment dispersions. (Although these dispersions could in principle be used with putty, they would slow the normally fast-drying putty too much.) If the filler is oil based, you can use either artist's oil colors or Japan colors, both of which are available from art-supply stores as well as finish suppliers. Oil colors are pigments ground in oil (usually linseed), while Japan colors are the same thing with heavy metal salts called driers added to speed up the curing time of the oil (see p. 101). It should come as no surprise that adding oil colors will slow down the drying time of the filler, whereas adding Japan colors may speed it up a bit. Since oil and Japan colors contain a binder (the oil) as well as pigment, you can add quite a bit without upsetting the mixture.

If, after all of my good advice, you feel you must color filler with a dye, use an oil-soluble one. No dye will do much to color the ground quartz that makes up most of the pigment, but at least an oil-soluble dye will tint the binder. But don't be surprised if the color bleeds.

Water-based filler

Water-based filler is newer, easier to use, smells better and dries much faster than oil-based filler. Like oil-based material, it is compatible over and under water-based dye stains, but it also boasts superior adhesion with water-based top coats as well as solvent-based materials. The pigment remains the same, but instead of oil as the binder and mineral spirits as the solvent, these fillers employ an acrylic-resin binder in a water emulsion. This means that they dry considerably faster. Some can be top-coated in as little as two hours, and most can be sealed by the following morning. Because these materials do not contain oil, there are no incompatibility or adhesion problems when they are put under water-based top coats, and the potential for a white-dot problem is non-existent. Thus, while presealing under the filler is still an option, it is not needed, even with mahogany.

Water-based filler can be handled just like oil-based filler, but its real advantage is that it can be squeegeed off almost immediately without creating concave pockets. Thin the filler as before, but this time use water for a fast dry, propylene glycol for slow, and a mixture of the two for medium. Brush it on, but instead of waiting for it to get hazy, immediately start to pack it into the pores of the wood with burlap. It will be much thinner than oil-based filler, more like a slurry than a mud. As soon as the pores are packed, you can squeegee off the excess from the wood surface. Any thin, flexible material with a straight edge will work, but my favorite type of squeegee is an old (or new) credit card (see the photo on p. 121). It is just the right size and thickness, flexible enough to conform to a bullnose edge, and comes free in the mail. Unlike other uses for this fine tool, removing filler with a credit card will not result in a hefty bill in your mailbox. I keep old cards in a drawer to cut into shapes for removing the filler in tight areas and moldings; the photo on p. 136 shows a few of these custom "tools."

Once the wet filler has been squeegeed off cleanly, leave it alone until it is dry. As with any water-based material, drying time will depend heavily on the relative humidity (RH) of the room, but at 50% RH, most water-based fillers will be ready to sand in two hours. The rest of the procedure is the same as with oil-based filler; scuff-sand with 220, restain if necessary, and seal with your choice of finish. After the water has evaporated, water-based filler is compatible under every common solvent finish, and is almost a must under water-based finishes. Instead of removing sanding swarf with a rag dampened with mineral spirits, use water. It's cheaper, smells better and is environmentally friendly.

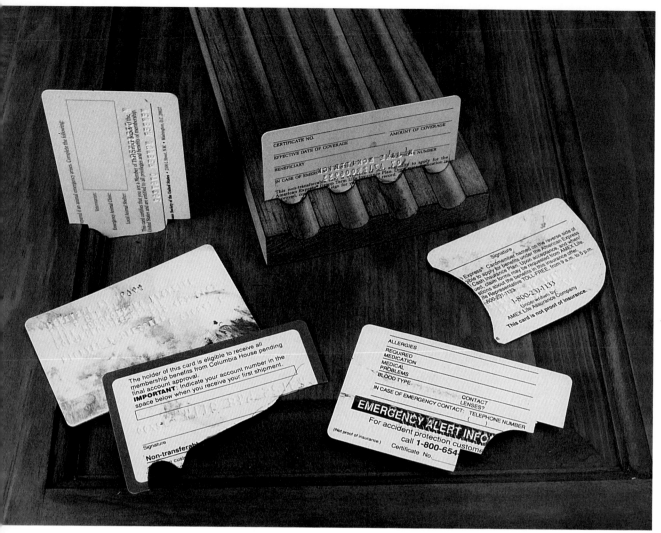

Extra credit cards can be cut to various profiles for removing filler on moldings.

Coloring water-based filler   With water-based filler, you can use universal tinting colors (UTCs). UTCs are pigments suspended in a solvent (usually a glycol ether) that is compatible with both water-based and solvent-based systems. (In fact, you can use UTCs with oil-based fillers too.) Because they often contain little or no resin (binder), there are limits to how much UTC you can add to filler, but since the colors are generally quite concentrated, you are not likely to get into trouble. Incidentally, when you go into a paint store that sells latex paint, you will notice a carousel of tubes, out of which the clerk dispenses colorant for mixing custom-colored paints. Those tubes contain universal tinting colors.

Primer and sealer

Primer and sealer are virtually synonymous. In the realm of wood-working, primer is regarded as the opaque version of clear sealer. Beyond that, the terms and materials are interchangeable.

To seal or not to seal?

When sealer is used, it is the first coat of finish that goes on the raw wood, but whether or not sealer is needed remains a judgment call. By understanding what sealer does and does not do, you'll be in a better position to make that call accurately. Sealer can be used to promote adhesion, act as a barrier coat, simplify sanding, or reduce finish absorption. Some sealers do more than one of these jobs.

Promoting adhesion   Wood is very porous, so most finishes adhere very well to it. However, wood is also somewhat lipophobic, meaning that it tends to repel oil. In order to convince wood to accept it, the oil must be made rather thin, or a sealer that promotes adhesion must be used. Heavy-bodied oil varnishes and polyurethane sometimes require the wood to be sealed first, with either a special sealer or a thinned coat of the same varnish.

Barrier coats   Often wood has resins, oils, waxes or stains in it that create problems for the finish coat. In some cases, the contaminant is naturally occurring, such as the waxy resin in rosewood that plays havoc with some oil varnishes, polyurethane and even a few lacquers. Vinyl sealer, a lacquer containing vinyl resin, does a nice job on this malady. Other contaminants are added by us, especially in the case of refinished wood, which may have been impregnated with silicone oil from furniture polish, wax from paint remover, or stain from a previous finisher. Shellac is an especially effective sealer for wax and silicone, and even works well with some stains, depending on their solvency. If the finish is to be a solid color, you can use a bleeder-seal primer to stop stains from walking up through the later finish coats.

Simplified sanding   Lacquers sold specifically as sanding sealer are, as their name implies, coatings that both seal wood and sand easily. The secret is the addition of soft pigment to the sealer, most commonly zinc or aluminum stearates; these soap-like pigments act as a sanding lubricant as well as a soft bodying agent. The stearates add loft to the sealer, causing it to build fast, so that one coat of sanding sealer seems thicker than an equivalent coat of lacquer. Their softness and self-lubricating properties cause them to sand quickly and easily with little heat buildup. But their softness can also be a liability. Too much sanding sealer under a fairly hard, brittle finish like lacquer can promote chipping of the top coat by creating a sandwich effect. The sealer gives under the pressure of a sharp blow, providing inadequate support for the brittle top coat.

Reduced absorption All woods are porous, but some are more porous than others. Some woods, like pine and lauan, are so porous that they seem to suck up solvent lacquer like a dry sponge. To save time and material, sealers that will halt the absorption in one or two coats are laid down first. These fall into two categories that accomplish the same end in different ways. Sanding sealers with high pigment concentrations act like liquid versions of pore filler, but on a smaller scale. Pores that are too small to fill with pore filler will be clogged up by the finer pigment in sanding sealer. Incidentally, pore filler is itself rather porous, so a coat of some type of sealer is almost always appropriate after grain filling. The other type of sealer acts more like a thin skin that bridges across the fine holes in wood, the way plastic sandwich wrap would form a barrier if you wrapped it around a porous brick. Shellac is a good example of this mechanism. Its cohesiveness, or ability to stick to itself, allows it to have enough integrity to seal out the top coat while it seals in contaminants like silicone and wax.

When to use a sealer

There are situations in which sealer is advantageous, and those in which it is a waste of time and material. When sealer is needed to act as a barrier coat or adhesion enhancer, the decision is obvious. For example, it is usually wise to put one thin coat of vinyl sealer on cocobolo or other rosewoods if your top coat is going to be lacquer, and always a good idea to use a sealer if a finish manufacturer insists on it. Likewise, shellac is almost always indicated when you are refinishing a piece of furniture. But when it is simply a case of deciding whether sanding sealer will save time, it is not so easy.

With very hard woods that are not particularly porous, such as maple and ebony, there is no real need for sanding sealer, and in some ways using sanding sealer is disadvantageous. Although it does sand easier than lacquer or varnish, the high pigment content will mean that the final finish will be softer and more likely to chip. There will also be a loss in clarity due to the light-diffracting properties of the pigment. Therefore, sanding sealer should be used only when it is needed, and then, only in small doses.

Woods like poplar, deal (any soft wood), lauan and some mahoganies tend to be so porous that if a fairly thin finish — such as lacquer — is employed, it will seem as if the wood is drinking it in endlessly. In these cases, one, or at the most, two coats of sealer should be used. These same woods also tend to fur up more after the first coat, and will require some sanding. The sealer will make the sanding job easier, and at the same time, the sanding will remove the excess sealer. Do not be tempted either to save time or to fill large pores by building a finish in sanding sealer. You will end up with an inferior, muddy-looking coating that chips and scratches easily and shrinks too much. Bear in mind that you have the option of a bridging sealer like shellac. It won't sand as easily, but it will do its job in one coat and will promote rather than mitigate clarity.

Application techniques   When it comes to applying sealers, the rule is the same as for other finish coats — put it on the most convenient way possible. Ordinarily, that will be in the same way that the rest of the finish is going to be applied, but there can be exceptions. Consider this: If you spray a 1-mil (.001-in.) coating of shellac evenly on a turned spindle, will it be evenly sealed? The answer is no. The spindle will absorb more shellac on the areas of exposed end grain than in the less porous areas of flat grain. When the dust has cleared, the end grain will be inadequately sealed, and the flats will be over-sealed. Now let's approach it from a different angle. Let's say we take some very thin shellac (½-lb. cut) on a rag or sponge, and flood the spindle with it. Then, before it has a chance to dry, we wipe off all the excess. The end grain will have absorbed all it can, as will the flat, but neither will have any excess on the surface.

This is precisely the way I seal most solid wood objects. The technique works nicely for turnings, carvings, raised panels, gunstocks and guitars, as well as with inlaid and multi-wood furniture that is made of woods of different porosity. The flood method works well with other materials besides shellac, provided they are thin enough and don't dry too fast. Just remember to don a pair of gloves before plunging your hands in solvent-based finishes, and that includes shellac.

CHAPTER 7
Puttin' On the Top Coat

By now you probably feel as if you've done it all. You have chosen the finish and applicators, stripped, sanded, puttied, stained and sealed, and at long last, are ready for the big event, the top coat. You've also learned the two great secrets of finishing: there's more to it than meets the eye, and the actual application of the finish is the least of the work involved. But after all those preliminaries, you don't want to run into any problems now. As is usually the case with woodworking, the place to start is the work area itself.

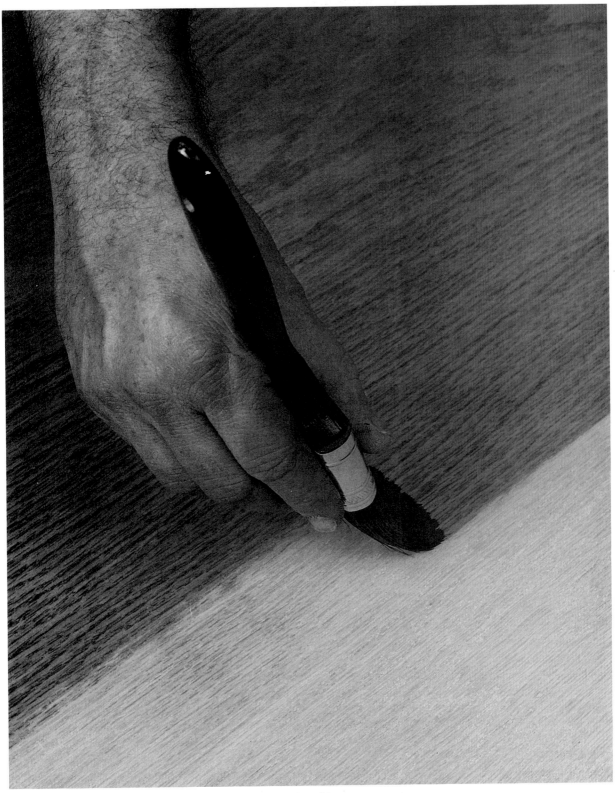

The correct brush stroke combines a comfortable grip with an appropriate brush angle.

The finishing-room environment

The finishing-room environment is critical to the success of your finish as well as to your own health. It should be as free from dust as possible, and should enjoy good ventilation in conjunction with stable temperature and humidity. Naturally, we can't all create ideal conditions. For that matter, most of us don't even have separate finishing rooms. But depending on which finish you choose, certain factors become more or less important. You have essentially two choices. You can control the conditions in your work area to conform to the finish you've chosen, or you can choose finishes that tolerate the conditions in your work area. Let's look at some of the factors and see how they affect coatings.

Temperature

When it comes to temperature, finishes are a lot like people. If it is a comfortable temperature for you to be working in shirtsleeves, it is most likely comfortable for the finish to be working as well. Although finishers usually talk about the temperature of the air in the room, you must also be concerned with the temperature of the finish and the wood itself. All three should be as close to one another as possible. If the finish has been sitting on a cold concrete floor in an unheated storage room, let it acclimate to the temperature of the workroom before you use it. The same goes for the wood.

All finishes have a Minimum Film Forming Temperature (MFFT), the temperature below which they will not work (see pp. 11-12). That temperature varies greatly from finish to finish and brand to brand, but we can still make some broad generalizations. Among the fussiest finishes are the water-based coatings, which generally have an MFFT of at least 60°F. Although a film will form at 60°F and above, most water-based coatings start laying out considerably better at about 10°F above the MFFT. Solvent systems like lacquer are generally formulated with lower MFFTs—usually 55°F or so—but will dry much faster in warmer air. With lacquers, you can effectively lower the MFFT by dumping in extra solvent, but that also results in less build per coat as well as a higher VOC content. Reactive two-package systems, like epoxies, often fall in this range as well, depending on the specific formulation. Oil varnishes frequently work as low as 45°F. Like lacquer systems, they will cure faster as the temperature rises.

In most cases, heat is less of a problem than cold. At high temperatures, some lacquers and varnishes may start to bubble, and lacquers may lose some inter-coat (coat to coat) adhesion. However, this usually does not occur below 90°F, and at those temperatures, most of us are busy looking for a cool drink and a hammock in the shade.

Relative humidity

Since temperature and relative humidity are so closely connected, it seems logical to discuss relative humidity (RH) next. Finishes are affected differently by RH. The most sensitive material is high-solvent lacquer: acrylic, nitrocellulose, CAB and vinyl solvent-release coatings. Most of these fast-drying coatings are sprayed on, and they are prey to blush due to moisture condensing out of the air (see the sidebar on p. 144). The obvious solution is to avoid spraying on days when the RH is too high, but that is not always possible. Instead, most finish manufacturers offer blush chasers or retarders that can be added to the lacquer on humid days. These are mostly slower evaporating solvents, and they will slow down the drying and curing time of the finish. The more retarder you add, the more drying and curing time you have to allow before handling or buffing the lacquer.

Relative humidity has little if any effect on oil varnish, but water-based varnishes and lacquers are another story entirely. Although manufacturers often brag that their water-based lacquer doesn't blush, it is still possible to get blush in fast-drying water-based lacquers. Water-based lacquers turn white when they are applied too heavily. The lacquer forms a water-trapping skin on top of the wet coat before the water in the emulsion has a chance to evaporate. This problem has more to do with the application than with the finish itself.

Crossover is a problem directly associated with relative humidity. Water-based varnish or lacquer contains water (the diluent) and tail solvents (the solvents for the resin). The tail solvents are supposed to evaporate more slowly than the water, remaining behind to knit the resin into a film after the water is gone. The problem is that water evaporates more slowly when the RH is high, and not at all when the RH hits 100%. However, RH has very little effect on the tail solvents. If the RH is high enough, the tail solvents evaporate before the water, and the coating never coalesces into a film; it just dries as separate little balls of finish resin. How high does the RH have to be for this to happen? That depends on the formulation. Some tail solvents are slower than others, but most water-based materials are designed to tolerate up to about 90% RH.

Ventilation

Ventilation is always important, but there are times when it is critical. By good ventilation I mean that a stream of air should be moving both in and out of the room. Moving air around in the room is not enough. You should be evacuating solvent-laden air and breathing fresh air. If you are spraying a high-solvent lacquer, a practice that is sure to load the air with solvents quickly, the air should be replaced just as quickly. But not all finish materials are that bad. Water-based lacquers may have only one-quarter of the solvents of solvent lacquers, and a lower air

What is relative humidity?

Let's start with absolute humidity, which is the amount of moisture (water vapor) in the air. This is a volume, and it is measured in grains of water. There is a limit to how much moisture air will hold, and that is called the saturation or dew point, because once the air is saturated with moisture, dew will form on anything that is even the least bit cooler than the air. Here's where it gets tricky. Warmer air can hold more moisture than cooler air. Relative humidity (RH) is the amount of moisture in the air in relation to the saturation point at that temperature, expressed as a percent. In other words, it's the ratio of the amount of moisture in the air to the amount the air could theoretically hold if it were fully loaded.

Let's say that at 60°F, 1 cubic foot of air can hold 4 grains of water, but at 80°F, the same cubic foot can hold 8 grains (these are not real numbers—I'm using them to make the math easy). Let's further assume that there are 2 grains of moisture in both the 60°F and the 80°F air. The 60°F air will be at 50% RH (it has 2 grains, but can theoretically hold 4), but the 80°F air will be at 25% RH (it has 2 grains, but can theoretically hold 8). Hence the same amount of moisture translates into a

different RH at different temperatures. For a given amount of moisture, as the temperature drops, the RH rises.

How does relative humidity affect you as a finisher? Let's assume that you are spraying lacquer in an 80°F room and the RH is 75%. To stick with the numbers we made up, that would mean the air holds 6 grains of moisture out of a possible 8. Let's also assume that at 70°F, the air can hold only 6 grains. That means if the temperature in your spray room drops just 10°F, the air will be at 100% RH, and dew will form on the furniture. Now you spray the wood with a high-solvent lacquer, content that everything is just fine. But as the solvent evaporates quickly from the wood, it cools the surface. (If you have any doubts about this, wipe some isopropyl rubbing alcohol onto your skin and see how cold it feels as it evaporates.) In fact, it cools the surface so much that the air

immediately above the lacquer film is now 69°F—just below the dew point. Moisture quickly condenses on the still-wet lacquer and gets trapped in the coating. The result looks like a hazy cloud, and goes by the quaint name of blush. Although the numbers I used are contrived, the process is not. This is precisely what is happening when lacquer blushes.

How can you avoid blush? The first step is to be aware of the RH in your finishing room. A simple device called a hygrometer measures the RH of the air. It would be a good idea to have one in the finishing area, especially if you are using fast-drying finishes (high-solvent lacquers are the most sensitive). Experience will tell you how much leeway you need, but as a rule of thumb, I don't spray lacquer above 75% RH without adding blush chaser or retarder to the mix.

Blush looks like a white cloud trapped in the lacquer.

flow is reasonable with these finishes. In contrast, pure linseed oil contains no solvents at all, and although it may smell oily, the danger from breathing the air is nowhere near what it is for solvent-release finishes. Be careful, though. Most oil finishes and varnishes do contain solvents.

Most shops are under-ventilated. The reason is that most people don't want to spend money heating or cooling air just to blow it outside. This is understandable, but that doesn't solve the problem. Besides, most solvent fumes are somewhat hazardous to breathe, and it is cheaper to pay heating bills now than medical bills later.

Dust

Woodworking makes dust, and finishing abhors it, yet the two activities always go hand in hand. It is a marriage made in...well, not heaven. Do your best. Try to let the dust settle before you put on a slow-drying finish. Use a tack rag to wipe down wood that is destined for oil or solvent varnish, and a damp cloth to tack off under water-based coatings. Do your finishing at the end of the day, so you won't be walking around kicking up dust while the varnish is drying. Yes, this time varnish is the problem child. It may be the most forgiving finish when it comes to temperature, relative humidity and even ventilation, but when it comes to dust, it is the pits. Fast-drying finishes tack so quickly that dust doesn't get a chance to settle, but slow oil varnish just sits there waiting to embrace every bit of airborne debris in the vicinity. If all else fails and you still end up with pimples in the final coat, relax. I'll tell you how to rub them out in Chapter 9.

Applying brushable finishes

Most woodworkers start their finishing career with a brush in their hand. Brushes are a satisfying extension of the hand, and although they are not the fastest way of applying finish, they certainly are efficient. (For more on brushable finishes, see pp. 9-14; for more on brushes and brushing techniques, see pp. 28-40.)

Once you've dipped your brush into the finish, touch the tip of the brush against the side or edge of the can to prevent drips, but don't scrape it across the metal edge unless you are trying to unload it. The top photo on p. 146 shows the appropriate brushing technique. Avoid the temptation to coat heavily. Several thin coats are much better than one thick one. Remember to presoak the brush in the appropriate solvent, and clean it as soon as possible after you've finished using it.

Keep the brush about 45° to the surface.

Don't flop the brush over the edge of the wood or the coating will drip down the adjacent side.

Oil varnishes (including oil-type polyurethane)

Classic slow-drying, thick varnish is the perfect mate to a brush. Its viscosity affords it wonderful handling properties, and the long drying time lets it flow out beautifully. Choose a good-quality natural China bristle brush, and clean up, presoak and thin with mineral spirits or naphtha. Because this reactive finish does not redissolve itself, you can pick up any runs, even on later coats, by unloading the brush and re-brushing the sagged or dripping area. The same technique works with excess puddles that form on inside corners, turnings and carvings. Coat them as dry as possible, but try not to scrub these recesses or you will get air bubbles and foam. On raised panel doors and wainscoting, coat the low-fielded areas first, then the frames and center panels last.

Cover a manageable area (1 to 2 sq. ft. or so) along the length of the grain, then spread the varnish evenly with short strokes diagonally or across the grain. Finish up by stretching it out with long, even strokes along the grain. When one entire top or side is coated, if the varnish is still wet (it should be), tip off the surface (see the bottom photo on p. 40). Remove all the excess varnish from the brush (yes, you can scrape it on the can this time) and holding the brush almost at right angles to the wood, drag only the tip of the brush through the finish. Take light, even strokes with the grain going from end to end along the entire surface. This graceful operation will help minimize the brush marks and knock out any air bubbles or specks.

Each coat will adhere to, but not remelt the previous one, so it is a good idea to increase inter-coat adhesion by scuff sanding between coats. Use nylon abrasive pads or fine (320-grit) stearated sandpaper, and wipe off the sanding dust with a tack rag. Varnish at the end of the day to keep the dust down, and limit yourself to one coat per day if you can. With oil varnish, patience is a virtue.

Paint pads are ideal for applying water-based coatings.

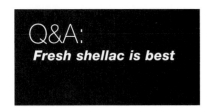

Q: I purchased an Empire sideboard that needed some refinishing. After cleaning the piece with steel wool and washing it lightly with turpentine, I applied a coat of thinned-down shellac, which went on nicely and looked good. The next day, I rubbed down the surface slightly with steel wool, wiped it down and applied a second coat of shellac; the finish instantly wrinkled up. Despite further cleaning and reapplication, the problem has persisted.

A: The most common cause for shellac wrinkling is the shellac being past its viable shelf life. After shellac flakes are dissolved in alcohol, the mixture starts a gradual chemical change that increases its flexibility but decreases its hardness. In time, the shellac will become rubbery and soft. This condition is usually not obvious on the first coat, but a second coat of finish will either crack or wrinkle from the movement of the first layer. This is why you must keep track of the age of any ready-mixed shellac finish. Buy cans that have been dated at the factory, and use up the shellac within six months of that date.

Better still, mix your own shellac. Buy dewaxed shellac flakes, which have an indefinite shelf life if kept cool and dry, and add them to ethanol or denatured alcohol. That way you can mix just enough for the job at hand.

Shellac and lacquer

Shellac and brushing lacquer are both evaporative finishes, and as far as application technique is concerned, they are the same. In fact, formulators think of shellac as a lacquer since it is a solvent-release finish. Because lacquer will redissolve itself, however, it requires a slightly different touch. The first coat isn't a problem, but too much brushing on the second or third coat will start moving the already dried lacquer around. Instead, each coat is flowed on, then left alone. No stretching out or tipping off is allowed.

Use a fairly short, very soft natural-bristle brush. I like fitch (skunk) hair because it is so soft that it barely leaves brush marks. For thinning, presoak and cleanup, shellac uses alcohol and lacquer takes lacquer thinner. How thin you cut the material is purely a personal matter. Thinner coats dry faster, but leave less material on the wood. Start with the shellac at a consistency somewhere between cream and a half-and-half creamer, and modify it from there.

Use a light touch to flow the finish on in the direction of the grain. You can go back over it to even it up, but do it quickly and don't scrub or cross brush the way you do with varnish. If you get a drip or run, catch it immediately. Otherwise, let it dry and sand it out later. The first coat will raise the grain a bit, so it is a good idea to scuff it once. After that, don't bother sanding, as each coat will melt into the last. There is no reason to sand between coats unless you need to remove flaws or flatten the surface. If you keep to fairly thin coats, you can put on two a day, but don't push it any faster than that.

With shellac in particular, it is possible to begin and end the finish with a rag, and use a brush only to build the middle up quickly. The easiest way to apply the first sealer coat is to take very thin (watery) shellac on a rag, flood it onto the wood, and wipe it off immediately with a dry cloth. This is especially effective with solid-wood pieces, because the shellac will soak into the end grain, resulting in a more even sealer coat. If you mess up, drips, runs, and areas that didn't get wiped in time can be evened up with a rag dampened with alcohol. The thin shellac dries very quickly, and is ready to scuff in an hour or so. For the next coats, switch to a brush, or a spray gun if you've got it, for speed. When the finish is built up sufficiently, you can wet sand with naphtha and 400-grit wet/dry paper, then top it off by French polishing the surface. This leaves a beautiful, deep, clear finish with that Old-World, hand-rubbed look of French polish, but with a fraction of the work. There's more on French polishing in the next chapter.

Water-based varnish (acrylic and polyurethane)

Water-based varnish is sort of a fence sitter. Technically, it is an evaporative system, like shellac. But because the level of solvent is so low, it acts more like a reactive system in that the coats adhere to one another without actually melting the previous layers. Therefore, the rules about drips and runs on successive coats follow oil varnish more than lacquer; pick them up, or it will take forever for them to dry enough to sand out.

The handling properties of water-based varnish are unlike anything else. Natural bristles are out of the question—they splay in water—so choose a synthetic bristle. I'd opt for 100% nylon, since it is the softest, and preload it with water. If the area is large and flat, try using a paint pad instead of a brush. As long as you scrape off most of the excess (paint pads hold a lot more finish than brushes), a paint pad will give you a smooth, even layout with almost no foaming or bubbling. If you do get foaming with a brush, try adding either one ounce per gallon of mineral spirits or half-and-half (the stuff you put in coffee).

Flow the material on in the grain direction without working it back and forth too much. Most clear latexes are very thin, so it won't be hard to keep the coat thin. Try to get it on right the first time. The more you brush it, the more it foams. Remember that water-based varnish is a coalescing finish. It will always look worst when it is first applied. Leave it alone, and it will get better by itself. It will dry faster than oil, but not as quickly as shellac or lacquer. However, unlike the

---

Thinning finishes

Manufacturers do their best to make coatings at just the right viscosity so they are not too thin or too thick, and flow nicely. But there are times when you want to take matters into your own hands and thin the material further. Usually, the can label will tell you what thinning solvent to use (generally the same thing used for cleanup), and it is wise to follow the advice. Occasionally, though, the label doesn't say. Below are some general guidelines for thinning solvents and amounts for common types of finish. As always, the label should supersede anything here.

Oils, oil varnish (including oil polyurethanes), spar varnish: mineral spirits, VM&P naphtha (naphtha evaporates faster than mineral spirits), or to slow down the drying time, linseed oil.

Shellac: any alcohol (but preferably ethanol) in any amount—shellac can be thinned indefinitely without affecting its ability to form a film.

Lacquers: lacquer thinner. Lacquer thinners vary, depending on the resins the lacquer contains. It is best to use the one formulated for your material.

Latexes: small amounts of deionized or distilled water (1 oz. per gal), small amounts of the resin thinner (lacquer thinner or glycol ethers for acrylics), small amounts of propylene glycol to increase flow-out and slow the drying time.

Catalyzed or crosslinked lacquers and conversion varnish: nothing. You often can't change these at all, but they rarely need changes.

How fast a solvent evaporates is directly related to its vapor pressure. High vapor pressure means fast drying. You'll also notice that most fast solvents have low flash points. Speed and flammability go hand in hand.

solvent systems, water-based materials dry much faster when the relative humidity is low. You should stick to one coat per day in areas with high humidity, but don't be afraid to put on two coats per day if you live in Arizona, or if winter heating has dried up the air indoors. After the first coat, you'll have to scuff-sand the furred-up wood, but after that sanding is optional. Incidentally, the first coat will dry lickety-split, so you don't have to count it toward the maximum of one to two coats per day.

The problem with water-based coatings is the water. Water has a high surface tension, so it would rather bead up than lay out smooth. The first coat goes on like a dream, because the accommodating wood soaks up the excess water, but each subsequent coat gets tougher to control. The formulae for these coatings are very sensitive, so you can't do too much playing around with the mix, and adding water doesn't help. If you are desperate, add about an ounce per gallon of propylene glycol, but be careful on vertical surfaces. The finish will flow out better, but it will also sag more easily.

Unlike shellac, lacquer and oil varnish, which are all more or less amber, water-based acrylics are perfectly clear, and the polyurethanes actually have a slight bluish cast. Except for very white woods, like holly and maple, most wood looks better, or at least more familiar, under an amber film. We are so used to seeing a wood like walnut through the amber filter provided by the finish that it looks somewhat pallid and washed out with a water-based polyurethane on it. Don't say I didn't warn you. Of course, if you are creative, you can always add a touch of water-soluble amber dye to the varnish.

Water-reducible varnish

Water reducibles are oil emulsions, so once the water is gone, the finish is a reactive oil varnish. They handle like other water-based coatings with a few minor differences. Water reducibles are amber, not water clear. They tolerate more brushing without foaming or bubbling, and they flow out better, mostly because they dry more slowly. If you like water-based evaporative finishes, you'll love water-reducibles.

Applying wipe-on finishes

Woodworkers must have a natural affinity for minimalism, because that's what wipe-ons are, finishing at its simplest. Choosing a finish always involves weighing options and deciding which elements are most important: durability, cost, drying speed, and so on. When it comes to a wipe-on finish, ease of application is clearly high on the list of considerations. Even though these ultra-thin finishes offer little protection to the wood, they still enjoy great popularity, and it can't all be attributed to the fact that they are quick and easy. That may have drawn us to wipe-on finishes at first, but their inimitable look keeps bringing us back.

All finishes are absorbed into the wood somewhat, but the major difference with wipe-on finishes is that we remove everything that did not soak in. Of course, a small amount remains on top to form a film, but it is so little that it is really not noticeable except that it keeps wood looking wet. This thin film will also stave off the oxidation that makes raw wood turn silvery or chalky, and help the surface shed water. Some wipe-on finishes offer a small amount of stain and solvent resistance, but they do almost nothing to protect against abrasion, heat or fungal growth. Some, like linseed oil, are actually food for fungus, and can promote mold rather than discourage it on exterior applications. (If you plan to wipe linseed oil on exterior shingles, add a commercial fungicide or mildewcide first.)

Repairability is a frequently cited advantage of a thin finish. You can repair damage by lightly sanding or rubbing with steel wool, then applying another thin coat of the same. It is not that these materials are inherently more repairable themselves. In most cases, they are thinner applications of the same materials we brush and spray. It's simply that it is hard to see a spot that was sanded and re-oiled when you are only allowing the newly sanded areas once again to take in what little they can before the rest is wiped away. In the case of oil-based materials, we are not so much reknitting the finish as we are fooling the eye.

Oils (linseed, tung and Danish)

The primary method for applying oils is to flood them fairly liberally onto the wood surface, allow them some time to sink in, then wipe off the excess unabsorbed material before the oil dries. Linseed oil and tung oil are the two most common materials used this way, and they both handle easily, but dry very slowly. Linseed oil takes several days to cure; tung oil is faster, but not much. As for the film they form, linseed and tung oil both form flexible, water-shedding, amber films that discolor over time with exposure to ultraviolet light. Tung oil is a bit tougher, but considering the thickness of the film, it makes very little difference. Neither absorbs into wood easily when cool (they both flow better when warmed).

Wood is by nature hydrophilic (it likes water), but somewhat lipophobic (it resists oil). To make oils dry faster and penetrate better, several modifications are offered. Boiled linseed oil is not actually boiled, but it does have metallic dryers added to it that cause it to cure faster. Driers don't work with tung oil. Instead, it is heat bodied, a process that partially polymerizes the oil, making it thicker and faster drying.

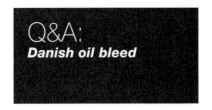

Q&A:
Danish oil bleed

Q: I applied a Danish oil finish to a 6-ft. red-oak kitchen bar top. After sanding it down to 220 grit, I applied the oil in accordance with the directions on the can. However, I had a hard time getting the surface dry without more oil bleeding out of the pores, and I had to continue wiping down the top for two days. Once the finish finally dried, I waited a few days, and then waxed it. However, the top doesn't seem to be very durable or resistant to stains. What should I do now?

A: Most Danish oil finishes consist of linseed oil cut with a large amount of mineral spirits and buffered with a small amount of alkyd resin. The problem you had with oil bleed was a result of overloading the oak's especially large pores with this mixture of mineral spirits and oil, which made it virtually impossible for the finish to dry. And you probably wiped off the lion's share of the finish you had applied, leaving little if any protective coating. Waxing the surface will do little to help.

Next time, put on at least three or four lighter coats of Danish oil, and let the film dry completely between coats. Better still, switch to a more protective varnish or polyurethane. Asking one coat of Danish oil to stand up to the daily rigors of a bar top just isn't realistic.

Another common option is to add thinners, since solvents dry faster than oil. Some manufacturers also add other modified oils—such as alkyds—to the mix. What evolves is a material that is a bit tougher than plain oil, penetrates better and dries faster. These modified oils are variously called "Danish oil finish," "teak oil" and several other similar names, and can be based on tung oil, linseed oil or other drying oils. It generally takes several coats of these oils before the wood is suf-

Tradition

The first time David called me it was to ask about an authentic, hand-rubbed oil finish. In my own defense, I must say that I did everything I could to talk him out of it, but he was an adamant traditionalist. I was certain that if I described the process to him, he would think I was pulling his leg, so I took him to meet Tony.

An old-world finisher and former teacher of mine, Tony had already passed retirement age at a gallop, but was still keeping shop hours in a cramped and cluttered New York walkup. The dusty old sample he showed us looked nothing like the one-coat wipes that pass for oiled walnut today. It was deep and rich and glossy, and I knew immediately that any hope of discouraging David was now lost.

In his heavy Italian accent, Tony described the arduous process. Start by sanding until the wood is perfectly smooth, he told us, then sand some more. When you are sure there are no scratches

left with 220 paper, start adding linseed oil and sand with finer wet/dry paper. He explained how sanding the linseed oil into the wood with 400-, then 600-grit paper would create a slurry of the oil and wood dust that would leave the surface smooth and start to fill the pores.

Finally Tony came to "the rule of two," and I was sure this would be the clincher. "Use your bare hand," he said, showing us a leathery, calloused palm, "and rub oil into the tabletop 'til you can't stand the heat no more. Rub it twice a day for a week, twice a week for a month, twice a month for a year, and twice a year for life. Keep after it, and it will always be beautiful." "That's not a finish," remarked David after we left the shop, "it's perpetual maintenance."

So when David called a second time for a traditional recipe, I was delighted he had chosen something simpler. He had heard of a home-brew mixture of beeswax, linseed oil and turpentine, and was hot to try it. I made it clear that this was not a durable bar-top finish; it is the sort of thing you use to wipe down exposed ceiling beams or other woodwork that needs to look good but takes no wear.

I also warned him of the smell. I told him to start by melting the wax, then mix in equal parts (1:1:1) of linseed oil and turpentine while the wax was still liquid. Finally I described how to wipe it on with burlap while it was still warm. At the time, it didn't occur to me to suggest a double boiler to heat the wax mixture.

Apparently, it didn't occur to him either. When I visited his shop a week later, my reception was on the chilly side. It was easy to see why. On his bench stood a one-burner hot plate supporting a rather blackened kitchen pot. Directly above on the otherwise white drywall ceiling was a sooty stain about the size of a deflated basketball indicating the spot where flames had recently danced toward the ceiling. "Did I mention anything about a double boiler?" I asked in my most innocent voice. David just glowered.

Shortly after that, I noticed that David had developed a curious fondness for modern, ready-mixed finishes, and an equally curious aversion to soliciting my advice.

ficiently saturated to satisfy the average woodworker. The cure time and number of coats vary greatly depending on the brand and formulation, but can labels are usually very informative.

As a thin finish, Danish oils are hard to beat. They are incredibly easy to apply, completely forgiving, repairable and good looking. In fact, they have only one real weakness. If a thinned oil is flooded onto wood that has very large pores—oak, for instance—it sometimes creeps back out of the pores and collects at the mouth of the pore. As the material dries, it forms small, hardened lumps of finish at the edge of the pores, leaving the surface of the wood feeling rough and pebbly the next morning. At that point, all you can do is scuff sand the surface and re-apply the oil. To forestall this problem, some people apply the finish early in the day and wipe the surface every hour or so to eliminate these pockets of oil as they collect, but before they harden. Another solution is to choose an alternative wipe-on finish when working on oak or ash.

Gel finishes

Gel coatings are oils that have been thickened to make them even easier to handle. They are sometimes buffered with other resins, like polyurethane, to impart more durability to what is essentially a weak finish. Like their thinner cousins, they are designed to be wiped on and off, and they leave a similar, fairly slow-drying film. They are even easier to apply, since they don't drip or run, and are not prey to the problem of pore lumps. All in all, gels are a rather nice improvement on an old favorite.

Water-based polyurethane

Although the technique is a little unorthodox, water-based polyurethane can be applied just like an oil finish. Just flood it on and wipe it off immediately. Polyurethane doesn't have the amber cast of oil, but it does look and act a lot like the popular Danish finishes, except that it doesn't repair as easily or nicely. Some water-based polyurethanes raise wood grain a bit, so you might want to scuff the wood and either re-apply or wax over the finish (I'll get to that in a minute). Naturally, there is nothing stopping you from using regular oil polyurethane varnish as a wipe-on finish, but you'll find that the water-based materials bite into the wood more easily.

Shellac, wax and a combination of the two

Either shellac or wax can be used as a wipe-on/wipe-off finish. With shellac, cut it very thin (almost watery), flood it on, and wipe it off immediately. It will raise the grain a bit, so plan to scuff it with very fine sandpaper (320 grit or finer), steel wool, or nylon abrasive hand pads. Paste wax can also be used as a finish in the same way. Smear it on heavily, let it sit for 10 or 15 minutes, and buff it off. Both of these finishes are evaporative, not reactive like the oils. They are both infinitely repairable, but neither one offers much protection.

A better alternative to shellac or wax is both together. Flood the wood with shellac, and wipe it off before it dries. If it looks like the shellac has soaked in and the wood still looks hungry, scuff the surface and add a second shellac wash. In a couple of hours when it is completely dry, apply a coat of paste wax with ultra fine (0000) steel wool or nylon abrasive pads. Let the wax set up for 15 minutes or so, and buff it off with a clean, soft rag.

For many years, a shellac/wax combination was a very popular finish for simple woodwork. It is easy to apply, dries very fast (it can be done in one afternoon), looks great and offers a surprising amount of protection for such a thin finish. It is sometimes called a museum finish (though not by museums) because it is so easily repairable and reversible and it looks like what you'd expect to find on itinerant or Shaker furniture. If you've never done more than wiped on Danish oil and you're looking for a finish to act as a springboard to launch you into "professional" finishes, this is the perfect place to start.

Applying sprayable finishes

By making finishes thinner, we can apply them with a spray gun and make them dry faster. Imagine taking a whole can of finishing material and running it through a carburetor so that a cloud of atomized liquid is blown toward a piece of furniture. That is precisely what is happening when you use a spray gun. It is the least efficient means of transferring material onto wood, and it fills the air with clouds of finish and solvent; but it is fast. That's what spray finishing is all about.

Spray finishes are designed to be applied quickly, and to dry just as fast. Consequently, they are mostly thin mixtures with a very high ratio of solvents to solids. Typically, lacquers contain only 12% to 24% solids, and it is rare to see one go above 35%. The recent VOC regulations are encouraging an increase in the solids content, with a parallel improvement in transfer efficiency, but both are still low compared with some of the brushable varnishes we use. The most salient characteristic of a low-solids, fast-dry finish is its ability to follow even the most subtle contours of the surface on which it is applied.

Whereas slow-drying coatings tend to flow out and find their own level, sprayed lacquer reveals everything beneath it from tiny wood pores to sanding scratches. The fast surface tack means that airborne dust is less of a problem, but ventilation is absolutely critical. If you get a run

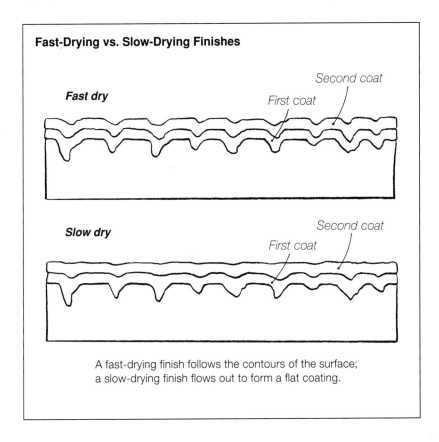

Fast-Drying vs. Slow-Drying Finishes

Fast dry

Second coat

First coat

Slow dry

Second coat

First coat

A fast-drying finish follows the contours of the surface;
a slow-drying finish flows out to form a flat coating.

with an evaporative finish, leave it alone and sand it out later. Touching it will put you through to the wood (see the sidebar on p. 5). But if you get a run with a reactive finish, it is usually a good idea to wipe it before it dries. At worst, you'll only mess up one layer.

Shellac

Like a bad penny, shellac keeps turning up in every finish application category. But shellac is more of an underappreciated old friend, for beyond being a finish unto itself, it plays a dual role as a lifesaver for refinishers who work with lacquer. Most refinished pieces have been contaminated with silicone oil from commercial furniture polishes. Solvent lacquers are particularly sensitive to silicone, reacting with fish-eyes as the lacquer chases away from the oily areas with low surface tension. Because lacquer is an evaporative system, once fish-eye shows up on one layer, it will re-appear in each subsequent one. The best way to deal with it is to remove as much as possible with solvents and surfactants during stripping (see p. 69), and then seal in the rest with shellac. Fortunately, shellac is both an excellent and compatible sealer coat under most lacquers.

Shellac can be sprayed at any consistency from heavy cream down to water, but it is easiest to control when it is thin and watery. Plan on two thin coats with a light scuff sanding in between, since shellac has a tendency to raise the grain of wood. If you're spraying with conventional compressed air guns (see pp. 46-53), go for a fairly low power air cap (one that draws about 8 cfm at 30 psi) and fluid nozzle (.050 in. to .070 in.). For high-volume, low-pressure (HVLP) guns, anything above a .035-in. tip at 3 psi is adequate. For the best layout, stick to thin, light coats. As with all evaporative finishes, sanding between coats is unnecessary unless you need to smooth the surface.

Old paint

The reason Gary and I became such fast friends is that one day he found me singing in the spray booth.

A spray booth is a noisy place. With the compressor running, the exhaust fan on and the air whooshing through the gun, you can't hear anything but yourself. There is a delightful sense of seclusion, probably the closest thing we blue-collar workers get to a private office. So even though I'm a lousy singer, I could warble at the top of my lungs with relative impunity, knowing that the din of the booth would hide me from exposure.

Of course, I had a reason for singing. Spraying is a very rhythmic activity. A good sprayer has to keep constantly in motion to apply a consistently smooth, even coating. A slight pause will usually translate into a run or sag, and a change in gun speed will mean a variance in film thickness. To maintain a constant fluid motion, I'd pace myself by singing as I sprayed.

Apparently, I wasn't the only one, for when Gary wandered in and discovered my secret, he admitted that he did the same thing. I knew then and there that he must be a good finisher, and I was right—he was. That's why it was so surprising when the job went haywire.

We had contracted to refinish six guitar bodies, matching the color to the original specs. Since we were sure that there would be silicone contamination, we decided to seal them first with two coats of shellac. As shellac ages, it turns rubbery, so we always mixed our own fresh. I found a full jug of shellac in the spray room, but I couldn't remember how old it was, so I mixed another and left it on a small table near the booth. Since we always used the same one-quart juice bottles to mix the shellac flakes with alcohol, we never bothered to label them.

By Friday, Gary had the guitars sealed, sanded and ready for the color coat. It was one of those rare days when everything goes right, and I had hit the color quickly without having to tweak the mixture until I had two gallons too many. In fact, when the spraying was done, we had less than six ounces of extra color left. We left for the weekend with light hearts.

As usual, Gary was in first Monday morning. "Better go look in the booth," he grunted. The guitars looked like mud flats with big plate-like cracks where the shrinking lacquer had split over the shellac. As I stood in shock wondering what could have gone wrong, my eye fell on the still full jar of shellac I had mixed the week before. Not far away was the jug of old material—empty.

Our momentum on that job never recovered. It took far longer to refinish those guitars the second time, and we ended up with about a gallon of extra top coat as we kept adding more in an attempt to get the color right. Gary stored the extra colored lacquer on a shelf with one of his hand-drawn labels on the can. The drawing on the label was an American Indian astride a pony, with the label "Old Paint."

Do remember that the solvent for shellac is alcohol, and the fumes are very flammable. Shellac should be sprayed only in a booth with an explosion-proof fan and lights, and non-sparking switches. When you are finished spraying, clean out the gun at once and run some lacquer thinner through it. Shellac will pit and corrode the gun's interior if it is left in too long.

Lacquers (nitrocellulose, acrylic, CAB, vinyl and urethane)

Virtually all solvent-based lacquers handle the same, since they are all evaporative coatings that can be thinned almost indefinitely. That means that they can be sprayed under a wide range of conditions and gun setups merely by altering their viscosity. The typical lacquer gun setup will accept a range of air caps that will move anywhere from 4 to 11 cfm at 30 psi coupled with a .070-in. fluid nozzle.

High-solvent lacquers are probably the most forgiving materials you can spray. You can apply them thin and dry, thick and wet, or anything in between, and the material will dutifully lay out for you. It's hard to imagine a more user-friendly spray material. For this reason, there are no really strict rules about applying, and you'll find finishers getting successful results with wildly contrasting application techniques.

I've listed a few common problems associated with spray lacquers, along with some solutions below.

Overspray Overspray is a pebbly texture that comes from the lacquer drying before it hits the wood. To eliminate the problem, spray wetter, lower the air pressure and/or reduce the fan width.

Overspray.

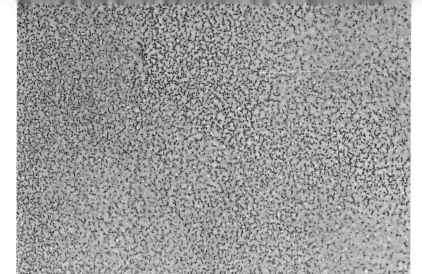

Orange peel.

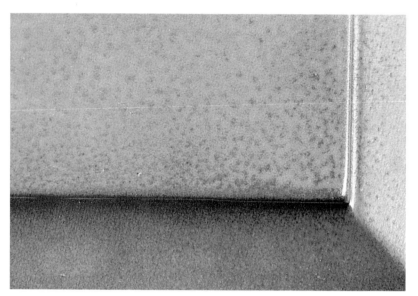

Fish-eye.

Orange peel If the material is too thick, it will not flow out smoothly, but will create a bumpy texture called orange peel. You can sometimes correct it by increasing the air pressure, but it is usually better simply to thin the material more.

Fish-eye Fish-eye is caused by silicone contamination of the wood. The best thing to do is avoid silicone in the first place, but if fish-eye shows up after the lacquer is on, sand the coat flat and add more silicone (fish-eye remover) to the lacquer. This is the classic case of fighting fire with fire. The silicone added to the lacquer reduces the surface tension of the material to match that of the contaminated spots.

Pin-hole   Many conditions can cause pin-holing (small pin-sized holes in the finish surface), but the most common one with spray lacquers is flooding material that is too thick onto open pores in wood. Prevent it by thinning the material and spraying lighter coats.

Spitting and unbalanced spray patterns   Spitting and unbalanced spray patterns occur when the gun is dirty. Stop, take it apart and clean it. While you are at it, make sure the packings are in good shape and the fluid nozzle is firmly seated.

Blush   White clouds caught in a finish are called blush. Their formation is due to moisture or to low active solvent levels. In either case, adding blush chaser or retarder solvents to the mixture will clear up the problem when you spray the next coat. For more on blush, see the sidebar on p. 144.

Water-based lacquer

I'd love to tell you that spraying water-based lacquers is as easy as spraying solvent-based ones, but sadly, that is not the case. Water-based coatings have oodles of advantages over solvent systems—higher solids content, low VOC, less toxicity—but all that is offset by one huge drawback. They are just plain ornery to apply.

To start with, you can't simply dump more solvent into water-based lacquers to solve any flow-out problems. On top of that, they have a higher surface tension, are more sensitive to both contaminants and temperature, are greatly affected by humidity, dry more slowly, sag and run more easily, and are even bothered by the amount of air flow your booth fan draws. All this adds up to the reality of water-based sprayables: it is much harder to get a good smooth layout. It can be done, though. Here's some tips to help you do it.

Start by downsizing your spray gun. For compressed-air guns, put in a small fluid nozzle (.040 in. to .055 in.) and a small air cap (5 cfm at 30 psi), and lower the air pressure to about 25 psi. Make sure you have a good filter on the air line to remove any oil or dirt. With HVLP guns, the fluid tip should be somewhere around .035 in. or .040 in. (air caps are keyed to the turbine output). If your HVLP gun is powered by a turbine, about half the problems associated with water-based materials are instantly eliminated. Water-based lacquer likes warm, dry, clean air. A turbine produces warm, dry, clean air. Water-based lacquer works best with low pressure and a gentle delivery, and HVLP guns deliver just that.

The temperature of the wood, the finish and the air in the spray room (as well as the air coming through the gun) should be the same, and preferably, above 70°F. The finish will lay out better as the temperature rises. Watch out for cool drafts cutting across the surface of the wood drawn by the exhaust fan. They can result in premature skinning that shows up as blush and orange peel. Since you are using less solvent, you might want to cut the fan back a little. Although they dry much faster in dry air, water-based materials will tolerate a wide range of relative humidity.

Make certain the wood is clean and free of oil, grease and wax. (I don't recommend using oil-based stains and fillers under water-based coatings. Opt for water- or solvent-based ones instead.) Spray light, thin coats to reduce sagging, runs, grain raising, blushing caused by trapped water, and a host of other problems. If you spray too heavily, the material tends to skin over, trapping water in the film. The resulting coat takes an agonizingly long time to dry. Keep to a slow spraying schedule—no more than two coats per day—to allow the finish to dry thoroughly between coats.

When a water-based lacquer first goes on, it looks like orange peel. Don't let that spook you into spraying on more. It will flow out in about two hours. If you still have orange peel in the dry coat, spray a little bit wetter on the next coat or, better yet, add a flow-out thinner if the manufacturer offers one. If you do get a run, wipe it immediately. You will not go all the way through the coats because the low solvent content doesn't let the material melt in that well. Besides, if you wait for a run to dry enough to sand out, you'll still be waiting when the cows come home.

In most cases, sanding between coats is not necessary, but since the solvent level is so low, you may want to anyway. If you use stearated (self-lubricating) sandpaper, make sure you remove all of the sanding dust before spraying. The stearates act like wax to create something similar to fish-eye. Wipe off the surface, but don't use standard tack rags because they often contain oil. Instead, tack off with a damp cloth. Avoid steel wool between coats. It may contain oil, and it always leaves metal fragments that can rust under the next coat. Use nylon abrasive pads instead.

Don't expect to be able to rub water-based finishes to a high gloss without running into problems. Once again, the low solvent level is responsible. Instead of remelting completely like solvent lacquers, water-based finishes form layers. If you cut through these layers while buffing, they may show up as witness lines. However, they rub up beautifully to satin.

If you add a crosslinker (see p. 20) to a water-based lacquer, the resulting finish will be much tougher, with better solvent and water resistance. However, the spraying characteristics won't change one iota.

Oil varnish

It is possible to spray oil varnish, but for the life of me I can't figure out why you would want to. It does not handle well through a gun, dries too slowly once it hits the wood, sags easily, and in short, has none of the characteristics that one expects from a finish designed to be sprayed. If you insist on trying, cut the varnish with a fast-drying solvent, like VM&P naphtha. Spray it as you would thin shellac, thin coats at low pressure through a small setup. From there you are on your own, but don't say I didn't warn you.

Crosslinked finishes (catalyzed lacquer, vinyl, CAB, conversion varnish and polyester)

With very few differences, crosslinked finishes handle exactly like solvent lacquers. They use the same gun setups and pressures, dry fast, and are extremely forgiving. In most cases, though, you can not add extra thinner, but because these coatings usually start out thinner, you don't have to. Once each coat crosslinks, the next will not dissolve it. Consequently, the finish forms layers like any reactive finish, and is prey to witness lines if you cut through cured layers. On the positive side, these finishes generally have much higher solids contents, so it is easier to spray a final coat thick enough to buff without rubbing through. As with all high-solvent materials, good ventilation is a must both to prevent fires and explosions and for your personal safety. I always wear a cartridge-type vapor mask when I spray such coatings. And with all crosslinked finishes, keep the pot life in mind. If the coating cures before you clean it out of your spray equipment, you will have a piece of sculpture instead of a functional spray gun.

Polyester is the only crosslinked finish that needs another word or two. Instead of scuffing after the first coat, as you would with any other solvent finish, let the polyester surface stay rough, and sand it back after you have built up two or three coats. That way you can avoid cutting through to the raw wood, an action that will result in more roughness. Some crosslinked finishes, including some polyurethanes, utilize an isocyanate kicker (initiator). Isocyanate is very hazardous and should be handled with extreme care. That means that gloves and a vapor mask should be worn while you are mixing the lacquer, not just when you spray. It is the concentrated crosslinking material that is the most dangerous part of the coating. Be very careful. If you are not sure of what you are doing, choose a different finish. I would.

CHAPTER 8
Repairing Damage

Finish repair really consists of only three things: removing excess or unwanted materials, filling spaces that should not be vacant, and changing colors that don't match. Drips, runs, dust and dirt occupy most of the first category. Pinholes, chips and dents fall in the second group. The third group is all about touch-up.

Drips, runs, dust and dirt

Wet finishes have an unfortunate knack for collecting all sorts of airborne debris. If something big, like an errant bug, gets into the finish, it is best to pluck it out with tweezers while the film is still wet. But in most cases, the small dust and dirt particles that embed themselves in the drying film will only result in small pimples on the dried finish. These will almost always flatten and virtually disappear during the light sanding stage of the rubbing process (see Chapter 9).

Drips, runs, and "curtains" (the wide runs that form on vertical surfaces) are a bit more work. In most cases, if you do not catch them immediately while the finish is still being applied wet, you will have to wait a good long time before you can fix them. These thick pockets of finish dry much more slowly than the area around them, and if you try to sand them flat before they set, the finish is likely to peel right down

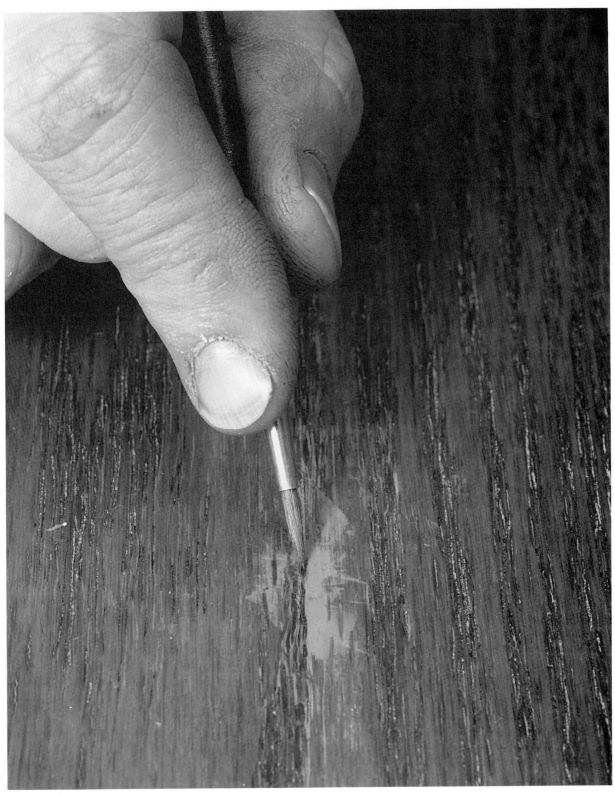

Touch-up is really a matter of fooling the viewer's eye with a replica of the grain.

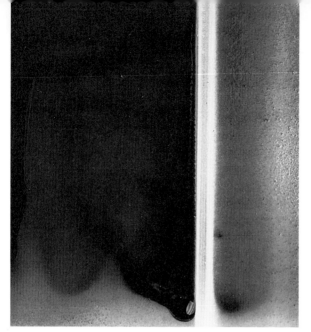

Spraying too heavily can mar the finish with drips, runs and curtains.

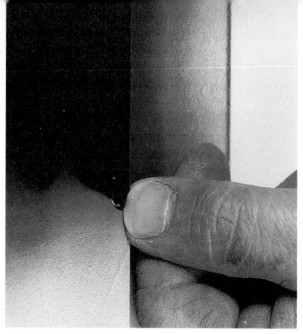

Press your thumbnail into the bulb of the drip to see if it's still soft. Don't sand it out until it's fully dry.

to the wood. It will almost always take several days for runs to dry sufficiently. Test the run by gently pressing your thumbnail into the thickest part. If it gives easily, let it dry some more.

Once the run is dry, you can go at it with a single-edged razor blade. If it is a very brittle finish (like nitrocellulose lacquer), use the blade like a tiny scraper to shear away layers of the run without cutting the surrounding area. If the finish is flexible (like spar or floor varnish), you can use the razor at a very low angle to slice off the bulk of the excess material. In either case, once you are close to level, you can start to sand. I like to use 400-grit or 600-grit wet/dry sandpaper with naphtha or soapy water as a lubricant. With the paper wrapped around a small (about 1-in. by 2-in.) flat block of hard neoprene, I gently sand until the area is completely flat. Once leveled, the finish can be rubbed to make the sheen uniform.

On occasion, you will sand too far and cut through the last coat into the one below. This is not a problem with evaporative finishes like lacquer, which by redissolving themselves form just one thick coat. But with reactive finishes like varnish and also with low-solvent water-based lacquers, it is common for faint lines to show where one coat is sanded through to the other. These marks, called halos or witness lines, are usually incurable except by recoating. Remove any wax, soap or oil film that might be on the finish from lubricants, and lightly scuff the entire surface with 320-grit sandpaper before you apply another top coat.

On a brittle finish, use the razor blade like a tiny scraper to remove a blemish.

On a flexible finish, slice off the run with the razor blade at a low angle.

After removing most of the run, wet-sand using water as a lubricant.

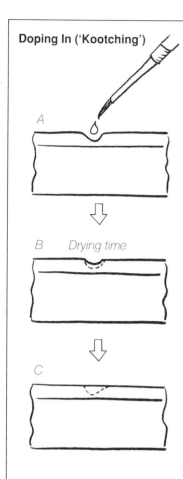

Doping In ('Kootching')

A

⇩

B *Drying time*

⇩

C

Place a drop of finish into the area to be filled (A). As it dries, the drop will shrink below the surface of the finish (B). Continue in this manner until the dent is brought to the level of the rest of the finish (C).

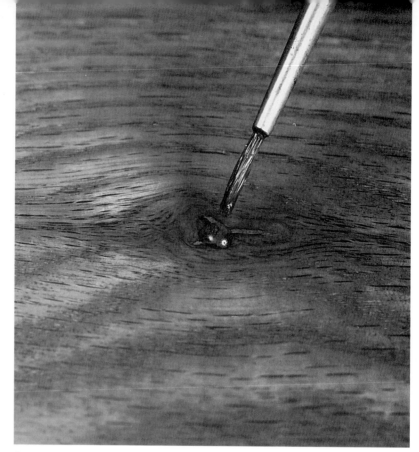

Adding a drop of finish to fill a hole in the surface is called doping in, or kootching.

Pinholes, chips and dents

Just as wood is prone to chips and dents, so is finish. But you can't steam up a dent after finish is in place, and wood putty would not look too good patching a chip in a clear finish. The two common ways to fill holes in the finishing process are doping in and burning in.

Doping in

Doping in (called "kootching" in some areas of New York) is the process of gradually filling a void with drops of the same finish. Using a very fine (000) brush or the tip of a toothpick, place a drop of finish into the area to be filled, whether it is a dent, chip or pinhole. At first, it will form a dome above the surrounding surface, but as it dries, it will most likely shrink below, especially with larger chips. Because of this, you may have to repeat the doping-in process two or more times until the dried spot is at or above the level of the surrounding finish. This can be very time-consuming, since you must wait for each drop to dry thoroughly before adding another. Once the level has been achieved, treat the spot like a low drip, wet-sanding it flush with a small block before rubbing out or recoating. It is always better if you fix these spots before the last coat of finish goes on, because that last film will help to blend out lots of imperfections.

Burning in

A faster but riskier way to fill a dent is to burn in the area. Burning in is the process of filling finish defects with hot-melt resins that look and act like clear, colored or tinted finish. Rather than requiring several applications and lots of drying time as with doping in, burning in takes only minutes and the surface is ready to work almost immediately.

Burn-in sticks are solid sticks of finish that will melt at fairly low temperatures, flow into a small defect, then reharden as they cool. Burn-in sticks come in clear, colors and transparent tints to match most coatings, and are sold by companies that specialize in finish-repair products. Because there are so many colors available (and because it seems that no matter how many you have, you never have the right one), there is a temptation to stock up. But like all finish materials, burn-in sticks have a shelf life, and a few heat waves will destroy them in short order. If the sticks start to get gummy or rubbery instead of liquidy when melted, or if they develop a crazed crack pattern on their surface, it is time to retire them. You can prolong their life a little bit by keeping them in the refrigerator during hot weather.

A small oven (background) heats three smooth-edged grapefruit knives and two Dragaway knives, which when touched to the burn-in sticks (foreground), cause them to melt and flow into a dent.

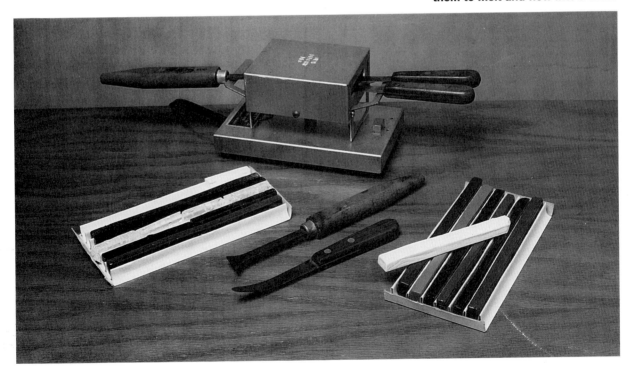

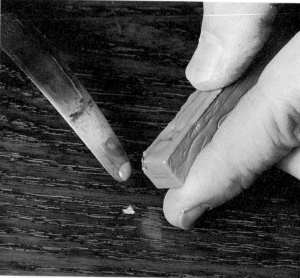

First, melt the appropriate color stick with a heated knife (left). If the stick bubbles, the knife is too hot. By melting only a little at a time, you can fill a spot without damaging the surrounding area (right).

Repairing a dent by burning in involves melting the appropriate color of stick with a heated knife or iron and letting it flow into the defect you want to fill. Once the blob has cooled, you can sand it flush just like a doped-in spot, and recoat with top coat. In theory this sounds easy, but in practice it requires some timing and restraint.

The first problem is heat. The range of heat that these sticks will tolerate is rather small, so the knife used to melt the stick must be just hot enough to do the job and no hotter. An overheated knife will cause the stick to bubble and burn, and leave air bubbles in the defect you're trying to fill. Suppliers of burn-in sticks sell rheostatically controlled electric knives, or heating ovens to be used with regular knives. These solve the problem of heat to a degree.

The second problem is that any amount of burn-in stick you apply over and above what you need to fill the hole must be removed. Unlike the doping-in liquid, this stuff does not shrink as it cools, and it is usually at least as hard as the finish. If you have too much to sand off easily, you are likely to cut through the surrounding finish while trying to level the bump. Once again, technology comes halfway to the rescue with a solvent (such as Mohawk's Brasiv) that will remove burn in without harming the surrounding finish — usually. But like all solvents, it will leave the surface of the burn-in uneven and soft.

There is a better way, of course. Let's start with the equipment. I use an oven loaded with three smooth-edged grapefruit knives and two Dragaway knives (Dragaway knives are made by Mohawk-Behlen; Starr calls its version "patching knives"). The thin knives both heat and cool quickly, allowing me to keep working by switching from one to the next, without slowing me down too much if they do overheat (the oven is good, but not perfect). I keep the knives clean by wiping them on a cotton rag before I replace them in the oven. I touch just the tip of the knife to the burn-in stick and transfer a very tiny amount of material into the defect by carefully pressing it in before the stick cools. If the stick bubbles, the knife is too hot. If it melts but does not bubble, then the knife can be quickly touched to the finish being repaired without risking burning or bubbling the area around the defect. By working with only a little material at a time, you can fill a spot without damaging the surrounding area or going overboard with the burn-in stick.

Now check out the Dragaway knives. It is essential that these be the right temperature also, but since they will be touching the finish before the burn-in stick, there is no feedback. How do you tell? I use pure, unadulterated experience. Practice on some finished scrap wood. It's not that hard. When the knife is the right temperature, you can pull the flat of the knife across the burn-in and it will level it perfectly. Keep the knife in good shape by cleaning it after use; now and then, square the leading edge on a sharpening stone. If the Dragaway works as it should, you will be able to do the final leveling with nothing more than 600-grit sandpaper and a little lubricant — light oil, naphtha or soapy water. Don't use the naphtha on the clear sticks, just on the colored ones.

Pull the flat of the Dragaway knife across the burn in to level it.

To protect the surrounding finish, you can mask off the area with tape before filling the spot (above), then remask for the knife (left).

Just in case you absolutely must do your first burn-in on a good piece, here are a couple of safety nets. One is a heat-blocking balm, which is sold under various names by finish-repair suppliers. It is smeared around the area to be burned in and will provide a little protection. The other is masking tape. You can bracket the spot with thin masking tape (like 3M Fineline tape) and run the knife on top of it. Neither of these methods is foolproof, but they may get you over the initial hump. But remember, tricks are no substitute for finesse.

Touch-up

Whenever customers watch a finisher do touch-up work, they invariably ask, "Do you paint as a hobby?" In my case, the answer is no, but I can readily understand the association. Good touch-up consists of nothing more than painting a convincing picture of wood on a spot of putty or burn-in.

Wood is not one color, but an amalgam of many hues that our eye averages into one general tone. If you look carefully at wood, you will see that even a small spot the size of the average puttied dent or burn-in contains a wide range of colors and patterns. There are grain, figure, pores and tonal variations in the background. On top of that, wood is somewhat translucent. Not only do we see colors on the surface, but also the effects of light going partway through the wood. The best way to duplicate a real wood look is to combine delicate patterns with layered color.

Blending color and grain lines

Start with a background of putty or burn-in that is a shade or two lighter than the lightest shade of the background coloring in the wood. When in doubt, go light. It is far easier to make a spot darker than it is to lighten it. In fact, it is next to impossible to lighten with touch-up. If you have to hide a dark spot, like a sap line in maple, you are better off gouging it out and refilling it with a lighter material.

To touch up a finish, choose a burn-in stick that is a shade lighter than the background color.

Q: My woodworking includes repair and refinishing of a variety of woods, but walnut and cherry seem to predominate. In many instances I have to repair gouges, scratches and indentations. Steaming cannot repair such conditions, and a filler is needed. The commercial filler sticks I have tried either have an unacceptable color or are not compatible with the wood finish to be used.

In desperation I am going to make up some "Shellac Sticks" from seedlac. My problem is that I cannot locate a source for about 5 lb. of seedlac.

A: Seedlac is nothing more than unrefined shellac with the wax, dirt, insect parts and branch remnants still in it. You might instead prefer to use a shellac that is slightly more refined; the price per pound is the same in spite of the fact that the dirt has been removed. Considering the per-pound price of shellac, seedlac turns out to be a fairly expensive way to buy tree bark and insect legs. Furthermore, I suspect you'll find that making your own burn-in sticks is a lot more difficult than you imagine. Considering the vast variety of colors and burn-in sticks, I've never had any trouble finding burn-in sticks to suit my needs.

Next, duplicate the fine grain and ray lines in the wood by painting them in with a very fine brush. Don't worry about the background color; you can fix that later. When the grain lines are in place, the overall color of the spot will appear darker as our eye "averages in" the spots of color. If you do the background first, odds are the added grain lines will make the area too dark. Try to match the character of the wood as closely as possible, but don't be afraid to be creative. If you are working on wood that contains knots or figure, it is sometimes easier to hide a defect by painting over it with a convincing-looking knot or grain pattern.

Once the pattern looks good, decide if the background needs to be tinted. If it does, mix a color with very little pigment in lots of vehicle so as to keep the color semi-transparent. By carefully applying light layers of this tint, you can gradually creep up on the right background tone without obscuring your graining efforts. As with filled spots, touch-up should be buried under another clear coat. If that is out of the question, consider French polishing (see pp. 175-178).

All right, I admit it. Touch-up isn't all that easy, but with just a little practice you'll be surprised at how well you can hide things in a finish. Remember that you are not trying to work miracles. Just break up the color so that it doesn't catch your eye. You will always see your own touch-up work, no matter how good it is, but you'll be surprised at how easy it is to fool others.

Filling nail holes

A common touch-up problem is how to fill finish-nail holes in prefinished moldings after they are installed. For these fill jobs, there are many colors of soft sticks designed to be rubbed or pressed into the hole, with the excess wiped or scraped off. In case you hadn't guessed, those touch-up sticks are nothing more than wood-tone wax crayons. If the hardware store doesn't have the color you need, borrow your kid's crayons. Be sure to ask permission first, and give them back when you are done. We finishers should set a good example.

Blush and water rings

Blush and water rings, two faces of the same evil, are caused by water or moisture coming in contact with a finish, and they are most common on evaporative finishes. In some cases, this white, cloudy aberration settles in the wax above a finish, in which case just removing the wax with naphtha will solve the problem. (Wax itself is also an evaporative finish, albeit a rather weak one.) Otherwise, the cure is to introduce a solvent that will soften the finish without removing it. About 90% of the time, a careful wipe with alcohol will do the trick. Dampen

Paint in the fine grain and ray lines with a small touch-up brush.

a rag and wipe it across the surface once. If you start rubbing with an alcohol-soaked rag, you run the risk of removing the finish or badly smearing it. Let the alcohol dry (it takes only a minute or two) and repeat the step if you need to.

If alcohol doesn't work, there is a stronger mixture of solvents called amalgamator that may, but it does take some practice to work with the stuff. You are quite likely to destroy the first few finishes you touch with amalgamator. In any case, even the alcohol is likely to leave the surface of the finish duller than it was, so expect to rerub or rewax the finish afterward.

Touch-up materials

Touch-up calls for a good set of brushes and an array of coloring materials. In my experience, the only type of brush hair fine and supple enough to afford the control needed to mimic grain lines is red sable. Although expensive, a set of topnotch red sable brushes is a must, and properly cared for, it will last for many years. Buy the best you can find in a range of sizes from no. 2 down to 000. A good sable brush should point (taper to a cohesive tip without splaying) and should be very springy. Clean and reshape the tip before you put it away, and store the brush so that nothing touches the tip. I keep mine upside down in a mug. To protect the hair, I dip it in shellac and shape it wet, then let the shellac dry like a protective mousse. When I need to use it again, I merely dip the brush in alcohol to redissolve the shellac, and I am ready to work.

Although you can touch up with almost any compatible coloring material, the range of colors and techniques demanded are more easily met with a color box. Mine is just a slab of wood with holes in it, and filling each hole is a different fresco powder. (At one time, I preferred sectioned plastic tackle boxes, but they never held up. The touch-up box in the photo at right on the facing page has been my constant and well-used companion since 1975.

Obviously, it makes up in durability what it lacks in appearance.)

The touch-up powders themselves are very finely ground pigments, so they will mix with almost any finish and won't leave little lumps when the touch-up line dries. Although you can mix the colors with whatever finish you are putting on, I usually use shellac or padding lacquer as my touch-up liquid. It is convenient,

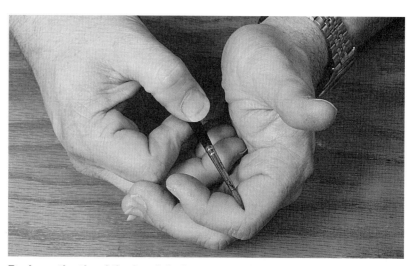

Reshape the tip of the brush before you put it away.

French polish

You've got your damage burned in and touched up, but you don't want to recoat the whole thing. Or perhaps, for some reason, it is just not feasible. Now what? You've got to seal the touch-up with something. Take heart. There is always French polish.

French polish is one of the most venerated, satisfying and tiring styles of finishing that you are likely to engage in. But it is an easy skill to develop, and will guarantee your membership in that exclusive club of serious finishers. And you don't even have to pay any dues.

mixes well with the powders, dries fast, and, in the small amounts used, is compatible with almost any finish.

How your color box is arranged is a matter of personal taste, but it is easier to use if it appeals to your sense of logic. Mine goes in

three ranks from light to dark. The center rank contains the pure mass tones: white, yellow, orange, red, and so on to black. The lower rank has the cool tones, from greenish white through raw sienna and raw umber. The upper rank has warm tones, from pinkish white and champagne through burnt sienna and burnt umber. Past black is a cluster of aniline dyes, which I rarely use. If you mix pigments and dyes and then top-coat the

touch-up, the dyes are likely to "walk out" (rise to the top of the finish) and mess up your coloring work. They are handy for work on dye-shaded finishes, though, so I keep them around.

The palette on which I mix my colors is simply a piece of glass or mirror. It is cheap, easy to clean, doesn't absorb or leak the shellac, and, being colorless itself, won't distort the colors I mix.

Brushes should be stored so that nothing touches the tips.

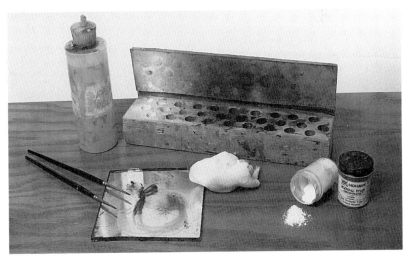

A touch-up box filled with various powders keeps all your colors at your fingertips.

To be precise, the term "French polish" actually refers to those shellac mixtures intended specifically for pad application. But most finishers use the term to cover the process of padding as well as all the various materials used, including both shellac and padding lacquer. Billed as "the modern alternative to French polish," padding lacquer is a ready-made shellac-based mixture buffered with at least one other (ostensibly more durable) resin, usually ethyl cellulose. In order to solvate the other resin, a different solvent package is used. Consequently, padding lacquer tends to bite into lacquer better than a straight alcohol/shellac mixture, and that may account for its popularity. Still, many purists prefer to mix their own fresh shellac to use as French polish. In my own work, I usually resort to padding lacquer, probably because I am more lazy than obsessed.

Whether you use shellac or padding lacquer, the process is the same. Make an application pad by filling a cotton or linen cloth with some absorbent material (it can be more of the same cotton cloth), making sure that the outer surface is smooth and free of creases or seams. My favorite pad material is washed, bleached tight-weave cheesecloth. Form the pad into a size that is comfortable for your hand. This is strictly a matter of taste. (Incidentally, I've heard these pads referred to by at least half a dozen official terms, but I've never noticed that naming them makes them work any better, so I don't bother.)

The solvent for French polish is alcohol. Alcohol is absorbed through the skin, and although it is not highly toxic, too much is not good for you. Before you begin working with French polish, it's a good idea to put on a pair of gloves.

Q&A:
Eliminating a perfume stain

Q: I have a chestnut-brown-colored ash dresser with a lacquer finish. Unfortunately, perfume was spilled on it. The perfume was quickly removed, but not before it damaged the finish, removing the lacquer's gloss in the area of the spill. What is the best way to repair the finish?

A: From your description, it sounds like the finish is still intact, merely dulled by the alcohol in the perfume. Fortunately, you can repolish the dulled lacquer with just about any automotive polishing compound. Just follow the directions on the can's label. Be sure to buy a "polishing" compound instead of a "rubbing" compound: The latter is usually a coarser grit and will not allow you to polish the finish to as high a gloss.

If the surface level of the finish in the perfume-affected area is significantly lower than that of the surrounding area, the repair will be much more difficult. The spot will require filling in some way, whether by burning in with a shellac stick (if it's a very small area), respraying the area with more lacquer or "padding in" more finish using the French-polishing method. You might want to check with a professional refinisher in your area before you begin such a repair, to make sure the job is not going to put you in over your head.

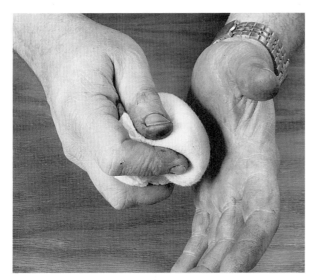

Make a pad by filling cotton cloth with absorbent material (above left), load the pad with French polish (above) and tamp the pad into your hand to spread the material (left).

Now load the pad with finishing material. You want it damp, but not too wet. If you get too much on, don't worry; simply squeeze out the pad as well as you can, and it will be about right. Many polishers like to tamp the pad when they add finish to it. You do this by patting it firmly against your other hand, and the idea is to distribute the finish evenly on the pad's surface. I don't know if tamping the pad actually spreads the finish or not, but it sure is satisfying. You will notice, though, that if you squeeze the pad, a little more French polish comes to the surface. This will come in handy soon.

Now move the pad across the surface of the wood without stopping, and it will apply an exceptionally thin layer of finish to the surface. The pattern or direction matters very little, but do try to cover the surface evenly, and alternate your direction to prevent curdling. Curdling looks like a series of ridges, and it forms when too much wet French

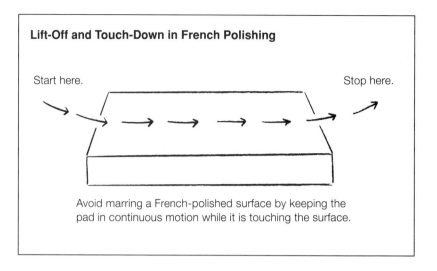

Lift-Off and Touch-Down in French Polishing

Start here.

Stop here.

Avoid marring a French-polished surface by keeping the pad in continuous motion while it is touching the surface.

polish keeps getting pulled in the same direction. If this does happen, stop, let the surface dry, and wet-sand the area flat with 600-grit sandpaper and naphtha before continuing.

As you rub, press lightly at first, and increase pressure a little as the pad dries. If the pad grabs too much, you can lubricate it with a drop of mineral oil, but keep it to a minimum. To lay on more material, squeeze the pad, but remember that you are pushing around liquid finish. That pad can take off material as well as put it on, so don't press too hard or get the pad too wet. Keep rubbing until the pad starts to dry out, then add a few more drops of finish and keep going. If the pad starts to cake or if the finish on it gets thick, add alcohol instead of polish. I like to finish off a French-polished surface with one thin coat in one direction, usually with the grain of the wood. Eventually, the surface will get shiny and smooth.

If you stop moving, even for a second, the pad will leave a mark by melting the finish, so you cannot begin or end your padding motion while the pad is in contact with the surface. You have to get the pad on and off the surface while it is moving. Think of how an airplane lands and takes off. It either lifts off or touches down while it is in motion. That's the way you have to handle the pad.

The rest is only practice and energy. If the surface starts to get too soft, give it a rest. It is not likely that you will be able to polish a surface in one shot anyway. Work it until you tire out, then go back to it later. There is no time limit. If you work dry and the surface is large, you can keep going for a long time. Or, you can come back to it an hour later, a day later, a week later or a year later. If you used oil as a pad lubricant, it may rise to the top and cloud the surface. You can "spirit it off" by lightly passing an alcohol-dampened pad over the surface.

The old shell game

"In-house" repair work—doing touch-up on furniture already in people's homes—is about as far from glamorous as you can get, but it pays well, and the environment changes every day. This home, however, was one that spelled trouble the minute we walked in. The matron of the house was loaded for bear and well cloaked in mistrust. Mrs. Needleman had already convinced herself that the water damage on her table was not repairable, in spite of anything we could say or do.

I was just 22 years old, and working one-on-one with Nat, a man my father's age, was giving me more than just an education in finishing. Being fairly sheltered, I had a lot to learn about human nature, and as luck would have it, our work provided ample learning opportunities.

The water mark was caused by a plant that had been sitting on one of two identical end tables that bracketed the living-room couch. Because the tables were a matched set, the owner did not want to refinish one for fear that the set would no longer match. We assured her that we could get the white ring out completely, but her skepticism outranked our powers of persuasion.

Nat convinced Mrs. Needleman that some of the materials we would be using were quite offensive, and that she would be safer if she left the house for at least two hours. It was one of several stories that he used to get customers out of his hair. There are few things more annoying than having someone watch over your shoulder while you are working on their precious furniture. In this case there was an added benefit. The actual repair would take only a few minutes, and he was sure that she would object to the fee charged if she found out how easy the job was.

Once the owner left, things lightened up considerably. We moved the lamp off the table and set to work. It took only a few quick wipes with alcohol to get the water mark completely out, and a light polish with paste wax restored the sheen to the top. Within fifteen minutes, the top was perfect, and no sign remained of its water mark. To make sure that the sheen on the two tables matched, we decided to wax the other one as well. That's when Nat hatched his fiendishly simple plot.

We switched the tables.

The table that had recently been cured of its water mark went into the far corner, and the undamaged one took its place. That way, when Mrs. Needleman scrutinized our 'repair,' she was sure to be satisfied; after all, that table had never been blemished. After carefully replacing the lamps, we sat down on the couch and Nat regaled me with stories of some of the shenanigans he had pulled on previous jobs.

When we heard the door open, we both jumped up from the couch and assumed our work positions. When Mrs. Needleman walked in, she saw me assiduously polishing what she assumed was the repaired table while Nat packed our tools. In reality, the polishing rag was dry and the table was an impostor. I tried to look exhausted as I stepped back, and soon the show began.

"Well, what do you think?" asked Nat as he pointed to the phony "repaired" table. Mrs. Needleman turned on the lamp and started studying the top. She crouched, turned, and looked at it from every angle as we watched in silence. Finally, she gave her verdict. "Hmm…, It's a very good job, boys. Of course, I can still see a faint ring where the water mark was, but really, it's just fine. After all, one can't expect perfection, right?" "Right," replied Nat as he handed her the bill, grinning smugly. Just as we had planned, none of us even looked at the real repair job.

I got out of there as fast as I could. I knew that in another minute I'd blow it and start laughing. Nat came out to the car a few minutes later, proud as a peacock and clutching a check. "I hope you learned something today," was all he said to me.

We never heard from Mrs. Needleman, even though I am certain that she discovered our ploy. How do I know we were found out? The tables were the square boxy type with a drawer for storage. And we hadn't bothered to switch the contents of the drawers.

CHAPTER 9
Rubbing Out the Finish

The allure of a hand-rubbed finish is both legendary and well deserved. There is a softness about the look, a sensual warmth associated with rubbing out a finish that makes even humble woods shine. It also sends woodworkers running for cans of rubbing varnish, confident in the label's promise of a film well suited for their expenditure of elbow grease. The irony is that virtually any finish can be rubbed, provided that it is cured and dry, and is thick enough so that it doesn't come off completely during the process. The process is essentially the same no matter what the finish material happens to be. Of course, some materials rub up easier, faster or glossier than others, but then, we're used to variations. After all, some woods sand and machine easier and faster as well. All in all, rubbing out a tabletop is simple and rewarding; you get a respectable aerobic workout and immediate results.

Whether a finish is wiped, brushed or sprayed onto wood, it will show a subtle texture on its surface upon drying. This unevenness results from a combination of factors, including the patterns caused by the application method and those caused by shrinkage or expansion of the finish during its cure. In addition, there may be "nibs" or "bitties" — specks of dust, dried finish or foreign matter that form tiny pimples projecting above the surface. This is particularly true of slow-drying or hand-applied finishes, but even spray application does not rule them out entirely.

When you are facing a tabletop the size of an aircraft carrier or an army of cabinet carcases, a mechanical buffer is the quick way to a high-gloss finish.

The object of rubbing a finish is to flatten the surface, both from the subtle undulations of brush or shrink marks and from the more abrupt dust pimples. The greatest advantage to a rubbed finish is how it feels —smooth, silky and level. The rubbing process is an abrasive one—it removes finish. Therefore, a finish that is to be rubbed must be slightly thicker than you want it to be when the process is completed. At the very least, it must be thick enough to allow a certain amount to be removed and still act as an adequate finish. Furthermore, all of the finish you'll be cutting through must be the same color. Cutting through a layer of glaze or tinted lacquer will leave a patch of lighter-toned finish. Even naturally tinted materials, like very amber varnish, may show up lighter if an area is rubbed too thin.

Abrading through a layer of colorless clear finish can also create problems with certain materials. If the finish adheres to the previous layer but does not dissolve it, very subtle outlines (witness lines) can develop where one layer has been cut through to show the previous one. Witness lines are a frequent problem with oil varnish, which will not generally dissolve itself once it is cured, and with water-based lacquers, whose low solvent levels mean that the coats do not melt together the way lacquer and shellac do.

In addition to flattening, rubbing leaves a scratch pattern on the now level surface. The difference between a finish rubbed to satin and one taken to gloss is merely the size and depth of the scratches. These small scratches control how much light is reflected off the viewed surface of the wood, and how much is deflected. Reflected light bounces off a surface at the same angle but opposite direction from where it enters. Deflected light bounces off the surface in any angle or direction. A glossier surface reflects more; a flatter or matte surface deflects

Cutting through a layer of glaze will leave a light patch in the finish.

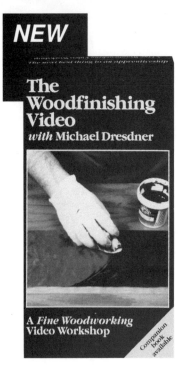

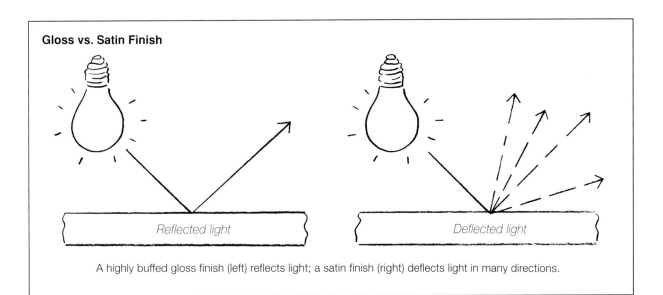

Gloss vs. Satin Finish

Reflected light

Deflected light

A highly buffed gloss finish (left) reflects light; a satin finish (right) deflects light in many directions.

The great perpetual-motion rubbing machine

Some years ago, I stumbled across a guitarmaker who, in his effort to combine tradition with conscientiousness, had somehow wandered into the twilight zone of finishing. Try as he might, he simply couldn't finish finishing. I'd better explain.

Being a staunch traditionalist, he had decided to finish his guitars using only French polish applied by hand with a pad. He mixed his own shellac formula, and spent hours on every instrument, careful to apply each layer as thin as possible. He was convinced that the ultra-thin finish was essential to preserving the bright sound of his handcrafted guitars. This was no mean feat. It took hours of time spread out over several weeks to build this beautiful but delicate finish.

But that wasn't enough. He was also committed to sparing no time or effort to achieve the perfect glossy surface. Although French polishing leaves the surface glossy, it has a certain satin softness to it, even when applied by someone with lots of experience, which he had not. To get that final fillip of gloss—the wet look that lacquer finishes achieve—he decided it was essential to rub and buff the shellac with several compounds, each finer than the last, until the surface was mirror-like.

Thus, he would carefully French-polish each guitar, wait for it to dry, and then just as carefully buff the surface by hand. Unfortunately, the combination of heat and abrasion created during the buffing process was enough so that at some spot or another, he would wear through the finish leaving a visible dry spot. No problem. After all, shellac is infinitely repairable, so back he would go to his trusty French-polish pad to repair the area. Of course, this left him with a slightly duller-looking patch, so as soon as the finish was dry, he'd go back to the compound and rub through a new spot, or, on particularly bad days, the same spot again. It was like watching some weird perpetual-motion machine that endlessly created and destroyed its own work.

I'm not sure how long this had been going on before I found out about it, but he did have a surprisingly large number of guitars that were completed— except for a few minor finish repairs.

Like all rubbed finishes, gloss surfaces contain scratches. The difference is that the size of the scratch is too small to register with our eyes. (This explains why it does not matter what direction you rub when buffing a gloss finish—you won't see the pattern anyway.)

We see only a small band of the range of light waves—between 400 and 750 nanometers (nm). (A nanometer is one-billionth of a meter.) Likewise, the light deflected by surface scratches is visible to us only if the size of the scratch is within a certain range. As it turns out, we can detect scratches down to about half the smallest size light wave we see. We do not see scratches that are made by particles smaller than about 200 nm. Thus, gloss rubbing compounds contain abrasive particles smaller than 200 nm.

more. Even buffed gloss finishes have scratches, albeit ones that are too small to register. Satin rubbed surfaces show their pattern readily. This is not a flaw in the process, but merely a characteristic of a rubbed surface.

A finish will even look different depending on the angle from which it is viewed. If you look down the length of the scratches, they will appear less pronounced than if you sight across them. This is why finishers try to rub low-luster finishes in the direction of the grain. It makes the scratches less obvious without making the surface glossier.

Rubbing up and rubbing down

If sheen is merely a function of the final rub, then it should not matter whether the finish is built in satin, gloss or dead flat matte, right? Well, no, but you do have a certain amount of leeway to change your mind after applying the finish. A gloss finish can be rubbed down to virtually any sheen, but it is not possible to raise the sheen of a satin or matte more than a small amount. The reason is that lower-luster finishes contain very finely ground pigments called flatting agents. These small bits of powdered mineral become part of the surface of the dried mate-

Satin or low-luster finishes contain finely ground pigment called flatting agent, which deflects light.

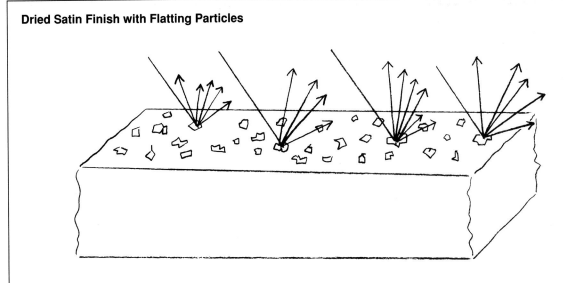

Dried Satin Finish with Flatting Particles

In a dried satin finish, small bits of powdered mineral (flatting particles) deflect light whether or not the surface is leveled by rubbing.

rial, making it slightly rough to our sight, but not rough to the touch. If we cut through these flatting particles with an abrasive, it may make the surface more level (and thus appear a bit glossier), but the flatting particles will still deflect instead of reflecting light. Therefore, it is best to start with a finish that is very close to the one you want to end up with after rubbing.

Some interesting effects can be achieved by bending the rules, though. One of my favorites is to rub a matte finish up to low satin. You start with a very low-luster finish, loaded with flatting powder, and rub it using a very fine abrasive medium, such as 0000 steel wool, with paste wax as a lubricant. The already dull and highly deflective surface will not show steel-wool scratches as readily as a gloss surface would, and the wax helps hide the scratches even more. The final step is to buff the wax with a soft cloth so that it takes on a gentle sheen of its own. The overall effect is an incredibly soft and uniform glow that does not glare, even under bright lights.

You can buy rubbing abrasives in powdered form or as premixed compounds.

Rubbing and polishing materials

The business of rubbing is done by abrasives, which are mineral, or by steel wool (which, when you think about it, is also mineral). You can buy the mineral in powdered form, or premixed into a liquid compound or paste slurry.

Powders

The old-timers in the world of finishing remember when all rubbing materials came in boxes and bags instead of cans and bottles. It is still possible to buy these powdered abrasives today, although they are getting scarce. The coarser powders are called pumice, and, true to their name, consist of ground-up pumice stone. They are graded on a one-letter scale, with F being the coarsest and FFFFF being the finest, similar to the steel-wool scale, which uses 0 to 0000. After the finest pumice, you graduate to rottenstone, a greyish powder that will yield a gloss finish. Fanatics can then go a step higher into fume silica, an ultra-fine sand powder.

To use the abrasives, you either premix your own slurry, or more commonly, mix it as you go. Pumice is commonly used with oil (any type), sometimes cut with a little mineral spirits to make it thinner. With rottenstone you generally use water, perhaps with a bit of soap in it for more slip. Load a soft absorbent cloth pad with the oil mixture, sprinkle a bit of pumice onto it, then have at it. The direction you rub is important only on the last grit you will use, since each graduation will, in theory at least, remove all previous scratches. As the pad stops cutting, add more pumice. If it starts to dry out or get too crusty, add oil and/or thinners. It's a good idea to store pumice in salt shakers. If you decide to try this, make sure the shaker has a closable lid that will keep out moisture.

Some finishers add finer and finer grits to one pad in the belief that the pumice breaks down to smaller particles with use. The more conscientious, however, carefully wipe off the wood surface and use a new clean pad for each successive grit. An intermediary wipe-down will also let you see your progress, since it is impossible to tell what's happening when you have a finish with the slurry on the top. You can keep going to finer grits until the finish is to your liking, or until you are too exhausted to care.

Premixed compounds

You are bound to find purists who swear by their own homemade pumice slurries. The truth is that the premixed materials are made from the same ingredients, and in general, are a good bit better and easier to use than anything you are likely to come up with on your own. It makes very little difference how or where you buy your favorite compounds. The only difference between what you buy in the auto-parts store and the stuff your industrial wood-finish supplier sells is in the size of the container (and perhaps the price).

When choosing a compound, there are two considerations to bear in mind. The first is the solvent in the mixture. If a solvent contained in the compound were to dissolve the finish it was supposed to abrade, disaster would result. Most commercial mixtures are water based or oil based; mineral spirits or naphtha is usually the strongest solvent involved. Most cured film-type finishes are impervious to these materials, but I have seen rare cases when naphtha will cut into some water-based coatings. If this happens, either switch to a water-based rubbing compound or find a more solvent-resistant water-based finish.

The second item to worry about is the presence of silicone or wax as lubricant. If, in the course of rubbing, you cut through the finish, you may find yourself wanting to back up and apply an extra coat of finish. If the rubbing compound has silicone or wax in it, it could cause fish-eye or wet spots in the next coat, and in extreme cases, might also inhibit adhesion. While this is not likely with oil-based varnishes, it is a common problem with both solvent-based and water-based lacquers. If you must recoat, wash the surface thoroughly with mineral spirits to remove any renegade silicone or wax. If possible, avoid silicone-laden rubbing compounds altogether. You may want to use pumice and rottenstone so that you'll have control of the vehicle medium.

The sheen of a finish is measured by the percentage of light that is reflected off the surface when viewed at a certain angle. The viewing is done by machines, which are somewhat less subjective than the human eye. The machine projects a measured amount of light at the surface at a given angle, then reads the amount that is reflected, reporting a percentage and an angle degree. A typical satin sheen callout might be: 35% sheen at 45°. Each manufacturer has his or her own idea of what constitutes matte, satin and semi-gloss, but as a general rule, matte usually ranges from 0% to 20%, satins run up to about 35%, semi-gloss to about 75%, and gloss may range all the way to 98%. It is virtually impossible to create 100% sheen, and you certainly can't go any higher than that.

Rubbing to satin

Rubbing to satin can be accomplished with an abrasive grit on a rag or pad, but more often is done with a non-abrasive lubricant and an abrasive pad. Fine steel wool (0000) or an ultra-fine nylon hand pad (such as 3M's Scotch-Brite brand) both work fine. The latter holds up better and generally produces a more uniform scratch pattern. The lubricants can be anything that reduces friction without dissolving the finish. Paste wax (either as is or thinned with minerals spirits), thinned light oil or soapy water all work well. Soapy water smells the best, while paste wax lets you rub and wax in just one step. This choice is up to you. Just to make things more confusing, there is another alternative that creates a sort of semi-gloss finish. By combining a rubbing compound as a lubricant along with an abrasive pad, you can achieve a sheen somewhere between a gloss and a satin.

Rubbing out a finish is comparable to sanding wood; you attempt to remove as little material as possible while making the surface flat and uniform. In fact, in most cases, the first step is a gentle sanding operation. To remove any nibs or unevenness in the surface, scuff-sand lightly with fine paper. I like to use 320-grit stearated sandpaper for this operation, and sand with the grain whenever possible—just in case. This operation will enhance any defects in seconds and give you feedback on how far you must go to sand.

After wiping or blowing off the dust, dip a piece of steel wool or nylon abrasive pad into your rubbing lubricant, and carefully rub the surface from end to end with the grain. On large flat surfaces, I like to catch the ends first with short strokes in the grain direction. This ensures that I don't miss these edges later, and also lets me avoid the corners of the piece; rolling the abrasive pad over the corners will quickly cut through the finish on the very sharp edge. Try to keep your hand flat, and stay away from sharp edges.

On your long strokes, overlap each pass, and try to go over each spot with at least six passes to ensure a uniform pattern. Try to keep the motion parallel to avoid curved swings that leave long, arched scratches. Don't be afraid to apply some pressure during this operation; after all, this is the aerobic part of this complete finishing sequence. To check your progress, squeegee an area with your thumb or a rubber pad, or simply wipe an area dry. When the surface looks and feels good, stop. Rubbing too much will only cause you to cut through the finish.

If you used soapy water, oil or rubbing compound as your lubricant, wipe the surface down carefully with paper towels or soft absorbent rags to remove all of the film residue. If you used wax, it may not wipe off quite so easily. You may find the surface taking smudgy fingerprints

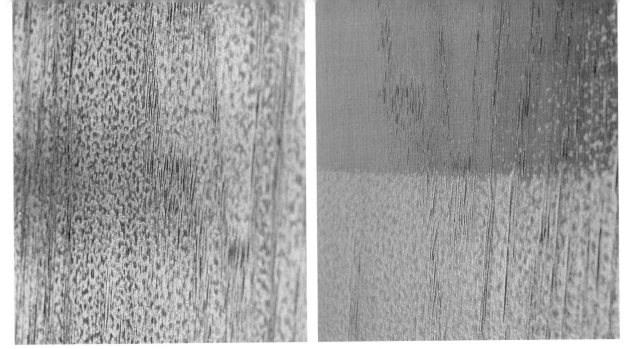

Scuffing will enhance any defects in seconds (left), but keep sanding until the surface looks like the one at the top of the photo at right.

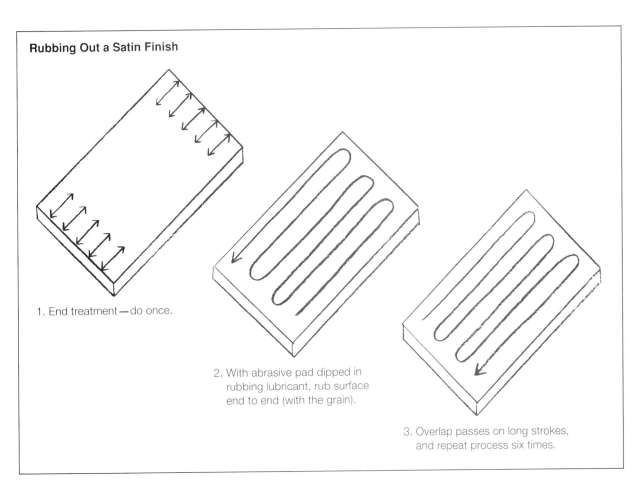

Rubbing Out a Satin Finish

1. End treatment—do once.

2. With abrasive pad dipped in rubbing lubricant, rub surface end to end (with the grain).

3. Overlap passes on long strokes, and repeat process six times.

due to an excess of wax. To remove the wax, sprinkle water lightly on the surface (it should bead up), and with a clean, new nylon or steel-wool pad, repeat the rub pattern once or twice, but this time, do it very lightly, applying no pressure beyond the weight of your hand. Take a look at the pad. It should be coated with wax, and the top should be clean and smudge free.

This satin finish is by far my favorite type of rubbed finish. It looks good, feels great, and works well with open pore woods. Besides, it hides a multitude of minor finish defects — not that any of us have flaws in our finishes, mind you...

Rubbing to gloss

Buffing a finish to gloss is not very different from rubbing to satin. It is impractical to buff anything but a fairly thick, filled-pore finish. Thin films will probably burn through, and open pores will hold rubbing-compound residue and look bad.

A gloss finish relies on several abrasive rubbing operations, each using successively finer grit. As before, the first step is to sand, but rather than stopping at 320-grit paper, make your final rubbing job easier by wet sanding to 600, or even 1200 grit. I like to start with 400-grit sandpaper using either naphtha or soapy water (just a tiny bit of soap this time) as my lubricant, then graduate to 600, then 1200 paper. It does not matter what direction you sand, since you will soon be removing all of the scratches anyway. Wipe off the slurry when you are finished sanding. The surface should look completely uniform, with the appearance of brushed brass.

Now it is time to pour on the elbow grease. With a soft, clean cloth, start rubbing every square inch of that finish with rubbing compound. Once again, the direction does not matter. There should not be any scratches left to see. When you've gone as far you can with the rubbing compound, wipe off the surface and graduate to polishing compound, which is a finer grit. Repeat the process, bringing the surface to an even higher sheen. This stage involves quite a bit of physical effort. By now you are probably starting to appreciate just how nice an easier-to-rub satin finish actually looks, but don't give up, you are almost there. Wipe off the polishing compound (there are actually several grits of this, and you are welcome to go through the succession of as many as your patience will tolerate) and take a look at the surface. You should be able to see yourself in the finish, and you'll probably look exhausted.

To remove wax used as a rubbing lubricant, first sprinkle water on the finish. The wax will cause the water to bead up (top). Now rub lightly with a clean pad (middle). When you are done, the pad should be coated with wax (bottom).

As you may have noticed, most of the shining up took place right before the compound dried completely on the surface. This is the point when most of the lubricant has flashed off, and the concentration of abrasive grit on the pad is highest. Be careful, though; it is also the stage that the greatest amount of heat is created, and on a particularly heat-sensitive finish, you could burn the finish or soften it so much that it curdles.

For a final extra shine, lightly rub the now glossy surface with a glazing liquid or non-abrasive polish, then rub it off with a clean soft cloth. Now go call a friend to look at your finish, and do try to act nonchalant. But in all fairness, you've got a right to feel proud. You have just built the *ne plus ultra*—the epitome of wood finishes—from start to finish.

Rubbing by machine

Machine rubbing does not lend itself to a satin rub finish, but virtually every step of a gloss finish can be done faster (and just as well) with machines. However, since either water or flammable solvents play such a large part in the process, the only safe sanding machines to use are air-powered ones.

Q&A:
Rubbed-out finish for a piano

Q: I'm refinishing a piano (ca. 1908). I've already used a high-gloss, fast-drying varnish over a mixed-oil stain and paste wood filler on part of the piano, and I'm not happy with the results. In spite of sanding between coats, I can't avoid sag/brush marks on the vertical surfaces, and sometimes the high gloss is too much. Should I switch to a spar varnish, which dries more slowly? How do I know which varnishes can be rubbed out?

A: Although brush marks are not unusual in fast-drying varnishes, there is no reason to get sags if you are using the varnish according to directions. Sagging or curtaining is often the result of thinning the varnish with too much solvent. Generally speaking, off-the-shelf varnishes are sold ready to apply by brush, and need thinning only if they are being sprayed. Check your can directions to make sure you are applying it properly, and use a good quality brush to help avoid brush marks.

A slower-drying varnish will allow brush marks more time to flow out, but it it will also make sagging on the vertical surfaces worse, so I would not suggest it.

Though you should get the best surface you are able to achieve before you start, you can certainly rub out any commercial varnish as soon as it is hard enough. Take your cues from the cure and drying times indicated on the can, and by testing the surface with sandpaper and a nail impression to ascertain when the film is cured. A satin rub will help smooth the imperfections, and it should solve your gloss problems as well.

For machine buffing, you can use a traditional lamb's-wool pad (left) or a thick foam pad (right).

Air-powered wet-sanding machines come in a variety of styles, but the most popular are the in-line single head "jitterbug" and the "double-header"—a squat workhorse that looks more like a lunar landing module than a woodworking tool. Unlike the typical small orbital vibrating sander, the heads on these machines go forward and back in straight line. Soapy water works as a lubricant to help you avoid overheating the finish surface, and to carry off the material being cut away. The sequence of sanding and rubbing steps is the same. Use a succession of finer grits, then switch to a buffer.

As if to prove that buffing direction is not an issue, power buffers are orbital; they spin around a central point. There are special buffing compounds available for use with machines,, but frankly, you can get excellent results with those designed for hand rubbing as well. Most auto-store compounds are designed to work well with either hand or machine rubbing. Again, the sequence of rubbing is the same—polish with a succession of finer-grit compounds, cleaning or replacing the buff with each new grit. The final step is a very light pass with a completely clean, soft head.

The type of buff (polishing head) is a matter of personal taste. The traditional buff is off-white lamb's wool, which will work with any type of grit compound and can be easily cleaned (I toss mine into the washing machine and dryer when they need it). Recently, though, a newcomer has arrived on the scene, a soft, thick foam head that purports to polish quickly without burning. With a little practice, you'll find that you can control either type easily to get a beautiful high shine.

The crenellated edge of a wet-film thickness gauge measures the depth of a freshly applied finish.

There are some things to watch out for when buffing by machine. As with all power tools, since the machine runs faster than a hand tool, it is easier to go too far. In the case of buffing, that means either curdling or burning the finish. Most finishes will get softer as heat is applied. With enough heat the finish will soften to the point of being rubbery. If that happens, any further action of the buffer will pull the finish in the direction of the moving head, causing a smooth surface to undulate, or curdle. Often, this is an indication that the finish is not dry enough for the amount of heat and pressure the buff is applying. On the other hand, if the finish is too thin, the buff can cut through the entire film and expose bare wood. This is called "burning through," and is most common on rounds and edges, where finish is frequently thinner. Therefore, when buffing with power tools, it is even more important to work on a finish that is both thick enough and dry enough to withstand the rigors of buffing machines.

How thick is thick enough? A lot depends on both the type of film and the expertise of the person behind the tool, but I would be cautious about machine polishing a finish much thinner than 5 mils, and I'd breathe easier if you start with 7 mils (a mil is one one-thousandth of an inch, or 0.0254 mm). For purposes of comparison, the page you are reading is about 4 mils thick.

Let me guess—you want to know how to measure the thickness of the film. Unfortunately, it is quite difficult to measure a dry film on wood, but you can measure the wet film easily, then calculate the dry from there. It is done with a very inexpensive device about the size of a credit card called a "wet-film thickness gauge." The crenellated metal plate is pushed into the newly applied finish to determine which of the steps clears the surface. The film thickness is somewhere between the step that clears the finish and the last one that doesn't. Most gauges are cut in 1-mil increments, so the readings are pretty accurate. This is a destructive test—it ruins the finish while measuring it—so it must be done to a scrap piece that was coated in exactly the same way as the one you want to measure.

Once you know the wet-film thickness, you can calculate the dry-film thlickness based on percentage solids (solids are what remains once the solvent evaporates). Let's say the wet coat measures 4 mils. The can label indicates that the material is 25% solids. That means the dry film will be 25% as thick as the wet coat, so the dry film will be 1 mil thick. The formula is: Wet-film thickness (mils) x solids (%) = dry-film thickness (mils).

In the example, one wet coat of material deposited 1 dry mil of finish on the wood. Multiply that by the number of coats, and you have the total thickness of the finish, in mils. Naturally, if you sand between coats, that will mess up your math, and you will have to extrapolate from there.

How dry is dry enough? This is a much more difficult question because so many variables are involved. How quickly a finish cures depends on the solvents involved, the film-forming action, the ambient temperature and humidity, the thickness of the film, the per-coat thickness, and the amount of drying time left between coats. You may have to rely on the manufacturer's recommendations—I say this knowing full well that reading the label directions is considered cowardly in male-dominated fields like woodworking. Generally speaking, I can't think of many air-dry finishes that are ready to rub before at least two weeks of curing time, and most—especially evaporative systems—will benefit from six weeks of curing. The longer you wait to rub it out, the easier it will be to buff the finish to a high gloss. Rubbing too soon will not only increase the incidence of burning and curdling, but will also require more effort and result in a duller surface. As Mahatma Gandhi once said, "There is more to life than increasing its speed."

KEY TO BRANDS

This key to brands lists products alphabetically according to product type in five major categories: finishes and sealers; paint and varnish removers; stains; pore fillers, putty, rubbing compounds and touch-up materials; and solvents. The key was compiled by surveying the major manufacturers of finish materials. Manufacturers are listed along with the products; their addresses appear on pp. 202-203.

Finishes and sealers

Solvent-release lacquers

Acrylic Modified / Pratt & Lambert

Brushing Lacquer / Behlen

Clear Wood Finish (gloss, semi-gloss) / Deft

Five Star Lacquer / Hood

Hi Solids Lacquer / Gemini

High Build Clear / Pratt & Lambert

Opex L61 Production Lacquer / Sherwin-Williams

Parks Clear Lacquer (gloss, satin) / Parks

Qualalacq 100E (gloss), 755 (satin) and 299 (flat) / Behlen

Sher-wood GP Lacquer Topcoat / Sherwin-Williams

Sher-wood Hi-Bild Lacquer / Sherwin-Williams

Sher-wood Moisture Resistant Lacquer / Sherwin-Williams

Sher-wood Water White Lacquer / Sherwin-Williams

Water White Lacquer / Gemini

Water White Lacquer / Hood

Wood-Kote Crystal Clear Interior Lacquer / Wood-Kote

Shellac

Bullseye Amber Shellac / Zinsser

Bullseye Clear Shellac / Zinsser

Shellac (orange, clear) / Parks

Shellac (orange, yellow) / Hood

Water-based acrylic lacquers

Clear & Clean Acrylic Lacquer / Wood-Kote

Clear Gloss Finish / AMITY

Clear Satin Finish / AMITY

Enduro Water-Base / Compliant

GemCoat Water Base Coatings / Gemini

Heirloom Crystal Clear Acrylic Varnish / McCloskey

Hydrocote Clear Wood Finish / Hood

Latex Urethane Acrylic / Benjamin Moore

Sher-wood Kem-Lac "W" Water Reducible Lacquer / Sherwin-Williams

Tabletop Gloss Finish / AMITY

Tabletop Satin Finish / AMITY

Varathane Elite Diamond Colors / Flecto

Water Borne Lacquer / Pratt & Lambert

Wood-Tex Water-Base Acrylic / Velco

Water-based polyurethane lacquers

Carver Tripp Safe & Simple Clear Poly / Parks

Carver Tripp Safe & Simple Super Poly / Parks

Clear & Clean Interior/Exterior Polyurethane with UV Absorbers / Wood-Kote

Enduro Water-Base / Compliant

Eurosheen Crystal Clear / Behr

Heirloom Crystal Clear Polyurethane / McCloskey

Hydrocote Polyshield / Hood

Hydrocote Polyurethane / Hood

PremaSeal Floor Finish / Behr

Resisthane / Hood

Safe & Easy Clear Wood Finish (gloss, satin) / Deft

Ultrastar Water Borne Lacquer / Pratt & Lambert

Varathane Elite Diamond Finish / Flecto Co.

Water-Based Zip-Guard Environmental Wood Finish / Star Bronze

Water-Base Urethane (gloss, satin) / Behlen

Wood-Tex Water-Base Urethane / Velco

ZAR Polyurethane / UGL

Water-based polyacrylic lacquer

Polyacrylic Protective Finish / Minwax

Water-Reducible Lacquer (gloss, satin, sealer) / Behlen

Waterworks (satin, gloss) / Waterlox

Tung-oil finishes

Minwax Tung Oil Finish / Minwax

Pure Tung Oil / Behlen

Salad Bowl Finish / Behlen

Tung Oil Finish / Behr

Tung Oil Finish / Hood

Tung Oil Finish / Savogran

Tungseal Tung Oil Finish / McCloskey

Waterlox Antique Finish (gloss, satin) / Waterlox

Waterlox Gym Finish / Waterlox

Waterlox Transparent / Waterlox

ZAR Tung Oil / UGL

Linseed-oil finishes

Moore's Interior Wood Finish
Scandinavian Oil / Benjamin Moore

Danish-oil finishes

Deftoil Natural / Deft

Oil/alkyd varnishes

Antique Oil Finish / Minwax

Clear Lac Semi-Gloss / Behr

Heirloom Varnish (traditional, VOS formula) / McCloskey

Oil/phenolic varnishes

Bar Top Varnish / McCloskey

Low VOC Door Varnish / Behr

Low VOC Super Spar Varnish / Behr

Man O' War Spar Varnish / McCloskey

PremaSeal Door Varnish (gloss, satin) / Behr

Rockhard Tabletop 4-Hour Water White Restoration / Behlen

Super Spar Varnish (gloss, satin) / Behr

Watco Marine Oil Finish / Minwax

Watco Teak Oil Finish / Minwax

Oil/alkyd polyurethane varnishes

C & C Marfin Velvet Varnish / C & C

Clear Wiping Gel / Bartley

Defthane (gloss, satin) / Deft

Ferrothane Plastic Finish / Flecto

Flagship Marine Finish with UV Absorbers / Wood-Kote

Heirloom Varnish / McCloskey

Helmsman Spar Urethane / Minwax

Liquid Plastic Polyurethane / Wood-Kote

Marine Finish in Colors / Wood-Kote

Master Gel Finish / Behlen

Minwax Polyurethane / Minwax

Tuff as Nails Polyurethane / Hood

Varathane Colors in Plastic / Flecto

Varathane Liquid Plastic Clear Finish / Flecto

Varathane Liquid Plastic Exterior Clear Finish / Flecto

Varathane Professional Clear Finish / Flecto

Woodmaster Polyurethane Clear Finish (high gloss, satin) / Glidden

XL-88, XL-89 (gloss, satin) / Waterlox

ZAR Polyurethane / UGL

Zip-Guard Clear Wood Finishes / Star Bronze

Water-emulsion varnishes

Moore's Silicone Wood Finish / Benjamin Moore

Crosslinked finishes: catalyzed lacquer (acid catalyzed, including CAB vinyl) and conversion varnish (including alkyd/melamine)

Catalyzed Lacquer / Gemini

Dymond-Cure Lacquer / Hood

Nitrothane / Behlen

Precatalyzed Lacquer / Gemini

Sher-wood Catalyzed Lacquer / Sherwin-Williams

Sher-wood Kemvar Conversion Varnish / Sherwin-Williams

Table Top Lacquer / Hood

Crosslinked epoxy systems

Super Gloss Build 50 / Behr

Crosslinked polyurethanes

Low VOC Polyurethane / Behr

Polane B Polyurethane Enamel / Sherwin-Williams

Polane Clear Topcoat / Sherwin-Williams

Polane HS Enamel / Sherwin-Williams

Polane Plus Enamel / Sherwin-Williams

Polane T Plus Polyurethane Enamel / Sherwin-Williams

Polane T Polyurethane Enamel / Sherwin-Williams

Polane 2.8 T Plus Polyurethane Enamel / Sherwin-Williams

Polyurethane (clear satin, clear gloss) / Behr

Water-based polyester

Resistol / Hood

Sealers and primers

Bullseye 123 Pigmented Acrylic Primer / Zinsser

Cabot Problem-Solver Primer / Cabot

Kover Pigmented Stain Primer / Zinsser

PremaSeal Sanding Sealer / Behr

Sanding Sealer / AMITY

Sanding Sealer #200 / Behlen

Scandinavian Clear Wood Sealer / Behr

Sher-wood GP Lacquer Sanding Sealer / Sherwin-Williams

Sher-wood Hi-Bild Lacquer Sanding Sealer / Sherwin-Williams

Sher-wood Lacquer Sanding Sealer / Sherwin-Williams

Sher-wood Vinyl Sealer 24% Solids / Sherwin-Williams

Ultra-Hide Quick Dry Sanding Sealer / Glidden

Varathane Elite Diamond Finish Sealer / Flecto

Waterlox Transparent / Waterlox

Crosslinked sealers/primers

Polane Plus Sealer / Sherwin-Williams

Polane Primer-Sealer / Sherwin-Williams

Paint and varnish removers

Refinishers (flammable solvent strippers)

Bix Stripper / Bix

Furniture Refinisher / Savogran

Master Furniture Refinisher / Behlen

Parks Liquid Strip / Parks

Parks No Drip Strip / Parks

Quick Strip / Bix

Raizoff Paint and Varnish Remover / UGL

Zip-Strip Furniture Refinisher and Liquid Remover / Star Bronze

Paint and varnish removers (DCM solvent, flammable)

Bix Stripper / Bix

Hoodstrip 276, 277 / Hood

Kutzit / Savogran

Strypeeze / Savogran

The Stripper / Behr

Paint and varnish removers (DCM solvent, nonflammable)

Bix Spray-On-Stripper / Bix

Flow-Dip / Pratt & Lambert

H₂Off / Savogran

Hoodstrip 281, 290, 888 / Hood

Master Fire Fly Remover / Behlen

Parks Pro Stripper / Parks

Super Strip / Savogran

Tough Job Extra Strength Remover / Bix

ZAR Paint and Varnish Remover / UGL

Zip-Strip Paint and Varnish Remover / Star Bronze

Zip-Strip Water Rinsable Paint and Varnish Remover / Star Bronze

Paint and varnish removers (NMP/BPO, nonflammable)

Woodfinisher's Pride Paint and Varnish Remover / Creative

Paint and varnish removers (DBE solvent, flammable)

Hydrocote Sure-Strip / Hood

Paint and varnish removers (DBE)

Bix Hydro Stripper / Bix

StrypSafer / Savogran

3M Safest Stripper / 3M

Paint and varnish removers (caustic)

Finish Off / Savogran

Flammable Solvent Finish Off / Savogran

Master PDE Paint Remover / Behlen

Stains and dyes

Pigmented oil-based stains (includes liquid and wiping)

Bleaching Oil / Cabot

Bleaching Stain / Cabot

Carver Tripp Wood Stains / Parks

Clear Tone Wiping / Pratt & Lambert

Decking Stain / Cabot

Eurocolour Wood Stain / Behr

EZ Wipe Stains / Gemini

15-Minute Wood Stain / Behlen

Gelled Wood Stain / Wood-Kote

Japan Color Stain / Behlen

Low VOC Scandinavian Oil Wood Stain / Behr

Master Gel Stain / Behlen

Minwax Wood Finish / Minwax

Moore's Interior Wood Finishes Penetrating / Benjamin Moore

O.V.T. Solid Color Oil Stain / Cabot

Pastels Wood Stain / Minwax

Pen Spray / Pratt & Lambert

Penetrating Stain / Gemini

Penetrating Stain / Hood

PTW Stains for Pressure-Treated Wood / Cabot

Scandinavian Oil Wood Stain / Behr

Semi-Solid Stains / Cabot

Sher-wood Wiping Stain / Sherwin-Williams

Sher-wood Wiping Stain Concentrate / Sherwin-Williams

StainWax / Cabot

Transparent Stain / Cabot

Tungseal Wood Stain / McCloskey

Watco Danish Oil / Minwax

Weathering Stain / Cabot

White Pickling Stain / Behlen

Wiping Gel / Bartley

Woodmaster Oil Wood Stain / Glidden

X-3D Wood Stain / Flecto

ZAR Wood Stain / UGL

Pigmented water-based stains (includes latex, liquid and wiping)

AMITY Water-Based Stain / AMITY

Carver Tripp Safe & Simple Wood Stain / Parks

Gelled Wood Stain / Wood-Kote

Hydrocote Penetrating Stain / Hood

O.V.T. Solid Color Acrylic Stain / Cabot

Varathane Elite Wood Stain / Flecto

Pigmented oil-water emulsion stains (includes liquid and wiping)

Heirloom Wood Stain / McCloskey

Plus 10 Semi-Transparent Stain / Behr

Plus 10 Solid Color Stain / Behr

Varathane Professional Wood Toner/Stain / Flecto

Oil-soluble polymeric dyes (contains binder)

Stain Concentrate / Hood

Tungseal Wood Stain / McCloskey

Zip-Guard Interior Wood Stain / Star Bronze

Alcohol-soluble polymeric dyes (contains binder)

Stain Concentrate / Hood

Water-soluble polymeric dyes (contains binder)

AMITY Tinting Colors / AMITY

Oil/water emulsion polymeric dyes (contains binder)

Zip-Guard Acrylic Wood Stain / Star Bronze

Oil-soluble non-polymeric dyes (includes unmixed powders)

Aniline Stain Oil/Lacquer (powder) / Behlen

Oil-Soluble Dye / Lockwood

Alcohol-soluble non-polymeric dyes (includes unmixed powders)

Alcohol-Soluble Dye / Lockwood

Aniline Stain (powder) / Behlen

Sher-wood Dye Stain / Sherwin-Williams

Solar-Lux / Behlen

Water-soluble non-polymeric dyes (includes unmixed powders)

Aniline Stain (powder) / Behlen

Smooth & Simple Wood Stain / Clearwater

Water-Base Stain / Behlen

Water-Soluble Dye / Lockwood

Pore filler, putty, rubbing compounds and touch-up materials

Oil-based pigmented fillers

Benwood Interior Paste Wood Filler / Benjamin Moore

Paste Wood Filler / Hood

Pore-O-Pac Paste Wood Filler / Behlen

Sher-wood Natural Filler / Sherwin-Williams

Wood Filler / Bartley

Wood-Kote Paste Wood Filler / Wood-Kote

Water-based pigmented fillers

Hydrocote Wood Filler / Hood

Wood-Tex Synthetic Wood Filler / Velco

ZAR Wood Patch / UGL

Water-based pigment/dye combination fillers

AMITY Water-Based Wood Putty / AMITY

Lacquer-based pigmented fillers

Wood-Tex Synthetic Wood Filler / Velco

"Clear" lacquer-based fillers

Quick Drying Wood Filler / Hood

Crosslinked polyurethane fillers

Polane Spray Fil / Sherwin-Williams

Polane 2.8 Plus Spray Fil / Sherwin-Williams

Latex putty

AMITY Water-Based Wood Putty / AMITY

Bix Stain Putty / Bix

Master Wood Filler / Behlen

3M Just Like Wood Wood Putty / 3M

Wood-Tex Solvent-Free Wood Putty / Velco

Alcohol thinning putty

Wood Repair Putty / Hood

Lacquer thinner/acetone thinning putty

Wood-Tex Wood Putty / Velco

Rubbing compounds

Deluxing Compound (rottenstone/carnauba/mineral spirits) / Behlen

Finish Rub (tripoli/mineral spirits) / Behlen

Polishing Compound / Hood

Rubbing Compound (silica/mineral spirits) / Behlen

Rubbing Compound / Hood

Non-lifting/non-shrinking burn-in sticks

Burn-In Sticks / Hood

Master Burn-In Sticks / Behlen

Wax sticks

Blend-Fil Pencils / Minwax

Master Fill Sticks / Behlen

Wax Sticks / Hood

Distressing sticks

Distressing Sticks / Hood

Pigment powders (fresco or earth powders)

Fresco Colors / Behlen

Fresco Powders / Hood

Master Furniture Powders / Behlen

French polish/padding lacquer

Padding Lacquer / Hood

Qualasole / Behlen

Ultra Qualasole / Behlen

Woodturner's Finish / Behlen

Clear aerosols

All American Polyurethane / McCloskey

Bullseye Clear Shellac / Zinsser

Clear Aerosol / Hood

Flagship Marine Polyurethane Finish / Wood-Kote

Helmsman Spar Urethane / Minwax

Jet Spray (gloss, satin, flat, sealer) / Behlen

Liquid Plastic Polyurethane / Wood-Kote

Man O' War Spar Varnish / McCloskey

Minwax Polyurethane / Minwax

Spray Zit Clears / Pratt & Lambert

Utilac Clear / Benjamin Moore

Wood-kote Crystal Clear Interior / Wood-Kote

ZAR Polyurethane / UGL

Colored aerosols

Colored Aerosol / Hood

Custom Packaging / Gemini

Jet Spray / Behlen

Spray Zit Shading Lacquer / Pratt & Lambert

Solvents

Lacquer thinner

Brushing Lacquer Thinner / Behlen

Lacquer Retarder / Pratt & Lambert

Lacquer Thinner / Gemini

Lacquer Thinner (fast dry/low temp., medium temp, high temp./humidity) / Hood

Lacquer Thinner / Pratt & Lambert

Parks Lacquer Thinner / Parks

Qualalacq 631 Brushing Lacquer Thinner / Behlen

Zip-Strip Lacquer Thinner / Star Bronze

Alcohol

Alcohol / Gemini

Behkol / Behlen

Denatured Alcohol / Hood

Methanol / Behlen

Parks Denatured Alcohol / Parks

Zip-Strip Denatured Alcohol / Star Bronze

Naphtha

Naphtha / Behlen

Naphtha / Gemini

Parks VM&P Naphtha / Parks

VM&P Naphtha / Hood

Acetone

Acetone / Gemini

Acetone / Hood

Parks Acetone / Parks

Zip-Strip Acetone / Star Bronze

Mineral spirits

Mineral Spirits / Behlen

Mineral Spirits / Gemini

Mineral Spirits / Hood

Parks Mineral Spirits / Parks

Zip-Strip Paint Thinner / Star Bronze

Turpentine

Parks Gum Turpentine / Parks

Zip-Strip Gum Turpentine / Star Bronze

Xylene (xylol)

Xylol / Hood

Parks Xylol / Parks

Xylol / Gemini

Toluene (toluol)

Parks Toluol / Parks

Toluol / Gemini

1,1,1 TCE

Parks Carbo-trichlor / Parks

Mixed paint thinners (mineral spirits/naphtha type)

AMITY Brush and Gun Cleaner / AMITY

Mixed Paint Thinners / Gemini

MANUFACTURERS' ADDRESSES

AMITY Finishing Products, Inc.
1571 Ivory Drive
P.O. Box 107
Sun Prairie, WI 53590
(800) 334-4259

The Bartley Collection, Ltd.
3 Airpark Drive
Easton, MD 21601
(800) 227-8539
(301) 820-7722

H. Behlen & Brothers
Route 30N
Amsterdam, NY 12010
(518) 843-1390

In Canada:
Lee Valley Tools Ltd.
Station J
1080 Morrrison Drive
Ottawa, Ontario K2H 8K7
(613) 596-0350

Behr Process Corporation
3400 West Segerstom Avenue
Santa Ana, CA 92704
(714) 545-7101

In Canada:
Behr Process Corporation
7510D Fifth Street SE
Calgary, Alberta T2H 2L9
(800) 661-1591

Benjamin Moore & Co.
51 Chestnut Ridge Road
Montvale, NJ 07645
(201) 573-9600

In Canada:
Benjamin Moore & Co.
139 Mulock Avenue
Toronto, Ontario M6N 1G9
(416) 766-1173

Bix Mfg. Company
Hwy. 12, P.O. Box 69
Ashland City, TN 37015
(800) 251-1098

In Canada:
Frank Schachter Sales Limited
6969 Trans Canadienne
Suite 7
St. Laurent, Quebec H4T 1V8
(514) 337-7741

Samuel Cabot Inc.
100 Hale Street
Newburyport, MA 01950
(508) 465-1900

In Canada:
International Paints Ltd.
19500 Rt Trans Canadienne
Baie-d'Urfé, Quebec H9X 3S8
(514) 457-4155

C & C Paints
P.O. Box 70328
Seattle, WA 98107
(206) 783-8835

Clearwater Color Co.
P.O. Box 197
Nazareth, PA 18064
(215) 559-0966
FAX (215) 559-1128

In Canada:
Waterbased Finishes
263 Adelaide St. W
First Floor W
Toronto, Ontario M5H 1Y2
(416) 586-9665

Compliant Spray Systems
23845 Helsinki
Mission Viejo, CA 92691
(714) 768-0615

Creative Technologies Co.
300 NCNC Plaza
Grenville, SC 29601
(803) 271-9194

In Canada:
Newron Sales
92B Carrier Drive
Etobicoke, Ontario M9W 5R1
(416) 798-3338

Deft, Inc.
17451 Von Karman
Irvine, CA 92714
(800) 544-3338

In Canada:
Newron Sales
92B Carrier Drive
Etobicoke, Ontario M9W 5R1
(416) 798-3338

Flecto Co.
1000-45th Street
Oakland, CA 94608
(510) 655-2470

In Canada:
Flecto Coatings Limited
Suite 203 South
1455 Lake Shore Road
Burlington, Ontario L7S 2J1
(416) 333-6545

Gemini Coatings, Inc.
P.O. Box 699
El Reno, OK 73036
(800) 262-5710

The Glidden Company
925 Euclid Avenue
Cleveland, OH 44115
(800) 221-4100

In Canada:
ICA
8200 Kelle Street
Concord, Ontario L4K 2A5
(416) 669-1020

Hood Products, Inc.
P.O. Box 220
Tennent, NJ 07763
(800) 229-0934

In Canada:
Waterbased Finishes
263 Adelaide Street W
First Floor W
Toronto, Ontario M5H 1Y2
(416) 586-9665

W.D. Lockwood Co.
81 Franklin Street
New York, NY 10013
(212) 966-4046

In Canada:
Lee Valley Tools Ltd
Station J
1080 Morrison Drive
Ottawa, Ontario K2H 8K7
(613) 596-0350

McCloskey
7600 State Road
Philadelphia, PA 19136
(215) 335-7330

In Canada:
Thornes
331 Chelsey Drive
St. John, New Brunswick E2Z 4E4
(506) 632-1000

Minwax Company, Inc.
15 Mercedes Drive
Montvale, NJ 06745
(201) 391 0253

In Canada:
Minwax Company, Inc.
245 Edwards
Aurora, Ontario L4G 3M7
(416) 513-4444

Parks Corporation
P.O. Box 5
Somerset, MA 02726
(800) 225-8543
(508) 679-5938

Pratt & Lambert
Paints/Chemical
Coatings/Adhesives
Box 22
Buffalo, NY 14240-0022
(716) 873-6000

In Canada:
Pratt & Lambert
P.O. Box 159
254 Courtwright
Fort Erie, Ontario L2A 5M9
(416) 871-4913

Savogran Company
P.O. Box 130
Norwood, MA 02062
(800) 225-9872

The Sherwin-Williams Company
101 Prospect Avenue, N.W.
Cleveland, OH 44115-1075
(216) 566-2000

In Canada:
Sherwin-Williams Company
170 Brunel Road
Mississauga, Ontario L4Z 1T5
(416) 507-0166

Star Bronze Company
P.O. Box 2206
Alliance, OH 44601
(800) 321-9870

3M Company
3M Center 515-3N-02
St. Paul, MN 55144
(800) 842-4946

In Canada:
3M Canada
P.O. Box 5757
London, Ontario N6A 4T1
(519) 451-2500

UGL
P.O. Box 70
Scranton, PA 18501
(717) 344-1202

In Canada:
Home Hardware
1 Brian Drive
Box 250
Burford, Ontario N0E 1A0
(519) 449-2413

Velco Inc.
3900 West 1st Avenue
P.O. Box 2280
Eugene, OR 97402
(503) 342-5738

In Canada:
Columbia Industrial Supplies
831 Shamrock Street
Victoria, British Columbia V8X 2V1
(604) 380-6395

Waterlox Chemical and Coatings Corporation
9808 Meech Avenue
Cleveland, OH 44105
(216) 641-4877
(800) 321-0377

In Canada:
Waterlox of Canada
Box 497
Bright's Grove, Ontario N0N 1C0
(519) 542-5453

Wood-Kote Productions
8000 Nelam Place
Portland, OR 97211
(503) 285-8371

In Canada:
Paint Sundry Products
209 Brunel Road
Mississauga, Ontario L4Z 1X3
(416) 890-1225

Wm. Zinsser Co.
39 Belmont Drive
Somerset, NJ 08875
(908) 469-4367

In Canada:
Paint Sundry Products
209 Brunel Road
Mississauga, Ontario L4Z 1X3
(416) 890-1225

GLOSSARY

The biggest problem with understanding finishing is that the materials we use are formulated by chemists, and chemists speak a different language than the rest of us. They talk about esters, ketones, polyols and resin weights, and we come away with the distinct impression that if they'd only stick to English, life would be much easier. Of course, we woodworkers are just as bad. Try talking to non-woodworkers about dadoes, mortises, raised panels and chamfers and see how quickly their eyes glaze over.

Since it doesn't look as if the chemists are going to change, I guess it's up to us to learn their language. Here's a guide to some of the most common chemical terms you may encounter as a wood finisher. Many of these terms are discussed more fully in the text; for page references, please consult the Index (pp. 210-213).

Acetone (dimethyl ketone)
A highly flammable solvent for paint, varnish and lacquer resins.

Acrylic
Many plastics, adhesives and coatings are based on acrylic resins, which may range from brittle to flexible. Plexiglas, for example, is an acrylic plastic, as are some ultra-durable commercial floor polishes. Acrylics have long been popular for car lacquers and latex paints because of their excellent exterior durability and resistance to yellowing. Many of the new clear water-based varnishes and lacquers are based on acrylic mixtures.

Acrylonitrile (vinyl cyanide)
A clear acrylic resin that is making its way into water-based coatings. Incidentally, it is the A in ABS (acrylonitrile-butadiene-styrene), the plastic used for plumbing pipes.

Alkyds
Modified oil resins used in varnishes and lacquers. Alkyds are oils modified by ALCohol and an acID (hence the name ALCID, or more phonetically, ALKYD).

Alkyd/polyurethane varnish
An oil varnish containing alkyd and polyurethane resins, more commonly called polyurethane varnish in the woodfinishing industry. See also Polyurethanes.

Alkyd varnish
Interior and exterior varnishes are frequently based on alkyd resins. Both fall into the general category of oil varnish.

Aniline dyes
Technically, a large class of synthetic dyes (soluble colorants), made from intermediates based upon anilines. In woodworking, the term is used generically to cover all soluble wood dyes, even if they are not specifically anilines.

Asphaltum
The paint industry's term for asphalt, a bituminous tar that makes an interesting wood stain and glaze when it is cut back with naphtha or mineral spirits. It is occasionally referred to as gilsonite.

Aziridine crosslinking additive
One of two common types of additive used to crosslink water-based coatings, especially floor finishes (the other is carbodiimide). Of the two, it is both more effective and significantly more hazardous. See also Carbodiimide crosslinking additive.

Binder
The non-volatile portion of the vehicle of a coating, which stays behind to form a film on the wood after the solvent evaporates. Generally the binder in a coating is referred to as the resin.

BLO
See Gamma butyrolactone.

Blown (oil)
Both tung oil and linseed oil are frequently thickened by a process called heat bodying or blowing, where heated air blown through the oil partially polymerizes it. The air bubbling up through the oil may be where boiled linseed oil got its name.

Blush
The whitish, cloudlike haze that occurs in fast-drying finishes, especially lacquer, when it is sprayed in very humid conditions. Blush is most often due to moisture (water vapor) trapped in the film or to bits of resin precipitating out of solution.

Blush chaser
The trade term for slow-drying or active solvents designed to be added to or sprayed atop lacquer to eliminate blush in humid weather.

Burning in
The process of melting lacquer or shellac sticks by touching them with a heated knife and using the resulting liquid to fill small voids in a finish.

Butyrate lacquer
A lacquer based on or containing cellulose acetate butyrate (CAB) resin. Because CAB is not as amber as nitrocellulose, it is often sold as water-white lacquer.

Calcium carbonate (gilder's whiting)
An extremely common natural white powder used in such diverse items as toothpaste, antacid, paper, whitewash, Portland cement, gesso and wood coatings. Calcium carbonate is used as a bodying agent in fillers, putties, primers, opaque paints and paint strippers.

Carbodiimide crosslinking additive
The less hazardous of two common crosslinking agents used in water-based finishes (the other is aziridine). See also Aziridine crosslinking additive.

Carbon tetrachloride (perchloromethane)

A nonflammable but toxic carcinogen that was once common as a household degreaser and cleaner. It is currently not permitted in products intended for home use.

Catalyst

Any substance or influence of which a small fractional percentage causes a significant change in the rate of a chemical reaction without either being consumed or undergoing a chemical change itself. In finishing, most catalysts are chemical (e.g., the heavy metals added to linseed oil to increase its drying rate), but even sunlight can act as a catalyst in some situations.

Catalyzed lacquers

A term used for a variety of crosslinking spray coatings, and more specifically, for those lacquers whose cure is initiated by an acid.

Cellulose acetate butyrate (CAB)

See Butyrate lacquer.

Combustible

Any material that will ignite (or whose vapors will ignite) at some temperature. See also Flammable. Nonflammable.

Conversion varnish

A curing or crosslinking varnish or coating.

Copolymers (polyacrylic and polyacrilonitrile)

Resins consisting of more than one class of polymer, such as polyurethane and acrylic (polyacrylic).

Crosslinked finishes

This term includes all reactive, conversion and catalyzed finishes, and refers to a finish that forms larger polymers (molecules) during its curing time after it has been applied to the wood surface.

Crossover

An undesirable condition that can occur in water-based coatings in very high humidity. Crossover occurs when the tail solvents responsible for merging the resin into a film evaporate before all of the water has left, preventing the material from forming the proper film.

Cyanoacrylate adhesive

A type of fast-drying, moisture-vapor-initiated, reactive adhesive with excellent polymerizing and bonding properties. Sold under trade names such as Krazy Glue and Super Glue, cyanoacrylate adhesives work on most substances, including many woods. However, because acid inhibits their cure, they do not work well on acidic woods, such as oak, unless the surface has been pretreated with an alkaline wash. Wiping alcohol on one side of a wood-to-wood bond will speed up the cure.

Danish oil finish

The general term for any of the various wipe-on finishes, usually consisting of some drying oil (such as tung or linseed) thinned with mineral spirits and bolstered with a small amount of resin (usually alkyd).

Dibasic esters (DBE)

Dibasic esters are derived from acids containing two replaceable hydrogen atoms per molecule. These compounds are being used in some of the new "safer" paint-remover formulations.

Diluent

A volatile liquid used to thin a mixture. A diluent is not a solvent for the resin or other components, but a liquid that the mixture will tolerate without precipitating the resin.

Doping in

The process of filling voids in a finish by adding drops of the same finish, then leveling the dried material. It is also called "kootching" in some areas.

Dyes

Soluble colorants used to make stains that do not scatter light, but absorb certain wavelengths and transmit others. Because they dissolve in their solvent, dyes afford deep, translucent color to stains and wood. See also Pigments.

Emulsion

A mixture of two or more immiscible liquids, in which small droplets of one (the dispersed or resin phase) are dispersed throughout another (the external or continuous phase). Many salad dressings are emulsions of oil in water, as is homogenized milk. Water-based finishes are emulsions of resin in water; hence, water-based resins are usually not water soluble.

Enamel

Originally this term implied a top coat that has the ability to form a smooth, glossy surface; however it is also used to denote a colored coating of any sheen. "Enamel" is an imprecise term that is virtually useless as a finish category.

Epoxy

Adhesives or coatings based on crosslinking resins which contain epoxide groups (an oxygen bonded to two carbons in a triangulated structure). This term is often used to describe any two-package curing finish or glue other than those initiated by a catalyst.

Ethyl cellulose

A resin used in wood coatings. It is softer and less brittle than nitrocellulose. Ethyl cellulose is frequently used as the coating on bowling pins.

Ethylene glycol

Although ethylene glycol is occasionally used in lacquers and stains, it is more familiar to us as antifreeze and brake fluid. Unfortunately, this toxic material has a sweet taste coupled with a low lethal dose. Antifreeze leaks have been implicated in the deaths of pets—especially dogs—likely to lap up the sweet spill.

Evaporative finishes

Coatings (also called solvent-release finishes) that form films by the evaporation of their volatile component, with no polymerization or other crosslinking taking place during drying. Consequently, they can be redissolved by their solvent at any time, even long after cure. Some examples are shellac and lacquer.

Excelsior
Fine, curled wood shavings used for packing fragile items, and as stuffing for chair seats. Once a trade name, but now in common usage.

Filler
A thick, opaque dispersion of ground pigment, silica, talc and/or other minerals used to fill the large pores in coarse-grained woods. Also called pore filler, it is designed so that once dry, it will not shrink under subsequent coats of lacquer.

Finish
Any protective coating applied as a liquid or gel.

Fish-eye
A finish anomaly usually caused by silicone or other oil contamination. It shows up as a distinctive pattern of dry spots and puddles created by the difference in surface tension between the contaminants and the high surface-tension coatings that are susceptible to it.

Flammable
Indicating a substance whose flash point is below 100°F. See also Combustible.

Flash point
The lowest temperature at which a liquid or its vapors will ignite in the presence of a flame or spark.

French polish
Originally, French polish was a shellac and alcohol mixture designed to be applied by hand with a cloth pad to produce a high-gloss finish. In current use, the term refers to both the material and the process of application.

Fume silica
A light powder consisting of finely ground silica, used both as a flatting agent in finishes and an abrasive for polishing.

Gamma butyrolactone (BLO)
A nonflammable (but combustible) compound, used in some of the new "safer" paint removers that do not contain methylene chloride.

Gilder's whiting
See Calcium carbonate.

Gilsonite
See Asphaltum.

Gloss
The measure of the percentage of light a surface reflects. With finishes, gloss is measured by shining light on the surface at a particular angle and reading the reflected amount at the complementary angle. Both the percentage of reflected light and angle are called out. A typical reading might be "35 sheen at 60°" meaning that 35% of the shone light was reflected at a 60° angle.

Hindered amine light stabilizers (HALS)
Free-radical scavengers added to coatings to protect against ultraviolet (UV) radiation. HALS work synergistically with UV absorbers to protect films from deterioration caused by the sun.

Hydrocarbons
Compounds containing hydrogen and carbon. Hydrocarbons are the building blocks of all organic chemistry and the backbone of finish and coatings chemistry. Aromatic hydrocarbons contain an unsaturated ring of carbon atoms; aliphatic hydrocarbons are composed of open chains or rings of carbon atoms.

Hydrolysis
A chemical reaction in which water reacts with another substance to form two or more new substances. Hydrolysis disables water-based crosslinkers, causing the lacquer to revert to its original state rather than cure.

Hydrophilic
Water-loving; absorbing or drawing toward water.

Hydrophobic
Water-hating; repelling water.

Japan colors
Pigments ground in boiled linseed oil or some other oil to which Japan driers have been added. These opaque colorants handle like oil colors, but dry faster.

Japan driers
See Metalllic driers.

Kootching.
See Doping in.

Lacquer
Any film-forming finish that dries by solvent evaporation alone. (The term "catalyzed lacquer" is an oxymoron.)

Latex
Latex has a variety of definitions, some of which are contradictory. In this book, the term is used (as is common in the coatings industry) as a synonym for emulsion.

Linseed oil
A reactive finish made from the seeds of the flax plant.

Lipophilic
Oil-loving; attracting oil.

Lipophobic
Oil-hating; a material that shuns oil. Also: lipophilic, oil-loving.

Lower Explosive Limit (LEL)
The minimum amount of a substance that must be in the air for it to be able to explode or ignite. It is expressed as a volume percentage in air.

Matte
A degree of sheen below satin and above dead flat, although it is sometimes used as a synonym for dead flat.

Melamine resin
A highly durable resin used in various coatings to increase hardness and solvent resistance.

Metallic driers
Also called Japan driers, these heavy metal salts or soaps are added to drying oils in order to speed up the cure. Their action is a true catalytic one. They initiate or speed polymerization without changing chemically or becoming part of the molecule. The metals remain trapped in the matrix of the dried film.

Metamerism
The phenomenon exhibited by a pair of colors that match under one set of lighting conditions but not under a different set.

Methyl ethyl ketone (MEK)
A flammable primary solvent for nitrocellulose lacquer, also used in other coatings.

Methylene chloride (dichloromethane)
A powerful, non-flammable solvent widely used in paint removers.

Micron (μ)
One millionth of a meter. The current preferred, but not yet common, term is micrometer (μm).

Mineral spirits
Nonflammable but combustible petroleum distillates that are used as solvents and diluents for a variety of coatings, especially oil-based coatings.

Minimum Film Forming Temperature (MFFT)
The lowest temperature at which a coating will coalesce into a film.

Miscibility
See Solubility/miscibility.

Moisture-cured urethane
Resins used for coatings and adhesives that cure by employing the moisture vapor present in air. In contrast to most finishes that simply adhere to wood, they form extremely strong covalent bonds with the wood itself.

Monkey
A trade term for a batch of resin that becomes cured and unusable during processing.

Mordants
Substances that are capable of binding a dye to wood or textile fibers.

Nanometer (nm)
One billionth of a meter, or 10 Angstroms. This unit of measure is used to describe the length of light waves and replaces the term "millimicron."

Naphtha
A common flammable solvent for oil-based coatings and stains consisting of aromatic and/or aliphatic hydrocarbons. Hi-flash naphtha is generally aromatic; VM&P (Varnish Maker's and Painter's) naphtha is mostly aliphatic.

Nitrocellulose
A flammable material used in explosives, rocket fuel, celluloid and nitrocellulose lacquer. Because it forms such a brittle finish, nitrocellulose is almost always modified with other resins and/or plasticizers when used as a wood finish.

N-methyl-2-pyrrolidone (NMP)
A solvent used widely both in "safer" paint-remover formulations and as a tail solvent in water-based polyurethane coatings.

Non-combustible
That which will not ignite at any temperature.

Nonflammable
That which will not ignite below 100°F. A substance can be both combustible and nonflammable.

Non-polymeric stain
A stain that contains no binder or resin. Because pigments require a binder to bond to wood, non-polymeric stains are generally dyes.

Oil-based finish
More or less a synonym for oil varnish.

Oil varnish
Any air-drying varnish based on or containing drying oils as the primary film former.

Orange peel
A finish flaw on sprayed finishes, where the coating does not lay out smooth, but takes on the texture of the skin of an orange. It is usually caused by spraying material that is too thick or poorly atomized.

Overspray
A dry, pebbly texture caused when sprayed finish dries in the air before hitting the wood. The droplets of finish adhere as dried particles rather than flowing out as a liquid.

Oxalic acid
A crystalline powder that mixes with water to form a bleach for wood. It is especially effective at removing stains caused by the contact of iron with woods high in tannin. In spite of the fact that it occurs naturally in rhubarb and spinach, it is both toxic and irritating.

Padding lacquer
Premixed, commercially made French polish. It frequently contains resins other than just shellac along with solvents other than alcohol.

Permissible Exposure Level (PEL)
See Threshold Limit Value.

Penetrating (oil-free) dyes
Solvent or water-soluble aniline-type dyes that contain no oils, resins or binders. They tend to color deeply, but must be coated with a finish to retain their color.

Penetrating oil stains
Oil-soluble dyes predissolved in oil and/or solvent.

Phenolic resins
The general term for a group of synthetic resins widely used in finishes and adhesives. Spar varnish is frequently an oil and phenolic-resin mixture.

Pickling stains
Pigmented wiping stains based on white or pastel colors. Left in grain, carvings and corners, they are used to create limed and pickled finishes.

Pigmented oil stains
Oil-based stains that use pigments (as opposed to dyes) as their coloring agent.

Pigments
In paint formulator's parlance, pigment is any dry particulate mineral added to coatings, stains, fillers, etc. The pigment can be colorless, like the fine silica added to clear coatings to reduce gloss, or it can be highly colored, like the pigments ground into oil to make Japan colors and paint. Although all pigments are opaque, their size and the amount added to the finish control their power to make the coating itself opaque. See also Dyes.

Pinholes
A finish defect related primarily to fast-drying sprayed coatings. Pinholes are created when tiny air- or solvent-vapor bubbles rise up through a wet coat of lacquer and break through the surface. If the film is sufficiently set, the lacquer cannot flow back over the hole, and a small cylindrical void representing the path of the rising bubble remains in the film.

Plasticizers
Solvents, resins or oils added to a brittle finish to make it more flexible.

Polyacrylics
Hybrid resins or a mix of polyurethane and acrylic resin molecules designed to offer better film properties than either one alone. Polyacrylics are tougher and more heat resistant than straight acrylics, and more stain resistant than straight polyurethane.

Polyacrylonitriles
Polyacrylonitriles are hybrid resins or mixes of polyurethanes and acrylonitrile resins, and are generally a bit more brittle and more amber than polyacrylic finishes.

Polyester resins
Highly durable and solvent-resistant resins derived from oils used to make plastics as well as finishes. Polyester finishes are generally acid catalyzed and some boast very high solids contents (some as high as 100%), resulting in little or no solvent emissions. However, their handling requirements make them much more suitable to industrial applications than home-shop use.

Polymeric stain
Any stain (dye or pigment type) that contains a binder or film former.

Polymerization
The formation of larger molecules (polymers) from smaller components (monomers and oligomers). This is the primary way in which reactive finishes are formed.

Polyurethane
An enormous class of resins and plastics derived from petroleum. As far as coatings are concerned, polyurethane resins can be divided into two classes: buffering resins, which are added to many types of film formers, including lacquers, water-based varnishes and oil varnishes; and self-curing or two-package crosslinked finishes. In both cases, the films formed have excellent hardness, gloss, flexibility, abrasion resistance, solvent resistance and adhesion (but not good stain resistance).

Pore filler
See Filler.

Primer
A barrier or coupling coat used to seal a substrate or to increase adhesion between the substrate and the finish coats. Primer is simply colored opaque sealer.

Propylene glycol (1,2 propanediol, methyl glycol)
A slow-drying tail solvent popular in water-based coatings. It also shows up in soda, syrup, medicine and vanilla extract.

Pumice
A volcanic rock. Finely ground pumice is used as a rubbing compound for satin finishes or as the first abrasive for gloss finishes.

Putty
A thick mixture of binder, solvent and colored or neutral pigment used to fill defects and voids in raw wood prior to finishing. Not to be confused with pore filler, which is essentially a thinner version of the same basic ingredients.

Reactive finishes
Finishes (also called thermoset finishes) that form a film by some means other than simply solvent evaporation, most commonly by polymerization. All oil-based varnishes and crosslinked or catalyzed coatings are reactive.

Relative humidity
A measure of the amount of moisture in the air, expressed as a percentage of the maximum amount of moisture the air is capable of holding at that temperature. Warm air can hold more water vapor than cool air.

Resin
The general term for any polymer or monomer that is used as the binder or film former in a coating. *See also* Binder.

Retarder
A solvent added to a coating, usually lacquer, to slow down the drying time in order to achieve better flow-out and gloss or to impede blushing.

Rottenstone (tripoli)
A finely ground natural limestone powder used as the final abrasive grit in creating a rubbed gloss finish.

Sanding sealer
See Sealer.

Satin
A degree of finish sheen below semi-gloss and above eggshell or matte.

Sealer
A barrier or coupling coat of finish designed to seal the substrate and/or increase adhesion of the top coat. Sealer is the clear version of primer. Sanding sealer contains added pigments, usually stearates, to make it build faster and sand more easily.

Seedlac
A form of shellac obtained from the original crude product. *See also* Shellac.

Shellac
The alcohol-soluble resin derived from the natural secretions of the female of the insect *Laccifer lacca*. Shellac has a long history in finishing, and still enjoys prominence as an effective sealer and the only resin of true French polish. There are many grades and refinements of shellac, from the crudest seedlac to dewaxed Kusmi aghani flakes.

Silicone
An outstanding lubricant, this low-surface-tension oil creates havoc if it contaminates wood or coats of certain finishes, especially high-surface-tension water-based and solvent lacquers. Curiously, the quick and dirty solution to silicone contamination in lacquer is to add more silicone to the subsequent coats of lacquer. *See also* Fish-eye.

Solubility/miscibility
The ability of one substance to blend uniformly with another. Solids are said to be soluble when they lose their crystalline structure and become molecularly or ionically dispersed. Thus crystalline aniline dyes break up and become ionic when dissolved, whereas pigments remain unchanged in liquid and merely become dispersed. In the case of liquids or gases in other liquids or gases, the term "miscibility" is used instead.

Solvent
A liquid capable of dissolving a resin or solid, and more broadly, the volatile portion of a coating mixture (even though it may contain latent solvents and diluents as well as true active solvents).

Solvent-release finishes
See Evaporative finishes.

Spar varnish (oil/phenolic)
Any oil-based varnish designed for exterior use. Spar varnishes frequently contain alkyds or oils buffered with phenolic resins, and are generally flexible (to tolerate wood movement through the seasons) and somewhat resistant to the elements.

Stearated
Containing zinc stearate, magnesium stearate or aluminum stearate. Stearates are soft, powdery soaps used both as a bodying agent in sanding sealer and as an anti-clogging lubricant layer on stearated sandpaper.

Surfactant
Any compound that reduces either surface tension between two liquids or a liquid and a solid. Surfactants include detergents, wetting agents and emulsifiers. In water-based emulsions, surfactants help keep the droplets of finish suspended in the water.

Swarf
Dust created by a cutting or grinding tool; a fancy name for sawdust.

Tail solvents
Slow-drying solvents used in water-based coatings designed to remain after the water has evaporated in order to coalesce the resin. Acrylic emulsions generally use glycol ethers as tail solvents.

Thermoplastic finishes
Filnishes that will resoften with the addition of heat, i.e., solvent-release finishes.

Thermoset finishes
See Reactive finishes.

Threshold Limit Value (TLV)
The maximum allowable exposure in an 8-hour period to a hazardous substance, measured in parts per million (ppm). Another term for TLV is PEL (Permissible Exposure Level).

Toluene (toluol, methylbenzene)
A widely used flammable solvent for nitrocellulose as well as many other resins and oils. It also shows up in gasoline and airplane cement.

1,1,1 trichloroethane (methyl chloroform)
A nonflammable degreaser/solvent with a TLV of 350 ppm in air. It is sometimes offered as a replacement for the now unavailable carbon tetrachloride.

1,1,2 trichloroethane
A nonflammable solvent for fats and oils with a TLV of 10 ppm in air. Because of its carcinogenic nature, it is not made available to the consumer.

Two-part epoxy coatings
See Epoxy.

Two-part water-based coatings (with hardener added)
Water-based coatings to which a crosslinker has been added to increase the durability, moisture and stain resistance of the film. See also Aziridine crosslinking additive. Carbodiimide crosslinking additive.

Ultraviolet absorbers (UVAs)
Compounds added to clear and colored exterior coatings to retard the destruction caused by the sun's ultraviolet rays. UVAs absorb photons, lower their energy level, and release them as less harmful heat energy. They work synergistically with hindered amine light stabilizers (HALS) and often appear together in paint formulations. See also Hindered amine light stabilizers (HALS).

Universal tinting colors (UTCs)
Pigments ground in a solvent or medium designed to be compatible with a wide range of coating resins and solvents, including both water-based and oil-based coatings.

Urea (carbamide)
The first organic compound to be synthesized (in 1824), urea is combined with other compounds such as melamine and formaldehyde to produce resins used in coatings and adhesives.

Varnish
At various times, the term varnish implied only clear coatings, only brushed coatings, or only oil-based coatings. It is currently used as a general term for finish. Some folks differentiate by calling reactive finishes varnish and evaporative finishes lacquer, and frankly, that's not a bad idea.

Vinyl
The term "vinyl" covers a huge range of resins and plastics characterized by a particular substructure in the radical $(CH_2:CH-)$. To generalize, vinyls are typically tough and flexible and are enjoying wider use as coatings for wood. Vinyl sealers are especially helpful as a first coat over resinous oily woods, such as rosewood, whose resins prevent lacquers and varnishes from adhering and drying properly.

Viscosity
The thickness of a liquid. High-viscosity liquids are thick, low-viscosity liquids are thin.

VM&P naphtha
See Naphtha.

Volatile organic compounds (VOCs)
Evaporative (volatile) organic (containing tetravalent carbon) chemicals, usually fast-evaporating hydrocarbon solvents. They have been implicated in contributing to the excessive tropospheric levels of ozone found in smog.

Water-based oil stains
Emulsions of an oil-based stain in water, water-based oil stains act like oil-based stains but have lower volative organic compounds (VOC) levels.

Water-based pigmented stains
Dispersions of pigment in water with a compatible resin binder (usually acrylic) and the necessary solvents, surfactants and other additives.

White titanium dioxide (TiO$_2$)
Titanium dioxide has the greatest hiding power of all white pigments, so it is widely used for white and pastel paints and pickling stains.

Wiping stain
Any easy-to-use or thickened stain, but more commonly a thickened pigmented oil stain.

Xylene (xylol, dimethylbenzene)
A widely used solvent for nitrocellulose and other lacquers and varnish resins. Flammability varies — some isomers are flammable and others are not.

INDEX

E

Earth colors. *See* Pigment powders.
Ease of use, of various finishes, 24-27
Enamel:
  characteristics of, 10, 24
  defined, 13
Environmental Protection Agency (EPA):
  and methylene chloride, 62
  and volatile organic compounds, 47-48
Epoxy finishes, temperature for applying, 142
Ethanol, safety of, 62
Ethylene glycol, hazards of, 62
Evaporative finishes:
  list of, 7, 13
  overview of, 4-5
  vs. reactive finishes, 7
  See also individual finishes.

F

Faux bois, discussed, 67
Ferrule:
  defined, 30, 32
  See also Brushes.
Filler:
  applying, 127-131
  for ash, 122
  brands of, 200
  homemade vs. commercial, 122-123
  for oak, 122
  oil-based, 127-134
  water-based, 135-136
Film formers, of various finishes, 24-27
Film thickness, measuring, 194-195
Finishes:
  brushable, 8, 24-25
  defined, 4
  fading of, 20-21
  qualities of, 7-8
  reversibility of, 21-22
  selection of, 7-8, 20-24, 24-27
  sprayable, 26-27
  for tabletops, 8
  wipe-on, 24-25
  See also individual finishes.
Finishing room:
  temperature in, 142
  relative humidity in, 143
  ventilation in, 143
Finish manufacturers, addresses of, 202-203
Finish repair:
  on brittle finishes, 164-165
  discussed, 162-170
  on flexible finishes, 164-165
  See also Blemishes.
Fish-eye. *See* Lacquer. Shellac.
Flammability, of various finishes, 24-27
Flash point, defined, 61
Flatting agents, in satin finish, 184, 185
Foam pad, as buffer, 193
French polish:
  as guitar finish, 183
  in lieu of refinishing, 21
  materials for, 176
  techniques for, 177-178
Fresco colors. *See* Pigment powders.
Fume silica, as rubbing medium, 186-187

G

Gel finishes:
  applying, 153
  characteristics of, 16, 25
Glazing, as staining technique, 113-114
Glossary, of finishing terminology, 204-209
Gloss finish:
  vs. satin finish, 183
  and scratch size, 184
  techniques for achieving, 190, 191
Gold leaf, brush for, 34
Gold size, brush for, 34
Gouges:
  vs. dents, 75
  filling, 78, 80

H

Hand-rubbed finish:
  advantages of, 180, 182
  materials for, 186
Heat resistance, of various finishes, 24-27
Hindered amine light stabilizers (HALS):
  defined, 20-21
  See also Ultraviolet absorbers.
Hydrocarbons, as health hazards, 46

I

Isocyanate, hazards of, 161

J

Japan colors, and filler, 134
Japan driers, discussed, 98, 101
Joint compound, as filler, 123

K

Key to brands:
  aerosol sprays, 201
  burn-in sticks, 200
  dyes, 200
  filler, 200
  finishes, 197-198
  padding lacquer, 201
  paint and varnish removers, 199
  pigment powders, 201
  primers, 198
  putty, 200
  rubbing compounds, 200
  sealers, 198
  solvents, 201
  stains, 199
Kootching. *See* Doping in.

L

Labels, reading, 8, 23, 125
Lacquer:
  applying, 148
  blush with, 159
  brands of, 197
  as brushable finish, 10
  brush for, 30, 148
  characteristics of, 10, 24, 26-27
  defined, 12-13
  fish-eye with, 73, 158
  heat resistance of, 8
  orange peel with, 158
  overspray with, 157
  pinholing with, 159
  as pore sealer, 133
  as sanding sealer, 137
  spitting with, 159
  solvent for, 5
  as sprayable finish, 17-18, 157-160
  temperature for applying, 142
  thinner for, 148, 149
  and ventilation, 143
  and volatile organic compounds, 17
  See also Padding lacquer. Water-based lacquer.
Lacquer thinner, brands of, 201
Lamb's wool, as buffing pad, 193
Latex, defined, 13
Linseed oil:
  applicator for, 44
  applying, 151-153
  as binder for pigment, 98
  brands of, 198
  characteristics of, 15, 25
  as exterior finish, 151
  and fire hazard, 15, 154
  raw vs. boiled, 15
  as wipe-on finish, 15
Lower Explosive Limit (LEL), defined, 22

M

Machine buffing, safety in, 192
Material Safety Data Sheet (MSDS), discussed, 23
Metamerism, discussed, 104-105
Methanol, hazards of, 62
Methylene chloride:
  and flammability of stripper, 60-61
  hazards of, 61-63
Mineral spirits, brands of, 201
Minimum Film Forming Temperature (MFFT), defined, 11-12
Moisture-cured polyurethane:
  characteristics of, 16, 25
  as wipe-on finish, 16
Moisture resistance, of various finishes, 24-27
Moisture Vapor Transmission Rate, defined, 12
Mordant, defined, 118

N

Naphtha, brands of, 201
Nitrocellulose:
  applying, 157
  characteristics of, 17, 26, 27
  and relative humidity, 143
  as sprayable finish, 17
  and ultraviolet degrade, 20
  water-based, 18
Non-polymeric stain:
  defined, 109
  using, 109-111

Publisher: JOHN KELSEY

Editor: ANDY SCHULTZ

Designer/Layout Artist: HENRY ROTH

Illustrator: M. JANE McKITTRICK

Photographer, except where noted: SUSAN KAHN

Copy/Production Editor: RUTH DOBSEVAGE

Art Assistant: ILIANA KOEHLER

Typeface: GARAMOND

Paper: WARREN PATINA MATTE, 70 lb., NEUTRAL pH

Printer: ARCATA GRAPHICS/HAWKINS, NEW CANTON, TENNESSEE